Mary Sparkes Wheeler

First Decade of the Woman's Foreign Missionary Society of the Methodist Episcopal Church

With Sketches of its Missionaries

Mary Sparkes Wheeler

First Decade of the Woman's Foreign Missionary Society of the Methodist Episcopal Church
With Sketches of its Missionaries

ISBN/EAN: 9783337097547

Printed in Europe, USA, Canada, Australia, Japan

Cover: Foto ©ninafisch / pixelio.de

More available books at **www.hansebooks.com**

OF THE

Woman's Foreign Missionary Society

OF THE

METHODIST EPISCOPAL CHURCH,

With Sketches of its Missionaries.

BY MARY SPARKES WHEELER.

INTRODUCTION BY BISHOP J. F. HURST, D. D.

NEW YORK:
PHILLIPS & HUNT.
CINCINNATI:
CRANSTON & STOWE.
1884.

PHILLIPS & HUNT,
New York.

TO THE
WOMAN'S FOREIGN MISSIONARY SOCIETY
OF THE
METHODIST EPISCOPAL CHURCH,
ITS
OFFICERS, HOME WORKERS, AND NOBLE BAND OF MISSIONARIES,
WHOSE
LOVE, LABOR, AND SACRIFICE
MADE THIS RECORD A POSSIBILITY,
THIS VOLUME
IS MOST RESPECTFULLY DEDICATED BY

THE AUTHOR.

PREFACE.

THE preparation of this volume was commenced early in the year 1878; but the work has been delayed longer than we anticipated, because of the time required to conduct the preliminary correspondence, extending, of necessity, to the ends of the earth. We have spared neither time nor pains to make the volume reliable.

In the preparation of the sketches we have made no statements without most ample warrant, either from the missionaries themselves or from their own personal friends; and we would gratefully record our especial obligation to these persons for their prompt and generous aid.

We propose to give our readers only a part of the history of our toilers in foreign fields. Just so much is presented as precedes and covers the first ten years of our Society.

Believing that a missionary should be divinely called to the work, and knowing the anxiety that young candidates have with regard to the nature of this call, we have, for the guidance and encouragement of such, entered, in some instances, into a detailed account of the religious experience and call of our ladies to missionary work.

It was our design to let the missionaries speak for themselves in relation to their work, and we had made ample quotations from their letters, but want of space, and the desire of the publishers to keep the dimensions of the work within certain limits, made it impossible to carry out the original plan.

We hope this will be a sufficient explanation and apology to the friends who have kindly furnished us material, for the non-appearance of letters and other papers which were sent to the writer to be embodied in the work.

We would also acknowledge our indebtedness to " Women of the Orient," and the " Heathen Woman's Friend," from which we have made some valuable quotations.

M. S. W.

COLUMBIA, *July*, 1880.

INTRODUCTION.

MY DEAR MRS. WHEELER: Your request to say a word of introduction in relation to the following History has reached me, and I have already examined your work with intense interest. It tells its own story of such tender and heroic romance as can be found only in the highest of all spheres—a profound religious experience, thoroughly enjoyed by the heart, and seeking expression in noble efforts to bring others to the same great joy.

I am glad to know that the first years of the life of the Woman's Foreign Missionary Society, with their singular record of sublime faith and far-reaching achievement, are not allowed to pass into dim and shadowy myth, or to be imprisoned in the official pigeon-holes of the centers where your work is managed, or to be limited to such loose and fugitive memoranda as have no bearing on the sympathy of Christian hearts the world over. Certainly ten such years have furnished enough material for a book, whether we take into account the beneficent response which the appeal of your Society has met with from the public; the character of the women who have borne the Gospel with glad hearts and strong hands to their less-favored sisters; or the direct and apparent results of your decade of evangelization and of woman's ministration in dark pagan homes. Napoleon used to ask, when a soldier's name was presented for promotion, "What has he done?" If the question be asked, What has the Woman's Foreign Missionary Society done? your pages contain such reply as ought to make all who have given their means for your better work double their contributions, and in their private devotions, more than ever, beseech our heavenly Father to give his increase to the pure seeds of truth that Christian women have been scattering, in the patience of strong faith, over many lands.

The work of the Society is not a novelty in Christian life. Its glory consists, not in that it is an invention of the century, but in the gratifying fact, that it has its place in the group of the inspirations and religious fervor of good women in all the centuries. Your Society has not originated its fundamental thought; it has simply found it, and has gone bravely to work to give it new drapery and a wider field. The elder sacred history abounds in rich illustrations of womanly interest in the great suffering world. Miriam sang the gladness of a nation, and Deborah knew as well how to rule a turbulent people as to destroy any army that might rise against them. That Christianity placed on womanhood a new emphasis can be seen throughout the Gospels. Whether it was the angel speaking to Mary, or Jesus lodging in the humble home of Lazarus and his sisters in Bethany, or the women watching in silent solitude the place where their crucified Lord lay, in all places and at all times it was the same—Christ was showing that whatever else his religion was to do, it was going to make happy homes, and women, to no small degree, the instruments of the regeneration throughout the world. Lydia, first of Paul's converts on the continent of Europe, became a bond of sympathy for scores of his small and feeble believing groups, around the classic shores of the Mediterranean. The names of Julia, Perpetua, and Felicitas will be ever associated with the fearless and all-suffering in martyrdom. When such women could not do any more for Christ, they simply sighed their prayers, as the pious Hannah, ages before, had prayed; "Only her lips moved, but her voice was not heard." Helena, mother of Constantine, was inspired with such missionary zeal that she built churches in neglected places, and organized missions from which the Gospel has never since been eradicated, notwithstanding the persecutions and wars, and the long and bloody rule of the Mohammedan chiefs. And later still, that Clotilda was the means of evangelizing the Frankish Empire, is only in harmony with the place which woman has always occupied in relation to the world's conversion.

So far as our own beloved Church is concerned, it was high time that our women should inaugurate special measures to enter heathen lands. No faith was strong enough to grasp the results we see to-day. Many a wilderness has been gladdened by their teaching, their medical ministering, and their bringing the young within the sunlight of the Gospel. The first ten years of success, however, have brought with them a great responsibility. There must be no falling off in sacrifice or popular response.

The number to reply in person to the Macedonian cry should be multiplied, and the means to send them should be prompt and ready from every part of the Church at home. Sad, indeed, would be the record of the future historian of the Woman's Foreign Missionary Society if she should have to write that the first decade was the best. The past proves what can be done, and should be only as the grain of mustard-seed to the future sheltering tree. How can these great results be reached? We cannot see the future, but we can trust Him who has its guidance in his hand:

> "I know not where his islands lift
> Their fronded palms in air;
> But I do know I cannot drift
> Beyond his love and care."

I congratulate you on the effort you have made in the following pages to make history teach by some of its modern heroines of faith. Beautiful as these characters are whom you have recorded, there are still more brave spirits ready to say, "Here am I; send me!" I sincerely trust that your book will tell its story of devotion and personal sacrifice to multitudes, and extend far out beyond their present limits the sympathy and the support which the Woman's Foreign Missionary Society so richly deserves.

JOHN F. HURST.

DREW THEOLOGICAL SEMINARY, MADISON, N. J.,
December 10, 1880.

CONTENTS.

	PAGE
INTRODUCTORY REMARKS	15
ORGANIZATION OF THE SOCIETY	37
ISABELLA THOBURN	47
CLARA A. SWAIN, M.D.	59
FIRST MEETING OF THE GENERAL EXECUTIVE COMMITTEE	70
FANNIE J. SPARKES	74
SECOND ANNUAL MEETING OF THE GENERAL EXECUTIVE COMMITTEE	93
BEULAH AND SARAH H. WOOLSTON	94
MARY Q. PORTER	101
MARIA BROWNE	111
CARRIE L. M'MILLAN	115
JENNIE M. TINSLEY	120
ACTION OF THE GENERAL CONFERENCE	124
LUCY H. HOAG AND GERTRUDE HOWE	128
LOU E. BLACKMAR	132
LIZZIE M. PULTZ	139
FOURTH ANNUAL MEETING OF THE GENERAL EXECUTIVE COMMITTEE	146
SALLIE F. LEMING	148
NANCY MONELLE, M.D.	153
LUCINDA L. COOMBS, M.D.	161
FIFTH ANNUAL MEETING OF THE GENERAL EXECUTIVE COMMITTEE	165
SIGOURNEY TRASK, M.D.	168
ANNA JULIA LORE, M.D.	179
LETITIA MASON, M.D.	189
SUSAN M. WARNER	193
MARY HASTINGS	195
JENNIE M. CHAPIN AND LOU B. DENNING	202
DORA SCHOONMAKER	209
SIXTH ANNUAL MEETING	213
LETITIA A. CAMPBELL	217
SEVENTH ANNUAL MEETING	231
LUCILLA H. GREEN, M.D.	235

	PAGE
NETTIE C. OGDEN	254
MARY F. CARY	258
OLIVE WHITING	264
EIGHTH ANNUAL MEETING	268
LEONORA S. HOWARD, M.D.	271
NINTH ANNUAL MEETING	274
MARY F. SWANEY	279
JULIA A. SPARR, M.D.	282
SUSAN B. HIGGINS	285
HENRIETTA B. WOOLSTON, M. D.	294
SALINA ALCESTA EASTON	295
MATILDA A. SPENCER	297
MARY A. HOLBROOK	299
EUGENIA GIBSON	307
MAGGIE ELLISON LAYTON	311
MARY ADELAIDE PRIEST	316
CLARA LOUISA MULLINER	320
CLARA M. CUSHMAN	322
MARY A. SHARP	323
TENTH ANNUAL MEETING	325
A TRIBUTE TO THE WOMAN'S FOREIGN MISSIONARY SOCIETY	331
CONSTITUTION OF THE WOMAN'S FOREIGN MISSIONARY SOCIETY OF THE METHODIST EPISCOPAL CHURCH	336
BRANCH LIMITS AND HEAD-QUARTERS	342
RECEIPTS OF WOMAN'S FOREIGN MISSIONARY SOCIETY	344
PAYMENTS TO WOMAN'S FOREIGN MISSIONARY SOCIETY	345
FORM OF BEQUEST AND DEVISE TO WOMAN'S FOREIGN MISSIONARY SOCIETY	346

Illustrations.

ISABELLA THOBURN	2
CLARA A. SWAIN, M.D.	58
FANNIE J. SPARKES	75

FIRST DECADE

OF THE

WOMAN'S FOREIGN MISSIONARY SOCIETY.

INTRODUCTORY REMARKS.

IT was Bishop Thomson who said, "Satan needed not to have troubled himself about Adam after he had captured Eve; nor will India be retaken from him until we imitate his tactics, and attack it at that side which, though weakest to our assault, is strongest for our defense; for woman is oppressed and depressed by idolatry. If she lost Paradise by her desire for information, may she not be induced to regain it by partaking of the same inviting fruit?"

The "assault" has, at last, been made on the right side, and the "inviting fruit," so long withheld from the millions of the hungry, starving souls of our heathen sisters, is now proffered to many of them—to all who hear the joyful sound—and multitudes are eagerly partaking. This fact has aroused the godly women of our land to a sense of their responsibility, and the importance of aiding in supplying the great needs of the heathen world.

It is a principle in God's economy that the elevation of a race shall come from the race itself. May it not be his will that the evangelization of heathen women shall be effected by women?

"Woman's quick susceptibility," said Bishop Wiley, " is an admirable trait in her character, adapting her to this great work. It enables her so readily to detect human sorrow and human need, it enables her to have a more vivid perception of the provisions made by redeeming love, and of the privileges flowing from it. She perceives the readiest mode of gaining access to the hearts of those whom she would benefit, and at the same time exercises a power of persuasion, which frequently prevails where other means have failed; and," continues the Bishop, " we often think that the hearts of women must sometimes really yearn to hear Christ declared by women's lips, to catch the inspiration in all its delicacy from a woman's heart."

Add to this, the fact, that the social customs and conditions of the heathen are such as to render millions of them unaccessible to men, as missionaries or teachers, and our duty, as Christian women, is imperative. This has led to the organization of our Woman's Foreign Missionary Society, whose *decennium* we now commemorate.

Our Society, though young, is not weak, for God is with us, and has wonderfully blessed our efforts in this direction, for the promotion of his cause. We have heard of a marvelous fig-tree near the Cape of Good Hope. It had a central stem, but the traveler told us he could not find it, for the limbs falling to the ground had taken root, at every point new trunks shot up erect, these, in turn, threw out new branches, which, arching, planted themselves in the earth, until the single stem had grown to be a forest, while, overhead, the leaves and fruit formed a canopy, which seemed like the roof of some vast cathedral, supported by innumerable columns. As we looked at this we thought, Surely here is a figure of our Society. It seems but as yesterday when the central stem was planted in the city of Boston. How small—how weak it appeared! But the godly women of the Church planted it with prayer, they watered it with their tears, Heaven blessed it—and how it has grown, until its branches reach from ocean to ocean, from New York on the east, to San Francisco on the west! Oceans themselves seem to be no barriers, for the arching branches have planted themselves in the lands beyond the seas, and we have a Woman's Foreign Missionary Society in India and one in China; and we expect, with the blessing of God, that this tree will grow and flourish until its arching branches shall encircle the globe, and its leaves, for the healing of the nations, spread from pole to pole.

The organization of the Society was hailed with delight by all our missionaries in the foreign field. Rev. Mr. Parker and Dr. Butler assisted in its formation, and, after his return to India, Dr. Butler wrote back, "I devoutly thank God for its organization." "The demand for such a society," wrote the Rev. James Baume, "was imperative, as it became increasingly evident that the godly women of the Church are yet to act a peculiar and glorious part in the conquest of the world to Christ."

Rev. S. L. Baldwin wrote: "It was with great pleasure that, from my distant post of observation in China, I noticed the formation of your Society. It will bring the Christian women of our Church into closer sympathy with the heathen women of China, India, and other lands. All the watchmen on Zion's outposts will hail with joy this new and powerful auxiliary in the world's conversion." "The Woman's Foreign Missionary Society," wrote the Rev. Dr. Thoburn, "was not organized a day too soon. There is a mighty work to be done among the women of India, which *only women can do*."

The missionaries' wives, with one accord, have done their utmost to advance the interests of the Society, by superintending and aiding in its work abroad, and by the contribution of valuable letters to the "Heathen Woman's Friend." Mrs. Parker and Mrs. Butler have manifested intense interest in all its various branches of work, and have been unceasing in their endeavors to assist it in its labor of love.

At home there has been one general rallying cry, "The Master is come, and calleth for thee!" Recognizing in this call the voice of Jesus, multitudes of elect ladies from all parts of the country have arisen, and, laying their wealth, talents, and accomplishments at the feet of Christ, have gone forth to labor for the evangelization of the world.

The officers of the Society—the presidents and corresponding secretaries of the various branches—are a noble band of Christian women, whose consecrated lives, pure hearts, and strong faith in God, together with their superior natural endowments, large culture, and brilliant talents, make them equal to any emergency connected with their work. The reflex influence upon the home-workers has been grand and glorious. A precious baptism of love and labor has fallen upon the women of the Church; and as they have been endeavoring to bless others, their own hearts have been watered from on high.

The clergy of our Church have also done much to advance the interests of the Society by their sympathy and co-operation, and our Bishops have been hearty and eloquent in their words of indorsement.

Auxiliary Societies have been formed, not only on the various charges, but at nearly all of the large camp-meetings, including Round Lake, Thousand Islands, and Ocean Grove. These are centers of influence, and have been wisely improved by the ladies, who are ready to seize upon every opportunity and to enter every open door of usefulness. The anniversary exercises, at these meetings, have been attended by large and enthusiastic audiences, and have been powerful agencies in creating missionary zeal and diffusing missionary intelligence.

At Saratoga and Clifton Springs successful auxiliaries are organized, and are a power for good, not only because of the money collected by them, but because of the influence exerted upon the multitudes who become infused with the missionary spirit, and go home to work for the cause. At Clifton Springs the ladies' missionary meetings have been seasons of wonderful interest. One of these, called by Mrs. Dr. Foster of the "Sanitarium," will never be forgotten. Over seventy delegates were in attendance from Geneva District alone. The programme was a most attractive one. At the close of the exercises Dr. and Mrs. Foster invited the ladies to supper, which was partaken of by more than two hundred persons. Here an interesting incident occurred, the account of which we take from the "Northern Christian Advocate:"

"After this delightful repast the company was called to order, and Bishop Janes was introduced and made some very interesting remarks. He said the scene before him was 'poetic.' He commended the Society, and said that as the parent Society and this were working together so harmoniously, and as the marital relation was the most sacred and delightful on earth, he proposed that the nuptials of the two be celebrated. Dr. Foster then said, that as the Bishop had 'gone courting,' and as no man, under such circumstances, liked to go away without an answer, he called for Mrs. Hibbard to reply, either accepting or rejecting. She replied that she had always been taught to be very honest in such matters, and she was too old to change her habits in this particular. She confessed that she saw two insuperable obstacles to the match: the first was, the two were *too near of kin*—the Bishop had just called one the *parent* Society; and, secondly, there was *too great a disparity in their ages*, the one being fifty years older than the other. She retired amid much applause, but the Bishop, undaunted, arose to say that a courageous man was not to be disheartened by one refusal."

The "Heathen Woman's Friend" says: "This *bonmot* given by Mrs. Dr. Hibbard, we venture to say, has not been paralleled in the history of our Society. For real wit and thorough truthfulness it cannot be excelled."

In the West the spirit of enterprise and progression with regard to missionary matters has pervaded the hearts of Methodist women to a remarkable degree. The annual branch meetings, district and quarterly meetings, held by the Society, together with the conference and other anniversaries, have been seasons of great interest, and have been attended by eager multitudes.

Our Methodist ladies have also organized a society called the "Woman's Missionary Society of the Pacific Coast," auxiliary to the parent Missionary Society, which appropriates from $1,500 to $1,800 yearly for the work among heathen women on the Pacific Coast. Mrs. Otis Gibson, Corresponding Secretary of this Society, writes:

"Upon the Pacific slope, where we are located, there exists a population of at least 150,000 heathen Chinese. They have reared their temples, set up their idols, and they fall down and worship the gods that their own hands have made in full view of our Christian Churches. The Churches saw their opportunity, and commenced schools among these people, and sent missionaries to tell them the story of Jesus and his love.

"But among these heathen were some two or three

thousand women and children who did not come to the schools, and did not attend preaching in the chapels. The Chinese women in this country are, most of them, bought and sold for vile purposes. The little girls are bought as servants, and when grown they are sold into a life of shame, without so much as asking their consent.

"There seemed no way of access to these poor women. It touched our hearts to know that these poor creatures lived, suffered, and died within sound of our church bells, and yet never heard that they were redeemed by the precious blood of Christ. Accordingly, the ladies of San Francisco organized for the purpose of carrying the Gospel to these Chinese women. Much good has already been accomplished, and many have been won to the Saviour.

"Thus the work has been spreading, and the end is not yet, for our God is marching on; and we believe that the women of our Church, having enlisted under the banner of the cross, and enrolled their names among God's embattled hosts, will never retreat until the Gospel is preached to every creature, and the kingdoms of this world have become the kingdoms of our Lord and of his Christ."

PRELIMINARY ORGANIZATIONS.

The institutions that are most efficient in the amelioration of the woes of mankind have not been known from the beginning in their present form, but are developments of ideas that have long existed without any crystallization. This is true of the various Missionary Societies that are now so successful in the spread of truth and the elevation of the race. The missionary idea has always existed in the Church of Christ, but only within a short time has the thought crystallized into its present shape. Woman's Missionary Societies are outgrowths of this idea—a later phase of the same work.

The great Author of human redemption made no mistake in his plan for the salvation of the world when he first revealed his resurrection glory to woman, and sent Mary forth to proclaim to the disciples and Peter the first message of salvation through her risen Lord. From that glad hour until the present time the missionary spirit has always possessed the hearts of women, and they have been among the first to tell the story of the cross and the sepulcher. The present form of labor in our Woman's Foreign Missionary Society is but the crystallization, for practical efficiency, of the Christian impulse that largely controls the hearts of devout and earnest women.

It would be interesting to trace the development of this thought from the earliest times, but we must confine our investigations to the limits of our own denomination. From our earliest history we have been a missionary Church, but our parent Missionary Society was not organized until 1819. So, from the beginning, the women of our Church have had the missionary spirit, but this spirit did not culminate in the organization of a permanent Society, embracing the whole extent of our Church, until 1869. Before this, however, there were indications of missionary life struggling for manifestation and organization.

FEMALE MISSIONARY SOCIETY.

July 5, 1819, about three months after the organization of the Missionary Society of the Methodist Episcopal Church, a number of ladies met at the Wesleyan Seminary, in Forsyth-street, New York city, for the purpose of forming an auxiliary society. Rev. Nathan Bangs presided, opening the meeting with prayer, and stating its object. At a subsequent meeting a constitution was adopted, and officers elected, consisting of a first and second directress, a treasurer, a secretary, and twenty-five managers. A large number of elect ladies, possessing, many of them, pecuniary and intellectual ability, united with this Society.

For more than forty years this Society continued its successful work, cheering the heart of many a missionary by its sympathy and aid. It labored among the unchristianized of our own country—the Indian tribes—and for the mission in Africa. Ann Wilkins, of precious memory, was among its noble representatives. The funds of the Female Missionary Society were paid over to the parent Board, but generally for a *specified* object, which, by mutual agreement, had been settled on beforehand. From a report made in 1861 we learn that this Society had, up to that time, raised and paid to the parent Society over $20,000. Besides this, it made contributions in clothing, bedding, books, etc., for the mission schools. Soon after that report the Society closed its operations.

WEEDSPORT MISSIONARY SOCIETY.

One of the earliest accounts of woman's work for missions in the Methodist Episcopal Church which we have ever heard, we gathered in part from the lips of an aged and saintly woman, who has from her earliest youth been a devoted member of the Methodist Episcopal Church—Mrs. Susan B. Fox, of Weedsport, New York. This dates back to the founding of the Liberia Mission, in 1832.

The appointment of the consecrated hero, Melville B. Cox, as our first missionary to Africa, awoke the spirit of missionary enterprise in the hearts of a few godly women of Weedsport, who banded themselves together for the purpose of devising means to aid him in his work of bearing the Gospel to the heathen. While unitedly praying for guidance in the matter, their hearts were *strangely warmed*—a baptism of love and power fell upon them—and, taking this as an evidence of divine approval, they set out with much enthusiasm to collect what they could for the enterprise. Mrs. Fox was the pioneer worker, and the inspiration of the others.

Without formal organization as yet, they began their efforts by personal *self-denial* and small savings. They went from house to house, begging missionary money. They met with great opposition and prejudice from the members of the Church. The objections now occasionally heard of " heathen at home," " poverty," etc., were then *fresh* and *rife.* Though often persecuted and rejected, they persevered. When money was refused they took whatsoever was offered them, provided it could be turned into money. They sacrificed their own ease, pleasure, and luxury. Those engaged in sewing sewed a little longer, and those at the spinning-wheel spun a little more, that they might have something to give to the cause. Whenever they met for deliberation and prayer the same divine power overshadowed them.

The first contribution from any *brother* of the Church was the sum of twenty-five cents. "This," says one, "was regarded as *remarkable*, and as a providential encouragement; and they rejoiced as though they had found great spoil." Like the early Christians, these women met in an upper room, in a sort of private way, where they labored, working with their hands, like Dorcas, making coats and garments for the poor and destitute in the mission fields. Many a box of clothing and other necessary articles was sent out from time to time in the progress of their work.

The first annual donation in cash was $7 sent to New York, to the treasurer of the parent board. A letter from Mrs. Fox, in her trembling hand, lies before us, in which we are assured that though her right hand is forgetting its cunning, her heart is still beating in sympathy with the missionary cause. Referring to the first offering, she says:

"We gave the money to the treasurer, baptizing it with our tears, and wishing it a hundred fold more. The next year we did better. Prejudice met us at every point, but by diligence and perseverance and the blessing of God, we prospered, our contributions increased, and prejudice gave way."

These ladies sent their first " Missionary Box" to Liberia. The capture of the slaver " Pons," with its living, dying cargo of nine hundred slaves, one hundred of the survivors of whom fell to the care of the Liberia Mission, was the occasion for a call to the Churches to furnish suitable clothing for these captives. This first mission box was a response to that call.

It is a source of great satisfaction now to know that some of the leading men of the Liberia government and nation at the present time were among the captives whom these ladies helped to clothe. Their contributions, in this form, were sent to Africa, Oregon, and South America.

The first formal organization of this Society was effected in 1840. Mrs. S. B. Fox was chosen President, which position she held until 1863, when, under advice from Dr. Durbin, the organization was blended with the parent Society. In 1869 they again organized, as auxiliary to the Woman's Foreign Missionary Society of the Methodist Episcopal Church.

The self-sacrificing and heroic Sophronia Farrington, the first unmarried woman sent by our Church to Liberia, had the same missionary fire burning in her heart before our mission was established in Africa. In regard to this she says:

" Ere the Methodist Episcopal Church started a foreign mission in Africa there seemed to be such a state of things as the messenger of the Lord described when he had been to and fro in the earth, and returned exclaiming, 'The whole earth sitteth still.' This state of things was so painful to me that I felt compelled to give myself to the Lord for work abroad, at the same time praying that he would open a foreign mission in the Methodist Episcopal Church, with a faith which amounted to an assurance that he would do it. With this faith I started for Boston to visit my friends early in 1832, where I waited till the way opened.

"Soon after Brother Cox's appointment he came to Boston and made arrangements, then went on to Africa, where he bought a mission-house, and made ready for us, and wrote for us to come on. But the evening before we started we received the intelligence of his death. Yet this did not shake my faith. I felt, as he said, 'Let a thousand fall before Africa be given up.' We arrived safely in Monrovia, January 1, 1834, but ere four weeks had elapsed our dear Sister Wright was no more; we had expected much help from her, as she was well qualified to do good.

"Soon a young Episcopalian, who arrived in another ship about the time we did, took the fever and died, and eight missionaries in all died within four months. Our superintendent now resolved to return to America with his wife and a colored minister, and wished me to return with them, as he thought he must give up the mission. The doctor said we could never endure the climate; but I felt an assurance that God was for the mission, and said I could never see it given up. They all left, and

I remained alone to trust in God; but he sustained me until a new recruit came, and established the mission.

"I taught a native school until my health failed so that I could not teach, and God seemed to say, 'Stay thy hand, and give way to the stronger ones who have arrived.' I now saw clearly that my work was to fill the vacancy and keep up the mission until the Southern help arrived, as those who could endure the climate. I then returned with the Rev. Mr. Seys, who was coming to America for his family."

Soon after the death of the eight of whom she speaks, Miss Farrington was seized with fever in a most malignant form, but, contrary to the expectation of her physician, she recovered. She was urgently persuaded to return to America, as to remain longer seemed certain death; but she would not relinquish her post. Her reasons are told by herself in another letter. She says:

"I was now seized with the fever again, which ran so high that, about the fourth day, I was given up to die. The pain extended all over my system, and was increasing. The doctor said mortification was taking place. After he had gone I prayed that the silver cord might be loosed and the golden bowl broken, if it were the will of the Lord. I was alone, except a little native girl, who was asleep in the room. The thought immediately came to me, Is there not some one to sympathize with me? At once Jesus seemed to stand by my side, with all his native sympathy, and showed me that it was not his will that I should die at this time, placing the mission before me as a reason why I should remain. I said, 'Then, Lord, remove the disease.' In a moment, sudden as a flash of lightning, the fever and pain all left me, and I was well.

> 'If half the strings of life should break,
> God can our flesh restore.'

The doctor said mine was the greatest cure he had ever wrought, to which I made him no reply. Mr. Spaulding now determined to return to America, and take me with him, and give up the mission. But I said, 'No; I can never see this mission abandoned. I can die here, but I will never return until the mission is established.' But he said, 'The Board will probably cut you off if you do not go.' I said, 'I will stay, and trust the Lord.'"

She did stay, and was the only white person on the coast to welcome John Seys, when he arrived to superintend the mission.

This saintly woman survived (the wife of Mr. George Cone, of Utica, New York) until after the close of our first decade, when she passed into the heavens.

WOMAN'S FOREIGN MISSIONARY SOCIETY OF THE WESLEYAN FEMALE COLLEGE, WILMINGTON, DELAWARE.

In the year 1846 one of the graduates of this institution (now Dr. Mary Dixon Jones, of Brooklyn, N. Y.) delivered an eloquent missionary address before the Alumnæ Association, which caused it to reorganize and form itself into a "Woman's Foreign Missionary Society."

This Society, though small, has exerted a widespread influence, and has contributed much to the cause of missions. The Misses Woolston, who have given twenty years' service in China, were graduates of this institution, and later Misses Easton and Layton, both teachers of this college, went to India, under the auspices of our Woman's Foreign Missionary Society.

Dr. Jones writes: "This little Society was organized in 1846, by the lady graduates of the Wesleyan Female College, all of them in their girlhood, blushing with the honors of the institution, and feeling the inspiration and enthusiasm of doing a great work. If the deliberations of that Society could be known, if their speeches could be told—little girls of fifteen and sixteen, who had scarce raised their heads from logic and conic sections, making missionary addresses!

"I notice among the officers of the Society at that time the names of Miss Augusta Durbin, daughter of Rev. Dr. Durbin, the great Missionary Secretary; Miss Maria Kennaday, daughter of Rev. Dr. John Kennaday; Miss Mary Tippett, daughter of Rev. Dr. Charles Tippett; and Miss Rebecca Bruner, now the honored wife of Rev. Dr. Dobbins. The Wesleyan Female College, of Wilmington, Delaware, was then probably the first and best school of learning in the country for young ladies, and has among its *alumni* some of the most finely educated ladies in the country. Contributions and collections were made regularly. I still cherish among my mementoes a Missionary Certificate, made at that early day, and presented me by the Society.

"This little Society did good, and sent a wave of influence in motion that will roll ceaselessly on to eternity."

LADIES' CHINA MISSIONARY SOCIETY.

This Society was organized in the city of Baltimore, April, 1848, its object being to aid in the formation and support of a Methodist mission in China. The subject of establishing such a mission in China was frequently brought before the Church, and was freely and fully discussed. In 1846 several individuals pledged annual subscriptions toward its support. During the same year the Rev. Judson D. Collins wrote to the Missionary Board his convictions and drawings toward this land. The Board replied that they had not sufficient money to establish a new mission. But this heroic man, moved by the same divine impulse as that which actuated Paul, when, "after he had seen the vision, immediately he endeavored to go into Macedonia, assuredly gathering that the Lord had called" him "to preach the Gospel unto them," wrote to Bishop Janes, "Engage me a passage before the mast; my own strong arm shall pull me to China, and support me when there." This appeal could not be resisted, and in 1847 the Bishop appointed J. D. Collins, with Rev. M. C. White and wife, to Foochow, China.

The Ladies' China Missionary Society was formed

for the purpose of aiding in the support of this new mission. The circumstances leading to its organization were these. In March, 1848, Dr. Stephen Olin preached a missionary sermon before the Baltimore Conference, which was remarkable for its pathos and power. The next day a lady met him at the house of a friend, and they entered into conversation with regard to missionary work in its various fields. This lady (Mrs. Anna L. Davidson) was deeply interested in the work of the Foreign Evangelical Society in Catholic countries. Dr. Olin asked her reason for working outside her own denomination. She replied, " Because there is no avenue for woman's work in the Methodist Episcopal Church." Said the doctor, "Create one." " How?" she inquired. " Organize an association for missionary work in China—that is just now open. Begin your work, form your Society, and I will speak at your first anniversary." She went home, considered the matter, prayed over it, and regarding the suggestion made by Dr. Olin as prompted by the divine Spirit, she immediately set about the work.

The organization was soon effected, and the first anniversary held January 1849, in the old historic Light-street Church, near whose site, in 1784, the Methodist Episcopal Church of America first received organic form. Bishop Janes presided, and Dr. Olin, true to his word, made an " able and effective speech." For ten years this Society collected and paid annually to the parent board about $300. An earlier writer says: " This feeble band of women

—feeble in one sense, but strong in faith and determination—struggled on through opposition and difficulties. An independent organization was considered an infringement, not only on Church usage, but the absolute rights of the Missionary Board; consequently official brethren, ministers, with a few honorable exceptions, gave it the cold shoulder. Nothing daunted, our little band quietly and steadily pursued their way, gathering and dropping small sums, as the widow's mite, into the treasury of the Lord."

In 1858 Dr. Wentworth, then missionary to China, made an earnest appeal to the ladies to raise funds for the purpose of establishing and supporting a female school in Foochow. He wrote: "It is a favorite scheme of mine, but I have already lost heart and hope on the subject. Teaching is a great aid to the diffusion of Christianity in all lands; witness the Sabbath-schools and Christian schools at home, and the anxiety of all Churches to obtain academic education, particularly the strenuous efforts of the Romanists, the greatest tacticians in the world on this particular line. We are surrounded by females degraded by custom, by ignorance, and vice. Such as escape drowning in infancy are immediately contracted in marriage, systematically crippled, and condemned to life-long seclusion. Our churches are full of men; our preaching is to men; only now and then a woman dares venture within sound of the Gospel, and these are the large-footed women; small-footed, or ladies of China, never. Their lords despise them as a class, and are ashamed to be seen abroad with them. Nothing in Asia or the East calls more loudly for reformation than the condition of women. In no department is missionary labor more needed than in this, and woman only can be reached by woman. Asiatics jealously exclude women from intercourse with men. Instead of here and there a teacher and a languishing school, China needs an army of Christian females, ready, if need be, to lay down their lives for their own sex and the Gospel. Your city is fond of building monuments, and certainly none could be more appropriate than one erected on this soil in the shape of an efficiently working female academy."

The amount desired was $5,000. This appeal came through the parent board, with its indorsement. Dr. Durbin, who at the time was Missionary Secretary, sent a communication with the following resolution:

"*Resolved*, That if the ladies feel heartily disposed to undertake this work, and have good hope they can accomplish it in a given time, the Board will accept their services in this respect, and execute their will."

The ladies *did* feel "*heartily disposed*," and undertook the work joyfully. It proved an inspiration to them, and to-day the Baltimore Female Seminary stands as a monument to their faith and zeal.

"In 1858 Miss Potter and the Misses S. and B. Woolston sailed with the present superintendent of the mission and wife, Rev. S. L. Baldwin. Miss Potter became Mrs. Wentworth." The Misses

Woolston remained in the school, faithful, successful workers, until recently, when they returned home for rest and change.

This Society continued its successful operations until 1871, when it united its name, interests, funds, and influence to the Woman's Foreign Missionary Society of the Methodist Episcopal Church.

ORGANIZATION OF THE SOCIETY.

TO Mrs. Rev. E. W. Parker belongs the distinguished honor of being the *originator* of this Society, the first person who made earnest and successful effort for its organization. In March, 1869, Mr. and Mrs. Parker returned from India to their home in New England. Their hearts were burning with missionary zeal. They were fresh from the field, where for years they had toiled unceasingly for the evangelization of the people of that land. As Mrs. Parker looked abroad over the millions of India's daughters uncheered by the light of life, oppressed by superstition and ignorance, her heart was burdened by the weight of responsibility which she felt to be resting upon her. The superior light enjoyed by the women of our own favored land only made, by contrast, the darkness of heathenism more dense. She felt that something more must be done to reach the *women* of India. As they could only be reached by women, *more women must be sent.* She said the missionaries' wives were doing all they could; they had already accomplished a grand and glorious work. They needed help, and she strongly advocated sending single women, who would be free from domestic cares, and who would be able to devote all their time to the one work of saving souls. She commenced her earnest appeals to the ladies

East and West to unite their efforts in forming a Woman's Foreign Missionary Society in our own Church, for the purpose of sending out these single missionaries.

Previous to this, however, some interest had been awakened in the hearts of many of our Methodist women by the success achieved by woman's missionary societies in other denominations. This helped to confirm their growing conviction of the necessity and feasibility of the thing, and gave promise of what could be done by the women of our Church; but up to this time no movement had been made toward any definite organization.

Mrs. Dr. Butler, the devoted and gifted wife of the founder of our India Mission, then a resident of Boston, joined heartily with Mrs. Parker in her efforts to arouse the women of the Church to a sense of their obligation to the heathen and their duty to God, who "hath made of one blood all nations of men for to dwell on all the face of the earth, and hath determined the times before appointed, and the bounds of their habitation;" and who, after finishing the work of redemption on Calvary, commanded his disciples to "go into all the world and preach the Gospel to every creature." Her appeals were soul-stirring, and such as could only be made by one who had seen with her own eyes the wants and woes of her heathen sisters. The interest began to spread. In different parts of the country the subject was discussed, and preparations made for following up the movement.

Mrs. Parker stated that the ladies of the West

said, in response to her appeals, "If the ladies of the East will start, we will follow." Mrs. Lewis Flanders resolved to commence, and Mrs. Thomas A. Rich enthusiastically joined in the good work. Mrs. Flanders first spoke to the ladies upon the subject of organizing a society in the Methodist Episcopal Church, at a Sewing Circle of Tremont-street Church. She had a constitution of "The Woman's Board of Missions," and as each lady arrived, she went and talked with her upon the feasibility of such a society in our own Church. The next thing she did was to call a parlor meeting, but the notices failing to reach the pulpit, only four persons came. Another meeting was called; notices were sent to the Methodist Episcopal Churches in Boston and vicinity, inviting all ladies interested to meet at Tremont-street Church, on Monday, March 22, at 3 P. M., "to consider the propriety of organizing a Ladies' Foreign Missionary Society."

The day came, and with it one of the most severe and forbidding storms of the season. Mrs. Parker was twenty-five miles from the place appointed for the meeting. Friends tried to dissuade her from making the unpleasant journey, telling her it would be in vain, no one would be there; but she, with a faith that

>Laughed at impossibilities,
>And cried, *It shall be done*,

said, "I must go to Boston." Mrs. Parker went, and found Mrs. Dr. Butler and a small company of ladies waiting. They addressed the meeting, having but nine auditors, namely: Mrs. Lewis Flanders,

Mrs. Thomas A. Rich, Mrs. Albert Ellis, Mrs. Thomas Kingsbury, Mrs. W. B. Merrill, Mrs. O. T. Taylor, Mrs. L. H. Daggett, Methodists, and two strangers, belonging to a sister Church, whose names are not known. A Constitution was drawn up and presented, article by article, for consideration, amendment if necessary, and approval; after which a board of officers was appointed.

Mrs. Bishop Baker, Concord, N. H., was elected President; Mrs. B. J. Pope, Boston, Recording Secretary; Mrs. T. A. Rich, Boston, Treasurer; and Mrs. Ruby Warfield Thayer, Newtonville, Mass., Corresponding Secretary. The meeting then adjourned to meet the following Monday.

At the next meeting, though the rain was again falling, more than thirty ladies were present. Their hearts were now thoroughly enlisted in the cause, much enthusiasm prevailed, twenty members were added to the Society, and six ladies became life members. A letter was received from Mrs. Thayer, assuring them of her sympathy and co-operation, but stating that on account of failing health she would not be able to serve them as secretary. The spirit was willing, but the flesh was weak. In a few months after she was called to her heavenly home.

The following ladies were then appointed to conduct the correspondence of the Society: Mrs. Rev. Dr. Warren, of Cambridge, Mass.; Mrs. Jennie F. Willing, of Rockford, Ill.; and Mrs. Rev. E. W. Parker.

Ladies were appointed from seventeen States to carry on this work by organizing auxiliary societies throughout the entire Church. Cheering responses came from all directions. Mrs. Parker gave direction to the work in New England, and Mrs. Jennie F. Willing created much enthusiasm throughout the West by her tireless and self-sacrificing efforts and eloquent appeals. Auxiliary societies began to multiply rapidly. In Brooklyn, New York, a Society was formed, having a most efficient president, in the person of Mrs. Dr. Harris, wife of one of our Missionary Secretaries, now Bishop.

On May 7 the Secretaries of the parent Board, Rev. Drs. Durbin and Harris, met the representatives of our Society in Bromfield-street Church, Boston, for the purpose of coming to a more definite understanding with regard to its object and aim. After thoroughly discussing the whole subject they gave the ladies their official approval, and "assumed the responsibility of publishing to the Church a statement of its objects and methods of work."

We quote the following from a report of the meeting:

"The whole subject was fully discussed, and the following conclusions reached:

"1. That such a Society is very much needed to unite the ladies of the Methodist Episcopal Church in increased efforts to meet the demand for labor among women in heathen lands.

"2. That this Society, though not auxiliary to the general Missionary Society, should work in harmony with it, seeking its counsel and approval in all its work.

"3. That a missionary paper might be published

by the ladies of the Society, with great profit to the entire missionary cause."

The Society, having received the recognition of the Secretaries of the parent Board, was thus authorized to proceed, and, with this encouragement, went forward in the prosecution of its work with renewed energy and zeal. All that the new Society now needed to make it an integral part of the Methodist Episcopal Church, was the formal recognition and authorization of the General Conference. It was understood that the Society, though independent of the parent Board, was to act harmoniously with it. Not as a rival at home or in the foreign field, but as a division of the same army, actuated by one spirit, controlled by the same general head, it should endeavor to aid in securing the conquest of the world for Jesus.

This Conference was a most satisfactory one. At its conclusion the Society made its first payment to Dr. Harris, for the support of a Bible woman in Moradabad, India. The circumstances connected with it were peculiarly touching and significant. It was the offering of a lady whose daughter said, shortly before, when dying, "If I do not get well, I would like to have papa give as much money to the missionaries every year as it takes to take care of me." There was such a sacredness about the offering as led the ladies to regard it as a smile of approval from the Lord of the harvest. Multitudes have since followed her example, and have cast into the treasury of the Lord their sanctified offerings, the price of tears and sacrifices, and in the name of departed loved ones are supporting orphans and Bible-readers in foreign lands.

"HEATHEN WOMAN'S FRIEND."

Previous to this meeting, on May 7, the ladies had cherished a plan of publishing a missionary paper, which should be the organ of the Society. They considered it important for the permanency and success of the enterprise that free communication should be opened between the home workers and the foreign field, thus bringing the heathen to plead their own cause at our very doors. But there were difficulties in the way. The Society was young and weak. It had no money to invest in this new departure. They felt that the funds raised by the Society must be kept sacred, and used only for the evangelization of the heathen abroad, and that this paper must eventually be self-supporting. However, so sure were they that it was the right thing to be done, that they at once set about the work, and their faith overcame every obstacle.

Five or six ladies became personally responsible for the expense of publishing the paper, and Mrs. Dr. Warren, Mrs. Rev. E. W. Parker, and Mrs. Dr. Butler were appointed to arrange for its publication. Mrs. Willing was shortly after substituted for Mrs. Butler.

The late lamented Mr. Flanders, of Boston, did much by his counsel and encouragement to aid them in this enterprise. His great interest and faith in the future of the Society will never be forgotten by its early workers. He opened his house most freely to every one connected with it. So convinced was he of the importance of their issuing at once a missionary paper that he pledged himself financially to help publish it; and his little son, "Freddie," commenced the work of soliciting subscribers, and secured thirty before a copy was ready.

We copy the following brief extracts from letters written by Mrs. Parker from Moradabad, India, to Mrs. Flanders:

"*September* 9, 1872.

"I remember with gratitude all the dear ladies who aided in organizing the Woman's Missionary Society, and who stood by it in its dark days and times of trial, but I remember you as the *first* one I talked with about it outside our missionary circle, and I remember how earnestly you went to work to carry out my wishes; and God crowned those efforts with abundant success, and now the little one has literally become a thousand. How wonderfully God has blessed our Society, so recently organized! I am sure you rejoice in it, and are thankful for all you have done, though you have had toils and trials in it as I have; yet in Christ's service we count all pain as pleasure, and rejoice that we are counted worthy to be co-laborers with him in the salvation of the world."

"*March* 26, 1874.

"You did a good thing when you helped to organize the Woman's Missionary Society. I always remember you as the *first* lady in Boston who said or did any thing to encourage me in this work. May God bless you abundantly in all things!"

"*May* 17, 1874.

"I love to think of the happy hours I spent with you, and of the encouragement you gave me in my work. You were really the one who set the wheels agoing that resulted in the formation of our Society, which is such a power for good in all the earth to-day. I am sure the good Lord must have put it into your heart. I often think of the tender tie that binds you to India. Does Freddie love the missionary cause still?"

OUR FIRST MISSIONARY.

"It is a significant fact, showing how on faith the corner-stone was laid, that the first missionary was appointed and preparations for her journey begun before the money was raised to send her."

On May 26 the first public meeting of the Society was held in Bromfield-street Church. Governor Claflin presided. Speeches were made by Dr. W. F. Warren, Dr. Butler, and Rev. Mr. Parker. Soon after, a meeting of the Society was held, and Miss I. Thoburn's name was presented as a candidate for foreign work. Her brother was already in the field, and so strong were her convictions of duty, that she had resolved, if not sent by us, to go as the representative of a sister Society. Not twenty ladies were present. They sat silent. They had less than three hundred dollars in the treasury — no more than enough for an outfit! "Presumption," said one. At last Mrs. Edwin F. Porter, with faith and courage exceeding all others, arose, and, with thrilling earnestness, spoke of the needs of the heathen and of the peculiar fitness of the one who had offered to go for us. "Shall we lose her," she asked, "because we have not the needed money in our hands? No, rather let us walk the streets of Boston in our calico robes, and save the expense of more costly apparel. Mrs. President, I move the appointment of Miss Thoburn as our missionary to India." Every heart responded Amen! and with united voice they said, "We will send her!"

On the following September Miss Clara Swain, M.D., was appointed medical missionary to India, and together these devoted women sailed as our pioneers—the first of the noble line which, as a strong and living cable, now binds the women of the East and West together in a bond which shall never be broken until the heathen shall be given to Christ for an inheritance, and the uttermost parts of the earth for his possession.

ISABELLA THOBURN.

MISS ISABELLA THOBURN has the distinguished honor of being the *first* representative of the Woman's Foreign Missionary Society of the Methodist Episcopal Church. Immediately after the announcement to the public of the organization of the new Society she offered herself as a candidate for work in India. Her appointment created great enthusiasm, and seemed to settle the pillars of the new structure more firmly on its foundations.

Miss Thoburn is a native of St. Clairsville, Ohio, and was blessed with the best of parents—Methodists from their youth up. Her brother, Rev. J. M. Thoburn, D.D., formerly a member of the Pittsburgh Conference, was appointed missionary to India in 1859. He is an earnest and indefatigable laborer in the cause of Christ, a most devoted missionary, whose labors have been crowned with great success. He has labored much among the natives, preaching to them in the vernacular tongue, and has also been very successful in the English work in Calcutta, where he has raised up a strong Church, and his ministry has been attended by multitudes. He was elected by the India Conference as their delegate to represent them in the General Conference held in Baltimore in 1876.

Her sister, Mrs. General Cowen, of Ohio, is Corresponding Secretary of the Cincinnati Branch of the Woman's Foreign Missionary Society, and is an elect lady of rare piety and culture.

. Miss Thoburn is liberally educated, being a graduate of Wheeling College, West Virginia. She also spent some time at the Academy of Design in Cincinnati, Ohio. After completing her education she taught for several years very successfully. She gave her heart to Christ and her hand to the Church early in life, and served God from principle rather than from impulse. Her conversion was not a sudden transformation from darkness to light. In her case the light shone as the morning; gradually, more and more unto the perfect day. From the time of her conversion she was deeply interested in missions, and, after her brother received his appointment to India, she looked toward that field with peculiar interest, and often longed to join him in his work—to have the glorious privilege of pointing the poor oppressed women of India to Christ.

When the Woman's Foreign Missionary Society of the Methodist Episcopal Church was organized she cheerfully laid on the altar of sacrifice all her literary and artistic pursuits and aspirations, and thankfully obeyed the call for missionaries, hailing it with joy, as an opportunity of fulfilling her long-cherished desire.

She sailed from New York, in company with Miss Swain, M.D., November 3, 1869, and arrived in India January, 1870. She entered at once upon her missionary work, and has now given ten years of continuous labor to the cause so dear to her heart.

Miss Thoburn is deservedly very popular in India. It is doubtful if any one sent out by our Society has rendered more efficient or valuable service, and none have succeeded in winning more effectually the hearts of the people, in all classes of society, who have come within the sphere of her influence. A missionary writes us: " Miss Thoburn's religious life is one of the most practical and symmetrical I ever knew. It has always seemed to me one of perfect obedience and of perfect faith. As an example of her way of doing I give the following incident: "When the renowned William Taylor was here in India, holding a series of meetings, he preached one evening on the subject of holiness, and announced that this would be his theme for the next morning's sermon, which would be followed by a prayer and consecration meeting. After we got to our room that evening Miss Thoburn said to me, ' What are you going to do about to-morrow morning's meeting? I see plainly what *my* duty will be—to follow all the new light given. I do not enjoy that blessing. I see I am not *entirely* consecrated, and if an opportunity is given, as there probably will be, to publicly avow my intention of seeking it, I shall have to take that step. If there is any thing in that experience that will make me a better Christian and more useful in the work, I want it.' She went forward for prayers the next morning, stated her position, said she intended to be henceforward, as never before, *all* the Lord's; that she expected him to be so to her, and to work in and through her as never before; and she has gone on steadfastly since that time, I believe, fulfilling, as far as it is possible for mortal to fulfill, the command, 'Walk before me, and be thou perfect.'"

The most important work done in the mission field by Miss Thoburn has probably been in connection with the Christian Girls' Boarding-School, in Lucknow, of which she has been superintendent. The first Annual Report of the India Branch of the Woman's Foreign Missionary Society, published in Lucknow, 1871, says: "This school was opened in April and continued until November, when it numbered twenty-five pupils. These were all from the city, except four, who were from out-stations, and boarded in the families of native Christians here. From knowing many native helpers and other Christians who have no opportunity to educate their daughters, a girls' boarding-school has been determined on for the coming year, something similar to the Amroha school, but of a higher grade. If we do any great and good work among the women of India we must show them the superiority of Christian womanhood, and we must have trained Christian women to work with us. The Orphanage has done much in preparing girls for usefulness, but it cannot reach all. Beyond its range is a field that must be occupied by boarding-schools, such as we depend upon for the education of girls at home. To meet this want we have organized the Lucknow Christian Girls' School."

This school has been steadily increasing in interest and numbers, and during the year 1879 one hundred and thirty-two names were enrolled. Though occupying a large share of her attention, Miss Thoburn's labors were not confined to this school alone. She was active in every good work connected with the mission field, and with a zeal which knew no abatement—a love for souls which no weariness could overcome, and a faith which would not shrink in the face of difficulties—she was continually reaching out into the regions beyond, and extending the field of her missionary operations. In addition to all her other work, she has organized several new schools, and superintended them until help could be sent from America. One of them is at Cawnpore, now managed by Miss Easton. From a private letter written by a missionary we make the following extract:

"I think there are but few Miss Thoburns living. I shall always be glad—glad through all eternity—that she was here when I came to India. What a record hers is! Captain Romaine, when describing General Holbrook standing on one side, and saying to the Indian chief, Joseph—pointing to General Miles—'There is the man you are to surrender to,' said, 'He is the one man in a thousand!' Isabella Thoburn is the one woman in a thousand. She began the Cawnpore school with nothing but her hands full of other work. She planned, she wrote letters, she did hard and distasteful work. For two years, in heat most intolerable, she made the weekly trips to and from Lucknow, and when the school gets, through her labors, a local habitation, a comfortable furnishing, and fifty pupils, she freely hands it over to another, and only hopes from her heart of hearts that the new superintendent may do more and better than she."

We close the sketch with the following extracts from a beautiful letter written by Mrs. Chandler, of Baltimore, who, with her husband, has just made the tour of the world—visiting our mission stations. It is full of interest, not only with regard to Miss Thoburn and her work, but as regards the general mission field, and must prove an inspiration to our home workers:

"What can I say to you of our dear Miss Thoburn which can in any wise convey to you all she is where she is? Going abroad, as we did, simply as tourists in search of health and pleasure, with no knowledge of the work of the Society, I did not know even the names of these noble women of ours. 'Home work' had been my rallying call for years, and amid the sin and shame and want and sorrow I found as I threaded the lanes and alleys of my city home, I turned a deaf ear to the cry coming across the sea. But conviction came to me at last. It forced itself upon me in China, with its millions of women bound hand and foot in chains of superstition and ignorance; in India, as I sat in zenanas and realized there the awfulness of the degradation of its women.

"But you wish me to speak of Miss Thoburn. Knowing her beautiful character, her *intense* shrinking from any thing which might shadow forth partiality or have a tinge of flattery, I find it difficult to moderate feeling into suitable words. But I shall write as I please about her work. There she is queen. On the evening of the 13th February Dr. and Mrs. Waugh drove me to the Memorial Garden, in Cawnpore, where the sod above English graves grows green, and where, under the pure white marble, a great company of Christian people, chiefly women and children, await the resurrection morning. From the cemetery we drove to the building, now our own property, in Cawnpore, and then under Miss Thoburn's charge, in connection with her school in Lucknow. With my mind filled with a vivid picture of that awful night of massacre—

'That waveless, sailless, shoreless sea of woe'

which engulfed and swallowed up so many of England's fairest daughters, I first saw Miss Thoburn. Her face is so peaceful; a sort of a benediction it was to me. Her presence is commanding. She is quiet in demeanor, but, I afterward found, quick to see, direct in decision, firm to act. The intense love that is poured out for her, and the deference paid her decisions by those with whom she is associated, prove her well-balanced mind and her superior judgment.

"Sitting there, the purpling shadows gathering, she pointed up the Ganges, directing my attention to an object swaying to and fro in the water. It was a human body, partially consumed at the burning *ghat* and then cast into the sacred river to find its heaven. 'Do you wonder,' she said, 'when from our very doors we look upon such things, our hearts' desire and prayer for them is, that they shall know and worship the true God?' Then, as we stood under the quivering peepul-trees and listened to the whispering leaves, she told me how the natives worshiped those trees, believing the constant motion, even when no breath of air seemed to be stirring, indicated the abode of the gods, who made those trees their home, and whose wives and children dwelt therein.

"The boarding-school was of wonderful interest to me. I think there were about sixty-five scholars. Some were young ladies and some were very small. They sang, 'Tell me the old, old story.' I thought how new it was to them, and how sweet to hear in that foreign tongue. There were bright faces there. Sunlight was in their hearts as they read the precious word, repeated texts of Scripture, and sang their glad song, *Esunam-u-de-poodo*—' The Name of Jesus.' Each class had its teacher, and was in its separate place. The lessons were progressing with as much regularity as in our best schools at home. It just made me cry to stand there in that land and hear these natives singing our songs, saying our prayers, and repeating our lessons. My heart sang its doxology of praise to God, from whom alone such blessings come.

"Then we went out for a walk, and there pressed upon us and followed after us the poor and maimed and leprous crowd, crying piteously, 'Backsheesh! mem Sahib, backsheesh!' Miss Thoburn said to us, 'I always realize more clearly as I walk these streets what our dear Lord meant when he said, "Give us *this* day our daily bread," for these poor wretches, many of them, have not one *pice* for tomorrow's bread.' And truly she appeared to me that day, with her pitying face, almost as an angel might who had left the music of heaven to dwell among wailing souls, sitting in the region and shadow of death.

"I expressed to her something of this thought in my mind, and asked her if she did not sometimes long for her own land of privilege? I shall never forget her look almost of reproach. She did not answer for awhile. We were out on an open elevation, and her eyes seemed to take in the whole sweep of the country, with its mosques and minarets, its shrines of pollution, and its people of degradation. With a kindling face she turned to me and said these words, 'Don't go home to excite sympathy for me. I am happy here in my work. I am busy here, and we all feel so. Our work lies here, and when sickness comes, and we turn our faces homeward, we leave our hearts behind.' O it is sublime—the lives and work of these women out there!

"In the evening there was a prayer and experience meeting in the Home, at which were the ministers and their wives, Revs. Cunningham, Craven, Mansell, Miss Blackmar, Miss Rowe, and others, whose names I have forgotten.

"O how precious it was, and how near seemed our God! I feared for Miss Thoburn's health. She was evidently overtaxing herself. If she could be prevailed upon to rest, it would be of great advantage to her and to us. Intellectually superior, morally heroic, of good *physique*, and splendid natural constitution, such a woman can seldom be replaced.

"I have never been the same woman since I trod those lands. Learning by sight what nations are without Christianity, and individuals without Christ, wakes one up to a responsibility of birth in a Christian land. Standing beside the banks of the Ganges, watching dying feet laved by its waves, while upon the brow, from which the light of life was fast fading, was its sacred mud, I made my vow of service to this woman's work for women.

"In bond of faith, in fellowship of labor,

"Yours, BELLE N. CHANDLER."

Clara A. Swain, M.D.

CLARA A. SWAIN, M.D.

THE Woman's Foreign Missionary Society of the Methodist Episcopal Church has the honor of sending the first medical lady who has ever gone as a missionary to the East, in the person of Miss Clara A. Swain.

This lady was born in Elmira, New York. She was converted and joined the Church at the early age of twelve years. Her conversion was marked by a clearness and a decision seldom seen in one so young, and this, with the intelligence, the maturity of thought which she evinced, led the Church to predict for her a life of rare excellence and usefulness. When only eight years of age she became impressed with the thought that some time in the future she would be called to carry the Bible to the heathen. This impression continued to follow her until she reached her twenty-fifth year. Then, as no way seemed to open for the accomplishment of this desire, she began to think perhaps she was mistaken, and strove to turn her attention in other directions.

Her education was received principally in Castile, New York. After this she was a student in Canandaigua Seminary. She then engaged as teacher in one of the public schools, in which she remained seven years. During her last term in this school she resolved to study medicine, and an opportunity was presented to her which she regarded as ordered of the Lord, and she immediately sent in her resignation to the school board, and accepted the situation offered. With an uncompromising faith in God, and a firm reliance upon her own energy and will, she pursued her four years' course, and graduated with high honors from the Woman's Medical College, in Philadelphia, in 1869. While completing her last college term the desire to engage in missionary work again filled her heart—her former impressions returned with such force that she was unable to shake them off. God, who was leading her, opened the way before her. His purposes concerning her began to unfold, and she was no sooner ready for the work, than the work was ready for her.

She was appointed medical missionary to India, and sailed with Miss Thoburn, November, 1869. After reaching that land she began her work in Bareilly. She was marvelously successful in winning the confidence and hearts of the people, from the lowest to the highest castes. Miss Swain was so intensely interested in her work, so self-sacrificing in her devotion to the suffering, and so ardent was her desire to open every possible door for the entrance of the word of life, that she toiled on incessantly, forgetting her own ease, and unobservant of the severe draft made upon her own energies, until her physical system was entirely prostrated by disease, and she was obliged to seek health and recuperation in her native land.*

* She has since returned to India.

She returned to America in 1876. While at home she lost no opportunity for advancing the interests of the cause; and when her physical strength would admit she attended and addressed large meetings, and, wherever she went, her presence, and her diffusion of missionary intelligence, proved an inspiration to the home work.

The account of her 'call to the foreign field, and her work in India, is so pleasantly told by herself in "Women of the Orient,"* that we give it, in part, to our readers.

"In a personal interview, Mrs. Sarah J. Hale, formerly President of the Ladies' Union Missionary Society, told me that more than twenty years ago she wrote an appeal to American Christian women in behalf of the Ladies' Medical Missionary Society, to aid in securing and educating women as medical missionaries. It had long been a cherished thought of Mrs. Hale's that a missionary lady with a knowledge of medicine might be able to enter the homes, and perhaps reach the hearts, of heathen women through the art of healing more effectually than in any other way. We are glad that this dear lady has lived to see her thought and plan for entering the Hindu zenana carried out, although not as generally as she could wish. In 1869, a few months before the Woman's Foreign Missionary Society of the Methodist Episcopal Church was organized, Mrs. Rev. D. W. Thomas, of Bareilly, India, wrote

* Taken from Rev. Ross C. Houghton's valuable book, entitled "Women of the Orient." Published by Walden & Stowe, Cincinnati.

to the Union Missionary Society of the Philadelphia Branch, requesting them to send out a medical lady for Bareilly, to instruct a class of native Christian girls, also to practice in the city as opportunity presented.

"In response to this call the ladies began at once to look for some suitable person who was willing to go. After three months of thought and prayer I accepted the call. I was a member of the graduating class of 1869 of the Woman's Medical College of Philadelphia. In the meantime, the ladies of the Methodist Episcopal Church organized a Foreign Missionary Society. As I was a member of that Church I preferred going out under the auspices of my own society. Upon application, the Ladies' Union very generously gave up all claim and granted my request. I sailed in company with Miss Thoburn, the first missionary appointed by the Woman's Foreign Missionary Society, November 3, 1869, and arrived in Bareilly, January 20, 1870.

"As I came out of my room the next morning after my arrival at Bareilly, I found a group of native Christian women and children sitting on the veranda, anxiously awaiting my appearance. I began my work at once among the women of the Christian village and in the families of the household servants living in the mission compound. Very soon it was noised abroad in the city and adjacent villages that a lady doctor had come from America and would go to visit any family that might desire her services, and any sick person coming to the mission-house would receive attention and medicine free. Accordingly, men, women, and children came.

"Not many weeks passed before I began to be called to attend patients in their homes. Within three months I attended the sick in fifteen different families in the city, five of which were high-caste families. Mrs. Thomas, or one of the native Christian women who understood English, always accompanied me and acted as interpreter.

"On March first I began teaching a class in medicine, consisting of fourteen girls from the Orphanage and three married women. In 1873, April 10, thirteen members of the class passed their final examination in the presence of two civil surgeons and Rev. Dr. Johnson, of our mission, who granted them certificates of practice in all ordinary diseases. Not long after these girls graduated they were all married except one, who proved to be a leper. She was sent to the Leper Asylum, in Almorah, in the Himalaya Mountains, under the charge of Rev. Mr. Buddan, of the London Mission. Lepers are much more comfortable in the mountain air than when subject to the heat of the plains. Most of the class married native ministers and teachers, who were sent out into the village to work. Their wives have had ample opportunity to use their medical knowledge. Some of them are doing a good work, while others make more intelligent women and mothers for having the advantage of medical knowledge.

"As my practice increased I found my room in the mission-house too small and inconvenient for our morning clinics, and the homes of the poor where I was called to attend the sick were so utterly destitute of comforts of any kind, that what little I could do for them seemed of very little use. I longed for a clean, comfortable place to offer them. Our need of a hospital each day grew more urgent, but just where we could purchase suitable grounds to build, and whether the Society could furnish the means necessary, were the two questions that needed first to be answered. The most convenient and suitable place for our buildings, and adjoining our mission premises, was owned by a Mohammedan prince. We had supposed that the purchase of this property was impossible. We were advised, however, to see if this could not be obtained, or at least land enough for our buildings. Through the advice of Mr. Drummond, Commissioner of Bareilly, Mr. Thomas decided to make personal inquiries of his Highness the Nawab, who lived in the city of Rampore, about forty miles from Bareilly. Through his highness' prime minister we gained permission to have an interview with the prince; also a promise to lay our *dak*, or, in other words, to make arrangements for our trip to Rampore, if we would notify him of the day we wished to go.

"Our party consisted of Mr. and Mrs. Thomas, myself, and a native Christian gentleman, who was formerly of the Mohammedan faith, and understood something of their royal etiquette. Informing the prime minister of the day we wished to go, he had every thing in readiness for us. Twenty-four horses, a grand old carriage, coachman, two grooms and outriders, were supposed to be necessary for these four humble people, who were to have their first experience with Eastern royalty. What a condescension for this king, who had made his boast that no Christian missionary dared enter the city of Rampore!

"We left home at five o'clock in the morning, changing horses every six miles. As we drew near, three cavalrymen came to escort us into the city. Passing through the gates, his highness' subjects made low salaams, and the children cried, 'Long life and prosperity!' We were driven through the main bazaar for about two miles to a house just outside the city, which is kept by his highness for the entertainment of European visitors and travelers. Here we found every thing necessary for our comfort. Breakfast was awaiting us, and servants stood ready to give us any assistance we might need. Mr. and Mrs. Parker, of Moradabad, who had been apprised of our intentions, were also awaiting us.

"His highness, on receiving the news of our arrival, sent his messenger to say he would not be able to see us until the next day, as he was especially engaged in his prayers. We were not sorry, as it gave us more time for rest and preparation for our anticipated interview. For our entertainment he sent two music boxes, which played very sweetly, and his trained men to perform for us. One man lifted a camel, another performed wonderful feats in rope-walking and climbing a pole. Then came a play—a burlesque upon English officials. They were well skilled in their profession, and not only showed their power of imitation, but their keen appreciation of the foibles and defects of others. To us it was not merely a source of amusement, but afforded us a valuable lesson. After dinner two fine carriages and horses were sent by his highness to take us for an evening drive.

"The next morning, early, the carriages were sent for us. We took our seats, and were first driven to several palaces and gardens, then came at last to the royal palace. As we entered the gate five royal elephants, beautifully caparisoned, made their salaams to us, by lifting their trunks and touching their foreheads in a very graceful manner. We were helped from the carriage and escorted into the presence of his highness. He arose and greeted us in a very friendly manner. His cordiality served to relieve our embarrassment as we took the seats which were assigned us and entered into a friendly conversation. After a few minutes the prime minister arose, advanced to his highness, and whispered something into his ear, to which he gave his assent. The prime minister then told Mr. Thomas to make his request known. Mr. Thomas said he wished to procure, upon some terms, the estate adjoining the mission premises belonging to him in Bareilly, for the purpose of establishing a hospital for women and children. Before Mr. Thomas had time to make a further statement, his highness said, 'Take it! take it! I give it with pleasure for such a purpose.' We were not aware that it is the custom of a Mohammedan prince never to sell any real estate which formerly belonged to his father's inheritance. If they consent to part with any of it, it is presented as a gift. Neither were we prepared for so generous a gift, and were not a little surprised when the announcement was made. We did take it with thankful hearts, not only to the Prince of Rampore, but to the great King of the universe, who, we believe, put it into his heart to give it to us.

"Our interview with the prince was short. Very soon after the matter of business was over he arose, bowed to us, and left the room. The prime minister then showed us some of the apartments of the palace, which were beautifully furnished and tastefully arranged. We were not invited into the women's apartments, much to our regret.

"Our gift contained forty acres of land and a house, well built but old, and needing some repairs to make it suitable to live in. This house the prince expected us to use as a hospital, but, owing to the style, we considered it unsuitable for native ladies, with their ideas of seclusion. So we decided to use it as a home for single missionary ladies and their attendants, and to build a hospital more on the plan of a native house. We began at once to repair the house, and had it ready to move into on January 3. A part of it was used for a dispensary, and a few rooms were reserved for patients whose caste would allow them to occupy a house with us, until we could put up more desirable buildings. A few native gentlemen, who were quite in favor of our efforts, promised to give us some assistance. Accordingly we drew up a paper, stating what we desired to do, asking for contributions, and circulated it among the native people. About seven hundred rupees (equal to $350) were subscribed. The estate was given to the mission, October 3, 1871. The dispensary building was finished May 10, 1873, and the hospital completed and ready for use, January 1, 1874. The expense of building, repairing the house already on the estate, making roads, setting out trees, etc., was $10,300. This was all furnished by the Woman's Foreign Missionary Society of the Methodist Episcopal Church, except the seven hundred rupees subscribed in India. The buildings are of brick, plastered inside and out, and whitewashed or tinted.

"Patients began to come to the hospital as soon as we could accommodate them; Hindus, Mohammedans, and native Christians, all having their own separate apartments. A patient seldom comes alone to stay in the hospital. If she is poor, she must bring her children, and, perhaps, her mother-in-law or widowed sister, who may be a member of her household. If the patient is of high caste, her husband and friends would consider it a disgrace for her to come alone. Often they not only bring their families and several servants, but a yoke of oxen, a horse and conveyance, a goat, their food, furniture, and cooking utensils. We are not always particular how many of the family come if they are willing to obey the rules necessary in such an institution, as we hope to do them good in a social and friendly way. They are no expense to us for food.

"The work of 1875, my last year in India, was more satisfactory to me than any year previous.

Possibly we had a more hopeful class of patients, and were able to do them more good. At one time, during the rainy season, the hospital was occupied by an American missionary lady and her children, Eurasian and Bengalee women, Hindus, Mohammedans, and native Christians, all with their own peculiar customs. With all these different people and castes there was never any trouble among the women and their servants, that I knew of. Twice a week as many of the patients and their families as were able assembled in one room for a prayer-meeting and religious conversation. These gatherings were often very interesting and profitable. Some of the women learned to read while they were with us; others, who were unable to learn, were always ready to listen to the reading of the Scriptures or to any other religious book.

"Sometimes the young women meet with great opposition from their mothers-in-law when they attempt to learn, or are in the least inclined to adopt any thing new. There are many difficulties to be overcome in all departments of our work, as there naturally would be among a people who have followed in the footsteps of their ancestors for two thousand years, without improvement either in art or science. There are years of hard preparatory work to be done in the homes of India before there will be any great change in the religious sentiment of the people. And this work must be done mainly through the agency of Christian women."

FIRST MEETING OF THE GENERAL EXECUTIVE COMMITTEE.

THE first annual meeting of the General Executive Committee was held at the residence of Mrs. Thomas Rich, Boston, April 20, 1870.

Previous to this, in order to make the Society more efficient in its operations, it was thought best to divide it into districts, similar to the missionary districts of the parent Society, each district to be represented by a branch Society. Accordingly these branches were organized in the following order: Philadelphia, March 3, 1870; New England and New York, March 10; North-western, March 17; Western, April 4; and Cincinnati, April 6.

The Executive Committee consisted of delegates from the six branches then organized, with the exception of Cincinnati, which was represented by Mrs. Parker.

In December, prior to this, a new Constitution, on an enlarged plan, arranging for these Branch Societies, was drafted and submitted to the Board of Managers of the Missionary Society, for their approval and sanction. The Board had previously referred the whole matter of ladies' missionary societies to a committee, who, on receiving the revised Constitution, recommended its sanction by the Board, which was freely given.

At this meeting of the Executive Committee Mrs. Dr. William F. Warren was appointed Editor of the "Heathen Woman's Friend," with a corps of editorial contributors. It is an encouraging fact that whenever a person has been needed to take charge of important trusts, vital to the interests of the Society, Providence has indicated the individual, and the position has been filled by the one prepared to bring the highest honor to God and his cause. The "Heathen Woman's Friend" is a power for good at home and abroad. By its general diffusion of intelligence, fresh from the foreign fields, it creates missionary enthusiasm wherever it goes. It is chaste, vigorous, and progressive. It takes the front rank as a missionary paper, and is appreciated and commended by the highest officials in our Church. In four years from the time the first number was issued it had reached a circulation of twenty-five thousand seven hundred. To Mrs. L. H. Daggett, the publishing agent, much credit is due for her superior business tact, and indefatigable zeal in superintending the financial interests of the paper.

The support of the Bareilly Orphanage, heretofore in charge of the parent Society, was now assumed by the ladies, and an appropriation of $3,000 made for that purpose. Miss Fannie J. Sparkes was accepted as a missionary candidate, to sail the next October for India, to engage in Orphanage work; and the following year she took charge of the institution. Steps were also taken with regard to extending our work into China and Bulgaria.

The first anniversary of the Woman's Foreign

Missionary Society of the Methodist Episcopal Church was held in Tremont-street Church, Boston, April 21. Mrs. William B. Skidmore read the Scriptures and offered prayer. The various Branches were then represented by the Corresponding Secretaries, after which addresses were delivered by Mrs. Dr. Maclay, of our China Mission, and Mrs. J. T. Gracey, of India. The meeting was one of great interest; and, encouraged by the reports of the year's work, the ladies went forth with renewed confidence and zeal to the labors of the coming year.

LINES TO MISS FANNIE J. SPARKES, MISSIONARY TO INDIA.

BY REV. W. W. RUNYON.

So fare thee well. We here thy voice no more;
   On rolling billows now thy bark is tossed.
The Master bids thee to far India's shore,
   There, like himself, to seek and save the lost.

Be thou, great King, her pilot o'er the flood;
   Propitious gales, breath on her from above;
Lead, angels, to the land of night and blood
   Your peer and sister, exile of her love:—

A darksome land in yon bright orient,
   Where hearts grow chill beneath the fervid skies;
Where human knees to stocks and stones are bent,
   And mighty gods from dust and slime arise!

In those rank jungles error builds her lair,
   Whose bleeding victims stumble, grope, and die.
Might Sinai's thunder shake the slumbrous air!
   Might millions wake to Calvary's mournful cry!

How long, O Lord, how long shall Buddh and Brahm
   Compel the incense of infernal fires?
Bid Sharon's rose, and Gilead's healing balm,
   Spring, phœnix-like, from out those smold'ring pyres.

Fly, angel of the glorious Gospel, fly!
   We shout, God speed you on your shining way,
Teach your fair hands to lift the cross on high,
   And pluck from fate's foul fangs the trembling prey.

O lady, prodigal of strength and ease,
   May India's sun pour benedictions down,
And those parched sands, beyond the pagan seas,
   Yield jewels bright to deck thy fadeless crown!

Thy virgin soul would give a nation birth;
   Thy glowing lips shall echo mercy's cry;
A myriad prayers escort thee round the earth,
   And myriad welcomes wait thee in the sky.

FANNIE J. SPARKES.

FANNIE J. SPARKES was the third person who responded to the call of the Woman's Foreign Missionary Society of the Methodist Episcopal Church. She went out the year following its organization, and was the first representative of the New York Branch. She was born near the city of Binghamton, New York, in the year 1844, and all the circumstances of her early life tended to mature and prepare her for her destined work.

Her father is an honored member of the Presbyterian Church in the city of Binghamton—a man of unblemished character and strict integrity, having the greatest reverence for God and unwavering faith in his word. He has devoted much of his time to Bible literature, and is the author of "Sparkes' Historical Commentary on the Eleventh Chapter of Daniel," and other works. Possessing great mental vigor, and having a clear insight to the spirit and tendencies of the times, he is always on the alert, watching the changes in the nations and calculating their influence upon the progress and destiny of the Church of Christ, which, with him, is the all-important element in the history of the race. At nearly seventy years of age, after a life of unceasing industry, he is calmly awaiting the summons of his Lord.

Fannie J. Sparkes.

Her mother is also possessed of rare intelligence, heroic faith, and indefatigable zeal in the cause of Christ. Her love for her children is only surpassed by her supreme love to God, to whom she consecrated them in their early infancy.

Surrounded with such influences, it is not surprising that Miss Sparkes early developed traits of character which, to those who knew her most intimately, seemed to promise a life of honor and usefulness. Patient, courageous, steady of purpose, untiring in effort, cheerful and buoyant in spirit, self-forgetting, yet always self-possessed, she found her greatest joy in blessing others, and her life was a verification of the sentiment

> "All worldly joys go less
> To the one joy of doing kindnesses."

Her early education was received in the schools of her native city, and she afterward pursued her studies with private teachers, receiving from them instruction in languages, music, drawing, and other accomplishments. At a very early age she commenced teaching, and for several years before going to India was principal of one of the largest graded schools in the city. She early evinced great thirst for knowledge, and gave evidence of an intellect of a superior order. While teaching others she was also striving, by every means possible, to perfect her own education; and, with an energy and zeal seldom known, she devoted every spare moment to the acquisition of knowledge, particularly the study of the languages. For this she seemed to have a natural aptitude, and she received marked commendation from her teacher, who said, when she afterward received her appointment to India, " She will acquire the languages of the Orient without difficulty."

Of her religious experience she says: " I cannot remember the time when I was not in the habit of occasionally, at least, going alone for prayer, even when I did not really desire to love God; but I could never bring myself to speak of these things to any one. When about eleven years of age, during a revival in the old Henry-street Church, Binghamton, New York, I became so deeply convicted for sin that for several nights I could not sleep. All that kept me from yielding to my convictions was the fear that because I was so young some might think I did not understand what I was doing, and started merely because others did. When I did finally decide to seek salvation I commenced the work most earnestly, and gave myself to Christ the best I knew how. I sought for weeks, but did not receive the assurance of my acceptance that I desired. I did not understand the simple way of faith. I had an erroneous though vague idea of the witness of the Spirit, and was looking for some wonderful instantaneous change to be wrought in my heart; and although I felt that I loved the Saviour and desired above every thing else to please him, I dared not say I was really a Christian. Soon after this I united with the Church, in accordance with the advice of my parents, pastor, and class-leader."

During the years that followed she was regarded by the Church as one of her most useful and exemplary members. She was faithful in her attendance upon the prayer and class-meetings, active in the Sabbath-school and all Church work, so much so, that when the call came for her to go to India the step was strongly opposed by many of her friends, who said she was doing as much and effective work here as she possibly could in a foreign field.

"Notwithstanding," she says, "I scarcely ever had the courage to profess myself a Christian unqualifiedly, because I could not tell just the time of my conversion. This was always a source of great temptation to me."

In the year 1869 she attended a camp-meeting at Spencer, New York. Here, after many struggles and heart-searchings, she entered into the sweet rest of faith, and received the clear witness of her acceptance with God. Before this she writes of having enjoyed communion with Christ, and of having received many remarkable answers to prayer. But now her joy was not interrupted by doubts and fears. Her peace was constant. She says: "I felt so thankful for *rest* after so many years of struggling that I thought it pleasure to do *any thing* for Christ. One evening, while engaged in secret prayer, the question was suggested, 'Will you go to India, alone, as a missionary for Jesus?' Then followed intense anxiety.

"The question I had to settle that evening was, If God calls me to India, can I refuse to go and still be his child? As a child I had for years cherished the hope of some day being permitted to carry the Gospel to heathen shores, but had long since given up the idea of ever being counted worthy: and now I found my heart so interested in other things, the sacrifice seemed greater than I could make. I struggled, yea, almost agonized in prayer, until three o'clock in the morning, pleading with God that he would not require this of me. The cry of my soul was, 'If it be possible, let this cup pass from me,' and I tried to say, 'Nevertheless, not *my* will but THINE be done.' Finally I was enabled to fully surrender myself to God for this work, if needed."

Soon after this, in a conversation with the late Rev. C. W. Judd, (returned missionary,) he told her he had been praying to God to direct him to some young lady for India, and he believed God was calling her to that work. This, in connection with the same opinion expressed by her pastor and presiding elder, Rev. H. R. Clarke, of Wyoming Conference, asking her to prayerfully consider the matter, and a letter from the Corresponding Secretary of the New York Branch, asking her to offer herself for India, led her to believe that God himself was opening the way.

"The *real* call I can never tell to any one; it was the voice of God speaking tenderly, yet commandingly, oft times and in oft-repeated tones to my inmost soul, and with such conviction and assurance as left no room for doubt or hesitation. I knew with all the certainty that I *then* knew I was his child, that God was leading me, and I dared not refuse to follow."

One thing that made the trial more severe was the fact that her parents, who loved her tenderly, and to whom she clung with all the affection of her young heart, could not feel that it was her duty to go. It was so early in the history of the Society, and Fannie was the first to go *alone*, (without any o her single lady as companion.) They feared she was not physically strong enough for such an undertaking, and they regarded it as mistaken zeal. To them it was a terrible sacrifice, and they parted with her never expecting to see her again in this life.

Referring to this, she says: "You know something of the trying circumstances under which I went, and that neither of my dear parents, notwithstanding they were most devoted Christians, could believe it my duty to go to India alone. I could never speak, not even to you, of the experiences of those days; they were to me days of most intense suffering, yet God enabled me, in a wonderful manner, to keep outwardly calm and cheerful. I knew my suffering, keen as it was, was less than that of my friends; for it is easier to go to a field of strife than see a loved one go; but the hardest part of my trial was, that I was causing those I so loved such sorrow, and yet I could not do otherwise. At times my whole soul went out to God in an agonized cry that he would suffer me to stay, at least until my friends consented to my going. I tried to believe that if *God* opened the way these obstacles would be removed; but the answer was always the same, 'This is *my* call; leave all and follow me.' God also gave me the assurance, in answer to prayer, that if I would obediently commit all into his care I should live to know that my parents both thought I was in the path of duty and would rejoice with me in all the way in which God had led me. That promise has been verified, as has been many others given me at that time."

A farewell meeting of great interest was held in St. Paul's Church, Newark, N. J. It was called by Mrs. Dr. Crane, wife of Rev. J. T. Crane, D.D., and niece of Bishop Peck, and was one of the most remarkable meetings ever held in the interests of the Society. Upward of two thousand persons were in attendance; hundreds left, unable to gain admittance.

September 20, 1870, a similar meeting was held in St. Paul's Church, New York.

Mrs. Dr. Butler gave a thrilling account of the death of Miss Boist, the first Methodist martyr in India, and of her burial under the rose-trees in her garden. The appeal in behalf of the women of India was emphasized by the presence of a Hindoostanee woman, who came to this country as nurse to the lamented Mrs. Waugh's children, and who was about to return to her native land. She was dressed for the occasion in the silks and ornaments of a high caste Hindoo lady, and her dusky brow was bent and her dark eyes cast down as she was introduced to the congregation. Mrs. Butler asked for her the earnest prayers of all present, that she might find the light she was seeking.

Miss Sparkes made a few remarks, and, as she was about to take her seat, Mrs. Dr. Olin, who presided at the meeting, presented her a basket of flowers given by the ladies of St. Paul's Church, saying that the perfume of the flowers would soon pass away, but the fragrance of their good wishes would be wafted over the ocean to her Indian home, and the incense of their prayers would continually ascend in her behalf.

Many friends were at the steamer the next day to bid good-bye to the departing missionaries. Dr. Durbin was there, and Mrs. Doremus, the President of the Union Woman's Missionary Society, and many others who have since gone up to join the ranks of the redeemed in heaven.

The group was a striking one as the vessel slowly left her moorings. Leaning against the rigging, the central figure was the Hindoostanee women, of low stature, with her dark face well set off in the frame of her white veil. Behind her stood Mr. M'Mahon, and on either side Mrs. M'Mahon and Miss Sparkes. At a little distance stood Mr. and Mrs. Parker and Mr. Buck; and so the good ship passed out of sight, amid tearful eyes and the waving of white tokens and the ascending of invisible prayers.

After a pleasant voyage she reached India, and stopped for a short time in Bombay, awaiting the coming Conference, which was to convene in January, 1871. Of her first impressions she writes: "I remember how great the difference seemed to me between heathenism and Christianity when I first reached India.

"I shall never forget our first landing at Bombay,

and the great moving mass about us. The streets seemed literally full of life; not the beauty and activity we usually associate with that word here, it was simply human motion, living misery, wretchedness, shamelessness, *darkness.*

"The city was as beautiful as magnificent buildings and wealth of foliage and flowers could make it, but the sights seen there were so different from those witnessed in Christian lands. Just at sunset I rode out in company with Mrs. Harding, of the American Board of Missions. When we had gone about half a mile out of the city we saw on our right hand the Mohammedan burial-ground; it was full of gay fantastically-shaped tombs, around which incense-lights were burning, and worshipers were bowing, offering sacrifices and prayers. Just across, on the left, lay the Hindu burning *ghat,* and from the smoke and flames arising from numerous funeral pyres we knew the bodies of the dead were burning; we had other reasons, too, for knowing it, for we were near enough to see with our own eyes the smoldering bodies, and to hear the prayers chanted by the nearest relatives, as they sat feeding the flames. Just above us, at the right, stretched the Malabar Hills, and we could plainly see on one of them what is called the Silent Tower, or great rocks, on which the Parsees leave their dead uncovered and uncared for. Round about us, on every side, were Parsees bowing in worship of the setting sun, (for they are fire-worshipers,) Mohammedans prostrating themselves with their faces toward their pilgrim city, Mecca, and Hindus crowding and pushing each other in their eager haste to reach their heathen temples at the ringing of the bell. The people seemed so far away from God, I wondered how they could be brought nigh. It seemed to me the little light a few Christians could hope to shed amid such great darkness, would be as a drop of water cast into the mighty ocean. I knew that the little light, like the oil which would not mix with the water, but, borne along on the waves, became lost in them, would remain clear and steadfast, but I feared it would be hardly perceptible amid the great darkness, and, for a little while, I thought we may as well go home, until I remembered the promise, 'I shall give thee the heathen for thine inheritance, and the uttermost parts of the earth for thy possession,' and the blessed words, 'Fear not, I will help thee.'

"As we returned the bell was just ringing for evening devotions. The servants and members of the mission-school near took their places with the members of the family, and listened attentively while a portion of God's word was read and a fervent prayer offered, and all the time voices of praise came floating in through the open windows from the homes of the native Christians living near, and I thought, already the promise is beginning to be verified.

"In the morning, which was Sabbath, we were permitted to worship with the company of native Christians assembled in the chapel near by. It was only a handful, you would think, but I thought I could realize something of the terrible darkness from which they had been brought into God's marvelous light; and as they sang in their own language to our familiar tune,

> 'The morning light is breaking,
> The darkness disappears;'

our hearts echoed the sentiment, and we felt strong and eager for the work."

At the Conference Miss Sparkes received her appointment to the Girls' Orphanage, in Bareilly, as teacher, Rev. Mr. Thomas being at the time superintendent. The following year she was herself appointed superintendent of that institution.

Rev. C. W. Judd says of Miss Sparkes: "From her first entering upon the foreign work, particularly the charge of the Girls' Orphanage, in Bareilly, she has shown that she was eminently qualified for that work, even more so than we expected; for she not only took charge of the educational department, but of the financial also, which included the purchase and preparation of food and clothing for nearly two hundred girls, besides the general superintendence of the buildings and grounds of the institution. Sister Fannie managed all this greatly to our satisfaction and the success of the Orphanage. An evidence of this is seen in the fact that she was appointed to the same work on her return to India the second time, after an absence of nearly two years. I might say much in commendation of her marked devotion to the mission, and her unselfishness in always taking upon herself the most difficult and unpleasant part of any work in which others were engaged with her, but I will only add that she has shown herself to be a true, devoted, unselfish worker in the foreign field."

At the close of an anniversary address, delivered before the Central Pennsylvania Conference, in Williamsport, the late Rev. J. D. Brown, returned missionary, arose and begged leave to make a few remarks. He said, "Miss Sparkes has been spoken of as having charge of the Orphanage, in Bareilly, but that does not half express it. 'I want to say that she is doing a grand and glorious work there; and is one of the most successful and effective missionaries in the field. She is doing the work of a male missionary, filling the place before occupied by the Rev. Mr. Thomas and Rev. Mr. Judd, and has been saving to the parent Society yearly $1,200 and a parsonage." He paid a tender and beautiful tribute to the noble and self-sacrificing women in India, who were laboring so devotedly for the redemption of their heathen sisters, and closed by commending the Society to the sympathy and support of the entire Church.

At the close of the year 1875 Mrs. Skidmore, Corresponding Secretary of the New York Branch, records, "Miss Sparkes has given five years of constant labor to the Girls' Orphanage in Bareilly. Reports of her work, together with letters received by patrons from the orphans, sixty in number, supported by this Branch, give satisfactory evidence that Miss Sparkes' ability in this department is unsurpassed."

As a consequence of this severe tax upon her body and mind she felt greatly the need of a change, and sought it by a journey, in the spring of 1874, to Paori, a little place in the heart of the Himalayas, and the extreme limit of the Conference appointments. She was accompanied by Miss Blackmar, who joined her at Moradabad, a distance of seventy miles from Bareilly. The long and difficult journey in conveyances peculiar to the country is graphically described by Miss Sparkes in one of her letters to the "Heathen Woman's Friend," published November, 1874. After a short sojourn in Paori she returned to her work in Bareilly, and continued at the Orphanage for nearly three years longer. But she became so worn with her labors and the debilitating effect of the climate, that she was obliged to seek absolute rest and change in her own native land. She sailed from Bombay, February 1, 1877, in company with Miss Pultz, who also had done faithful service in India for nearly five years, and was returning in quest of health, leaving the Orphanage in charge of Miss Cary.

Arriving at her home in Binghamton, after the first greetings her father said, " Let us all sing, ' Praise God, from whom all blessings flow.' " Rev. H. Wheeler, her brother-in-law, commenced singing, and the whole family joined with glad hearts and moist eyes in singing this doxology of praise. She was most enthusiastically greeted by the Church and Sabbath-school. The following Sabbath the church was beautifully decorated with evergreens and flowers. In the rear of the desk were the words WELCOME HOME! in illuminated letters. "All hail the power of Jesus' name" was sung, the Twenty-third Psalm was read, after which the school sang "Come, let us be joyful to-day." Addresses were made by the clergy and Sabbath-school superintendents. Miss Sparkes spoke briefly, and closed by repeating the Lord's Prayer in Hindoostanee.

While at home she exerted a wide-spread influence upon the home-workers and Societies, sparing neither time nor labor in answering the numerous calls that came for addresses in the interest of the Society. She was fresh from the field where she had been laboring for seven years, and could speak from personal experience and observation.

A friend of the Society writes: " Miss Sparkes is a lady of fine presence and rare culture. She went from city to city, from camp-meeting to camp-meeting, from Conference to Conference, and by her earnest and eloquent appeals awakened intense interest in the work of the Society, and was the means of obtaining a large increase in its cash receipts. She has created and established a bond of union and interest between the Church at home and the Church in India which can never be broken, and which will be fruitful of earnest prayer for her safety and success. It is probable that the eighteen months spent at home was as fruitful of good as the same time could have been in India."

At the anniversary of the Round Lake Auxiliary, held August 2, 1878, Miss Sparkes spoke. The Holy Spirit was present in a wonderful manner. At the close of the addresses a lady sent up a note pledging herself to pay $600 the next year for Miss

Sparkes' salary. A traveling drinking-cup was sent up with a note saying it was from a poor man who wanted to do something for the cause, but had no money. The cup was sold to the highest bidder, the money put into the treasury, and the cup given to Miss Sparkes. The tide of enthusiasm rose high, and in all about $1,050 was received as the result of the meeting.

Miss Sparkes addressed more than one hundred missionary meetings during the last year spent at home, and four public meetings in her own church, on which occasions the church was densely crowded, and hundreds went away for want of room. It is only just to add that this part of missionary work was entirely unexpected to her; and when first asked to represent the cause in a public meeting her whole soul shrank from it, and it was only after many prayers and heart struggles, and a strong conviction of duty, that she yielded to the wishes of the home-workers, regarding the call of the Church as the voice of God.

After spending about a year and a half in America, and regaining in some measure her health and strength, she resolved to return to her chosen field of labor.

A farewell meeting of great interest was held in her native city. The last meeting in which Miss Sparkes participated was in Central Church, New York, November 7, 1878, just before sailing. After addresses by Bishop Andrews and others, Dr. J. P. Newman, pastor of the Church, arose and said: " On the banks of the Susquehanna is a quiet Christian home, where competency waits on honest industry, where the Bible spreads its banquet of wisdom and love, and where prayer bears on high the desires and gratitude of the heart. Within that tranquil home is a venerable father, of sturdy piety and heroic faith, whose robust intellect and large culture, whose familiarity with the sacred prophecies and acquaintance with great authors, dead and living, have enabled him to give to the Church and the world a rare book on the 'Origin and Fall of the Turkish Empire,' as foretold in the eleventh chapter of Daniel and in the other parts of the prophetical Scriptures, and which book should be in the hand of every pastor in the land who desires light on the Eastern question, which now occupies so much of public attention. And within the sanctities of that dear home is a Christian mother, intelligent, restful, and devout, who has reared her sons and daughters for God and his Church, and who has taught them to add new charms to the family circle by their mutual and reciprocal love. That home is a typical Church—it is a type of heaven.

"Forth from that home on the banks of the flowing river comes one who is among the brightest and best of the sisterhood of the Church; whose beautiful character, cultured mind, and devout spirit would make her a delight in the highest circles of society; whose love for Christ and for those ready to perish is stronger than life itself. On the part of her revered parents Fannie J. Sparkes is their immense sacrifice placed on the missionary altar: but on her own part she is a free-will offering to the Lord. In the presence of such a sublime fact let us never mention our missionary gifts as sacrifices. When compared to it they are as nothing. It was my happiness, in the winter of 1874, to visit Bareilly, where I found Miss Sparkes surrounded with one hundred Hindu girls, whose young womanhood had been consecrated to Christ. To those who pray for her speedy return she goes with a dry eye and a glad heart. On Saturday next she sails for her home in India; but ere she leaves us she will speak a few words to cheer our hearts. It is my great pleasure to present to you Miss Fannie J. Sparkes."

In fitting words she took her farewell of the audience. " Saying good-bye is not all sacrifice," she said. " There is so much of joy in the thought of carrying the light of life to heathen women, that had I a thousand lives I would gladly lay them all upon the altar of this service."

Miss Sparkes reached India about the 1st of January, in time for the Conference, and was reappointed to superintend the Orphanage in Bareilly. We leave her to pursue her work under the guidance of that Providence that has been her protection amid the dangers of sea and land, and with the divine promise as her best heritage, " Lo, I am with you alway."

SECOND ANNUAL MEETING OF THE GENERAL EXECUTIVE COMMITTEE.

THE Second Meeting of the General Executive Committee was held in Chicago, May 16, 1871. Delegates from the six Branches were in attendance. Reports showed that the interest and zeal of the ladies were unabated, and the work was enlarging and spreading itself out in all directions.

The Ladies' China Missionary Society, of Baltimore, which had been in the same kind of work for twenty-three years, at their anniversary, March 6, 1871, passed a resolution of co-operation with the new Society, and on the 10th of the same month organized the Baltimore Branch. During this meeting of the Committee they were taken into the Society, with their assets, "comprising the support of the Boarding-school at Foochow, and of the Misses Woolston, who had been teachers therein for twelve years."

Misses Mary Q. Porter and Maria Brown were also appointed missionaries to Peking, China; and Misses Carrie M'Millan and Jennie Tinsley were appointed missionaries to India.

BEULAH AND SARAH H. WOOLSTON.

HIGH up on the shining list of brave and consecrated spirits, who cheerfully laid on the altar of Christ their youth, culture, and talents, willingly sacrificing ease, comfort, health, country, friends, and all, for the sake of rescuing those who were ready to perish, are the names of Beulah and Sarah H. Woolston.

In the year 1858 the Missionary Society of the Methodist Episcopal Church, taking into consideration the importance of reaching and educating the female population of China, in order to establish the principles of Christianity among its inhabitants, sent the two sisters Woolston to labor among the women and children of that land.

Their home was in Trenton, New Jersey. They were well educated, being graduates of the Wesleyan College, Wilmington, Delaware. "For several years these sisters had cherished a strong desire to work for Christ in a foreign field, but when they announced themselves ready to respond to the call from China, their friends were astonished, and no wonder. China was farther removed from us then than it is to-day. There was no Pacific railroad to reduce the months of sea voyage to only a few days; no telegraph to cheer the exiled ones with messages from their native land. And here were two young ladies exchanging cultivated society and bright prospects in a Christian land for pioneer work in a land of which but little was known, and that little enshrouded in uncertainty.

"They went in the dewy morn of youth—the 'time of promise, hope and innocence, of trust and love'—when their hearts were glowing with vital ardor, and when the joys of earth seemed most inviting; but they cheerfully relinquished every fond ambition, every dream of worldly ease or pleasure, and went forth to proclaim the tidings of salvation to the benighted women of China."

We remember how the Church at home was thrilled at the announcement of their appointment, and how she sang,

> "March on! brave youths, the field of strife
>   With peril fraught before you lies;
> March on! the battle-plain of life
>   Shall yield you yet a glorious prize.
> Unfurl your banner to the breeze,
>   Emblazon truth on every fold,
> And, nobly shunning selfish ease,
>   Tread down the wrong, the right uphold."

Miss Isabel Hart, Corresponding Secretary of the Baltimore Branch of our Society, says in a private letter: "Probably no two persons ever shrank more from publicity or observation, but 'their works praise them in the gates.' Let them eat of the fruit of their hands. We must remember they were the pioneers in the work when it was a most unpromising experiment—when a passage to China meant several months in a sailing vessel, when transit and tidings were not easy and rapid as now, when they were not sustained by the organized efforts and overflowing sympathy of more than fifty thousand women. Plain, practical, quiet women—all honor to them! They remind me of what Charles Dickens said of some one doing all the good he could and making no fuss about it. Faithfulness, persistency, practicalness, I should regard their essential traits. They have stood at their post to this day, and never dream of deserting it. It is their life-work, calmly and soberly undertaken. They do not seem impatient of results, but do their duty and trust in God. They have learned to labor and to wait."

These ladies sailed from New York, October 14, 1858. There were on board of the same vessel other missionaries: Rev. S. L. Baldwin and wife, and Miss Phebe Potter, who were also going out to re-enforce this mission. The reader will pardon us if we stop to pay a passing tribute to one of the passengers on that voyage—the beautiful, the cultured, the gifted Nellie Gorham Baldwin, a personal friend of the writer. We stood by her side as she gave her last testimony for Christ in her native land. She said, "I do not regret the step I have taken. I go cheerfully, fully determined to do all the good I can, believing that God will go with me, and that the prayers of these dear Christian friends will follow me across the waters to my far-away home." The last time the entire family knelt around the altar was a season of painful interest; rising from her knees, she seated herself at the piano and played

"The Missionary's Farewell." With a clear voice she sung,

> "Yes, my native land, I love thee!
> All thy scenes I love them well;
> Friends, connections, happy country,
> Can I bid you all farewell?
> Can I leave you,
> Far in heathen lands to dwell?"

When she finished the hymn her eyes alone were tearless. She was then but nineteen years of age. Her missionary life was short, but eventful. She reached China, acquired the language, entered upon her duties as a missionary, but the debilitating effects of the climate, together with her arduous missionary labors and the care of an infant daughter, began to wear upon her constitution. Her health failed. Physicians advised her to return home. She, hoping to regain her health, and anxious to continue her missionary labors, desired to remain longer. At length she sailed with her husband for America, and died at sea, March 16, 1861, on board the ship Nabob, when four days out from New York. Her remains were interred in the beautiful cemetery in Binghamton, New York, near where our own loved ones lie sleeping. The shadow of her monument falls daily upon the graves of our own precious children, and as we visit the spot, and read upon the tomb-stone, "Nellie; died at sea, aged 21 years," and underneath, the simple but beautiful inscription, "She hath done what she could," we think, when our life's labor is ended, we would sooner have this truthfully inscribed on our tomb than the most eloquent eulogy that earth could pronounce.

The Misses Woolston arrived in Foochow March 16, 1859, having had a sea-voyage, by sailing vessel, of one hundred and forty-eight days. It was during this year that the "Baltimore Female Academy" was founded, and it was given into their charge. In a week or two after their arrival they had engaged a teacher and begun study; also a cook, and commenced housekeeping, using only the Chinese language in communicating with either. In the fall of 1859 temporary quarters were secured for their boarding-school.

One year later they report fifteen girls as having entered the school, only eight of whom remained—the oldest thirteen, the youngest eight years old—all of them obedient, and quite contented to be away from their homes. Two of these eight, on first entering the school, were exceedingly careless and stupid, but have greatly improved. Five of the girls are from heathen homes.

October, 1861, the report says: "During the year we have made many efforts to induce the Chinese to place their girls in school, but with little success beyond promises for the future. Since January two who have been with us from the beginning have been taken home. One was stolen away by her mother, who wished to bind her feet; the other was taken under pretense of making a visit. Her parents, after numberless excuses to continue her stay at home, said she should not return, because she would be instructed in the Christian doctrine, and would then refuse to marry the one to whom she was betrothed."

In 1862 fifteen girls are reported as diligent, obedient, and truthful. " Most of the larger ones understand that the object for which they are admitted into the school is, that they may become acquainted with Christianity, and on their return to their homes will be expected to teach the same, as far as practicable, to their people. They already realize that there is great power in prayer, and some of them have the habit of frequently retiring for private devotions. The first scholar baptized is Hü Süng Eng. She was received into the Church March 9, 1862, since which time she has maintained an exemplary Christian deportment, and her influence over the other girls is most salutary. The school seems to be slowly gaining the confidence of the Chinese, and we hope to obtain in a few years as many pupils as we can take charge of."

1866, report says : " The term closed with twenty-seven pupils ; eight are members of the Church. During the year two—having completed a term of five years — returned to their homes. Both are members of the Church, but have gone back to heathen homes, where they expect to receive no encouragement in their Christian life, but, instead, opposition, and probably persecution."

1867, report says : " At the close of the term the number of pupils was twenty-eight. During the year four were dismissed. Two, having finished their term of years, returned home. The school is almost daily visited by Chinese women and children. They frequently come in companies of eight or ten ; occasionally in crowds of twenty or thirty. They are pleased to receive portions of Scripture, and are attentive to the reading of chapters from the Gospels and other books. On leaving, they are invited to come again and bring their friends with them, which many of them do."

Though at first meeting with opposition on every hand, the ideas and customs of the people being utterly opposed to the education of women, they toiled on heroically, energetically, until, with the blessing of God, their school was at last established on a permanent basis.

Of those who have already graduated from this school some are the wives of native preachers, others are married into heathen households, where their influence may be exerted for good, others are teaching day-schools. All are spreading the gospel news far and wide.

March 4, 1869, after ten years of patient and persevering toil, the Misses Woolston returned to the United States to recruit health, leaving Mrs. Sites in charge of the school, numbering thirty-three girls.

In December, 1871, after nearly three years' absence, they returned and resumed charge of the school, now under the auspices of the Woman's Foreign Missionary Society. They were at this time transferred from the parent Society to ours.

The Misses Woolston have been among our most faithful and efficient missionaries, laboring on unremittingly to the close of the first decade of the Society; when, feeling the need of rest and a change of climate, they returned again to America, November 25, 1879.

MARY Q. PORTER.

THE first missionary sent out by the Western Branch of the Woman's Foreign Missionary Society was Miss Mary Q. Porter. The Branch may justly be proud of so honored a name. Few have given their time and best labors with such devotedness and singleness of purpose to the cause of missions, and few have been so efficient and useful in their chosen sphere. Miss Porter was born in Alleghany City, Pennsylvania, October 20, 1848. Her father was a man of marked ability and sterling integrity; her mother a woman of rare intellectual endowments, and a successful and popular practicing physician. Her home and home influences were well calculated to develop in her young heart the spirit of purity, benevolence, and heroism.

Her education was received in part at home. Afterward she attended school in Blairsville, Pennsylvania. In 1858 her family returned to Pittsburgh, where she continued her studies. She had the reputation of being unusually bright and quick, as well as patient and persevering in acquiring knowledge. In 1860 she removed with her family to Davenport, Scott County, Iowa. Here she entered the high school, from which she graduated. For several years after she was engaged in teaching, and had charge of a class in Latin.

Very early in life she gave her heart to Christ, and united with the Methodist Episcopal Church. She was zealous in winning souls, and active in every good work, and was at one time appointed Sabbath-school superintendent by the unanimous vote of the school. As her religious life developed her mind was strongly directed to the foreign missionary work. After thinking much on the subject, and prayerfully asking divine direction and guidance, she became thoroughly convinced that it was her duty and privilege to consecrate her life to this cause. It was no halt or blind sacrifice which she thus brought to the Lord, nor was it a heart crushed with disappointment and blighted hopes; but in all the freshness, beauty, and purity of her young womanhood, with all the promising possibilities of a brightly opening future, she brought her most precious gifts and laid them at the foot of the cross.

Miss Porter anticipated some objection on the part of the Woman's Foreign Missionary Society on account of being under the age required by their rules; but after an interview with her the ladies were so much pleased with her personal appearance and the high character of her testimonials that they determined to waive their arbitrary rule, and secure her services at once. Her thoughts had been directed to Egypt and India as her future field of labor; but when the ladies wrote advising her of the urgent call to establish a girls' school in Peking, China, and asked if she would go there, without hesitation she signified her willingness to do so.

She left home October 14, 1871, and set sail from

San Francisco November 1, in company with Miss Maria Brown as her co-laborer, and Misses Sarah H. and Beulah Woolston, who were returning to their missionary work in Foochow after a visit home. She was peculiarly cheerful and happy in her disposition, encouraging her friends sometimes amid the deepest trial or the greatest perplexity, by saying, "Do not be discouraged. If we do the best we can and trust God for the rest, it will all come out right; *I know it will.*" There was never a cloud in her horizon so dark that she could not see its silver lining—no affliction so great that she could not realize that it was working for her good. This calmness and serenity of spirit possessed her when parting with friends and all that she held dear in her native land.

About the time Miss Porter started for China the following beautiful poem appeared in the "Central Christian Advocate," entitled,

OUR MISSION AND OUR MISSIONARY.
BY MRS. H. B. CRANE.

A feeble company we stand,
Yet to the ministering Hand
  Our calling high we own:
Our souls have talked with God, and he
To us hath spoken graciously;—
  Not in loud thunder-tone,
Or fire, or storm, or earthquake's shock,
Which rends the solid mountain rock;
  But breathing still and low,
In the hushed spirit's waiting ear,
When to the throne faith brings us near,
  As sweetest music's flow.
He whispers, "Many mansions fair
Within the Father's kingdom are,

Awaiting multitudes
Of earth-born souls redeemed from sin:
Would'st thou for me these ransomed win
    To high beatitudes ?
I give thee love divine ; no bound
To love's unfailing source is found ;
    Go, in this armor shine !"

    *   *   *   .*   *   *

This is our mission ; we are blest
Obeying holy Love's behest :
    In His sweet name we send
Glad tidings to the lands afar,
That rays from our Prophetic Star
    With their night shades may blend.
Our messenger, a woman frail,
No arméd guards with coats of mail
    Her weakness to defend ;
Yet clothed in mighty panoply,
Unseen, yet strong for victory
    She dares our wily foes.
With faith-nerved courage may she bear
To the dark field our banner fair ;
    Its radiant folds disclose
To opening eyes of sin-bound souls ;
And on Immanuel's army rolls
    Hosts of new names inscribe.
O Father ! we before thy throne,
With loving hearts present this one
    Of princely Israel's tribe,
Whom to the Gentile world we send ;
O wilt thou not in fire descend,
    And clothe her with thy power?
And may the gift of tongues be hers,
Rightly to speak the thought which stirs
    In the propitious hour.
Like winged seed borne on the wind,
A distant soil and home to find,
    O may the seed she bears,
Of gospel fruit, find ready soil,
And, springing up, repay her toil
    Despite all weeds or tares.

> And from the lovely garden bloom,
> Of Christian graces and perfume,
>   The "Flowery Land" may bear
> From sisters saved and borne above
> Their darkness, to the light of love
>   A precious harvest there.
> A fadeless crown when life is done,
> And China to the Saviour won,
>   May our dear sister wear;
> And when with sheaves the reapers come
> To shout with joy the harvest home,
>   May we the glory share.

Miss Porter was unable to reach her destination before spring, so she remained in Foochow until March, then went to Peking, and, in company with Miss Brown, entered at once upon the difficult task of establishing a girls' school. The buildings needed repairs and additions, and this, with the amount of labor and patience necessary to overcome the prejudice existing against foreigners, and inducing the Chinese to let their girls come to school, the new experience of housekeeping with servants unacquainted with the ways of "foreign barbarians," and the difficulty of teaching in a language which the new missionaries themselves did not perfectly understand, made the task a formidable one. But the God in whom she trusted gave her courage and grace to overcome every obstacle. He aided her in establishing the school, and thus made her his honored instrument in gathering souls into his kingdom. The first and eldest girl admitted to the school was named for the Branch Secretary, Mrs. Lucy Prescott. She, with several others, embraced Christianity, and was baptized. She remained in the school until she was married to a Christian Chinaman. During Miss Porter's visit home Lucy sickened, and died a happy Christian, and went home as the first-fruit of the faithful labors of the missionary ladies of the Peking school.

Miss Porter is a very fine musician and a beautiful singer, having a very sweet, clear, strong voice. Her musical talents have been a wonderful help to her in her missionary work. She has been the main dependence as an organist and in leading the singing, both in school and chapel service. Her work is not confined to school duties alone, she and her assistants having in charge the religious services for Chinese women. In prosecuting this part of the work they are under the necessity of visiting the "Southern City," (or Chinese city proper, they living in the Tartar, or northern division,) to hold service in the chapel there.

They go twice a week, riding, or rather jolting, over the rough streets in the "mission cart," a two-wheeled vehicle, clumsy and heavy, in which they have to seat themselves on the floor, with risk of serious injury to their heads from the sudden jolts and clumsy motions. It is wadded inside to afford some protection from these.

All the letters written by Miss Porter while in China breathe the same spirit of consecration to Christ, and undying love for the souls of the heathen around her. Her many pressing duties during the day led her to do most of her writing at night. In this way she overtaxed her eyes, until they became exceedingly painful and gave her serious trouble.

In 1877 she returned to America and consulted an eminent oculist, who assured her that no serious disease existed, and that with rest and proper care they might be perfectly cured. This assurance filled her heart with joy and thankfulness, and she at once began to turn her attention backward toward her school and other missionary work in China.

The ladies of the Missionary Society made her return home the occasion of a delightful reception in the First Methodist Episcopal Church, Davenport, Ia., December 16. The attendance was very large. Many of the members of the various Churches of the city, with their pastors, were present. After devotional exercises Rev. Mr. Anderson, who was Miss Porter's pastor when she left home for China in 1861, extended to her a hearty greeting and welcome to the home where she was "born in the Church and born anew unto God."

One of the city papers says: "Miss Porter's response was earnest and affecting. In a clear, sweet voice, with a countenance beaming with love, she thanked those before her for the welcome. She then gave a very interesting account of the missionary work in Peking—its methods, its trials, its pleasures, its discouragements, and its successes. She concluded by singing a sacred hymn in the Chinese language."

Miss Porter was present at the Eighth Annual Meeting of the General Executive Committee, held in Minneapolis, Minnesota. At the anniversary, held Wednesday evening, May 17, she gave a most interesting account of her work, and sang exquisitely a Chinese translation of the hymn—

> "When He cometh, when he cometh,
> To make up his jewels."

While in this country she did much pioneer missionary work for the ladies' Society, besides visiting auxiliary Societies and anniversary meetings. Her unpretending modesty of deportment, her eloquent utterances, her youthful appearance, her quiet self-possession, her sweet face and pleasant voice and manner, won all hearts, and left a lasting impression in the minds of those who were so fortunate as to hear her.

During her absence from the mission, Miss Campbell, (who had been sent out after Miss Brown's marriage,) together with Mrs. Davis, (formerly Miss Brown,) labored indefatigably in the school and chapel work, and it was on this account that Miss Porter, contrary to the wishes of her friends, decided to return to Peking in the autumn, instead of waiting until spring to rest and recuperate, saying: "I owe it to Mrs. Davis and Miss Campbell to return as soon as possible and relieve them. I fear Miss Campbell will kill herself; she is not strong, and often taxes herself beyond her strength in her zeal and anxiety for the success of the work."

The Corresponding Secretary of the Davenport Auxiliary says: "She came with no complainings of trials endured, but with an earnest solicitude for a vigorous carrying forward of woman's work for woman in China. She has left us with health reestablished, and a cheerful confidence of future success in her labor of love, for Christ's sake."

The last sociable before leaving was a very pleasant occasion both to Miss Porter and her friends, saddened only by the thought of parting. Many were present to give her greeting, and then, with a prayer for prosperous journeyings and safe return, and a benediction on the labors of the years that must intervene, to say, Farewell!

On the evening of the next day, five o'clock, September 20, Miss Porter took final leave of her friends and family, and started *en route* for Peking *via* San Francisco. After reaching once more her chosen field of labor, she wrote back to her friends at home: "If I ever had any doubts as to my call to the missionary field, they are all removed. I am perfectly happy in my work, and feel it to be more glorious than ever."

During the prevalence of the famine in North China many refugees from the stricken districts crowded into the city, and, as a consequence, the typhus, or "famine fever," as it was called, broke out, and several of the missionaries fell victims to the disease, Miss Campbell among the number. This sad affliction was a serious loss to the mission, and Miss Porter was left alone in the school work. This trial was increased by the removal of her loving friend and faithful co-laborer Mrs. Davis, who, with her husband and children, went to the Tientsin Mission, eighty miles from Peking. Her duties now were most arduous, with the additional labor and increased responsibility; but, claiming the promise, "As thy day, so shall thy strength be," she labored on cheerfully until Miss Cushman came to the rescue, bringing the needed aid and comfort to the patient and persistent toiler. With this additional efficient help, doubtless the work will be still more successful, especially as a larger number of girls have been added to the school on account of the reduced circumstances of their families through the famine and the disease following.

We leave her in her far-away home in China, happy in the consciousness that she is obeying the will of Him who hath sent her, and doing her part to usher in the glorious time when earth's remotest nation shall be illuminated with the light of the ever-blessed Gospel of our Lord Jesus Christ.

MARIA BROWNE.

THE life of this lady has thus far been quite romantic and full of interest. She was born on the Atlantic Ocean, of Irish parents, as they journeyed to this land of promise. Subsequently she was taken from an orphanage, and adopted by a lady in Melrose, Mass.

> " Here began a new existence,
>   Quickly youth's glad currents run,
> And her inner life unfolded
>   Like a flower before the sun."

New hopes and aims and aspirations began to spring up within her heart. She was fond of study, and at eighteen years of age she was graduated from the high school in the town where she resided. The next six years of her life were spent in the family home, with the exception of the time spent as teacher of the school from which she was graduated. At thirteen years of age she was converted, and joined the Methodist Episcopal Church, of which her foster-mother was a member. Although so young she was an earnest and devout Christian, and at once began her missionary work among those of her own age, many of whom she led to Christ.

With regard to her call to the foreign missionary work, Mrs. Daggett, of Boston, agent of the "Heathen Woman's Friend," writes:

"We were greatly in need of a suitable lady for Peking—had been looking for one in a quiet manner, for we have always been a little fearful of saying aloud—that is, too loud—'We want a lady for missionary work,' lest the one least fitted should be the first to say, 'I'll go!'

"One day a lady called at the Mission Room with names for the 'Heathen Woman's Friend.' With her was a young lady of quiet mien, who, after a few words when introduced, sat silent until they left; but all the while I was conversing with the other I was studying the silent one. I did not think of her as a future missionary at first, but her face intensely interested me, and its expression did not leave me when she left. In a few days the husband of the lady who came on business called, and I made careful inquiry about the young lady who called with his wife. (He was a superannuated preacher.) To every question his answers were definite, and, without exception, highly commendatory. I learned from him of her early history, and the circumstances surrounding her, which had an influence in developing her character; and I could see how by experience and discipline she had been each day fitting herself, though unconsciously, for the work the Lord had in store for her. When I told him what I was thinking of, and asked, 'How would she do for a missionary?' he started up from his chair, and said, 'Why, if she would go, you would not find a better one if you were to search the world over!' I told him of the difficult language she would have to learn, the thousands of hair-breadth sounds to distinguish between, and the contortions of the tongue to be practiced. He said, 'She has a most wonderful memory; after listening to a sermon or lecture can repeat nearly the whole of it.' All his commendations were in the superlative degree. I asked if he had ever heard her speak of entering the foreign mission work. He had not. I then asked him to get his wife, with whom she was very intimate, to talk with her, and if she had any inclination to the work to let me know.

"In a few days she called, and during conversation said, she had thought she would like to go, but had never felt any call. I asked her what she meant by a call. She said she had never felt, 'Woe is me if I go not.' I asked her if she was willing to go if the Lord should *call* her. She said, 'O yes, I am willing, or I think I am, to do any thing he will help me to do, if I know he wants me to do it.' 'Then,' I replied, 'it is not necessary for you to feel the woe of which you speak. What would you think of a mother who would say to a perfectly obedient child, who only needed to know her mother's wishes to comply with them, "Child, if you do not perform this duty I shall punish you severely?"' I asked her to go home and ask God to make plain his will in this matter, and listen carefully for the answer; cautioning her not to take our call for God's, unless it should be made known to her that he was calling her to this work through us, or by human voices; and let me know the decision. If I had not felt pretty sure as to how the question was to be settled I am afraid I should have undertaken to 'steady the ark' a little. I should be loath to have the best woman in the world go to a foreign field without feeling sure the Lord wanted her there as well as we; but I was satisfied that she was our missionary to Peking in embryo."

After prayerfully and conscientiously considering the matter, she fully decided to go. She sailed from San Francisco, November, 1871. A most pleasant farewell meeting was held, October 9, at her home in Melrose, Mass. Appropriate and earnest words were spoken by Rev. Dr. Haven, Mrs. Dr. Monroe, and Mrs. Hon. E. F. Porter. Miss Browne followed with words which will long remain in the hearts of those who listened to them.

Miss Browne's record in China has been one of devout, earnest, faithful, successful labor. After serving the ladies' Society for a number of years as a single missionary she was married to Rev. G. R. Davis, of the parent Board, and with united effort they are still laboring for the redemption of China. Mrs. Daggett says, "Mrs. Bishop Wiley wrote me of her appreciation of Mrs. Davis as mother, housekeeper, and missionary, while she was on her visit to China."

CARRIE L. M'MILLAN.

CARRIE L. M'MILLAN was one of the early missionaries of the Woman's Foreign Missionary Society, having been sent out the third year of its organization. She is a native of Gettysburg, Pennsylvania, and was born October 23, 1844. In 1862 she graduated from the Gettysburg Female Seminary, after which she spent some time in teaching. Her father's brother, Rev. G. W. M'Millan, was a missionary to India. He was sent out by the American Board, (Presbyterian,) and spent nine years in Dindegol, Southern India. Her mother's sister was the wife of Rev. James Curran, whose son is now a member of the Central Pennsylvania Conference, and her sister married Rev. M. L. Drum, of the same Conference. While Carrie was an infant her mother died, leaving her children the rich legacy of a saintly life. Her father was a "good man, full of faith and the Holy Ghost." He dedicated his children to God, and they were all brought into the Church in early childhood.

Of her religious experience and call to the mission field she says: "I cannot remember when I first began to understand the plan of salvation, or felt the burden of an unrenewed heart. I was often deeply convicted of sin, and at the age of seven years I was clearly converted. All alone, out in the fields, I wept and prayed until the light and love of the justified and pardoned came into my soul. Long as the cycles of eternity roll I think I can never forget the joy of that hour. At night, when alone in the darkness, I seemed to see the loving angels hovering over me, with wreaths of flowers in their hands. I cannot tell you how early this one thought entered my heart, and filled my whole soul—*that my life-work was in India!* I can recall no incidents—nothing—that could have influenced my mind or turned my thoughts in that channel. It came gently, imperceptibly as the dew of evening; and yet so grew with my growth, and filled and thrilled me, that I seemed to live a charmed life. Some years after I came across those well-known lines, 'The Missionary's Call,' by Dr. Nathan Brown. I cannot describe my feelings as I read them. They seemed to be telling the story of my inner life, for I had felt indeed,

> 'My soul is not at rest; there comes a strange
> And secret whisper to my spirit, like
> A dream at night, that tells me I am on
> Enchanted ground. Why live I here? The vows
> Of God are on me, and I may not stoop
> To play with shadows, or pluck earthly flowers,
> Till I my work have done, and rendered up account.'

"As a school girl I studied with reference to this one object. In tracing out these Eastern nations on the map, or noting the paths across the oceans, I would think, 'My school-mates and teachers little think I will see those places.' These longings of my early life were never forgotten; and, when, at last, I revealed them to my pastor and his wife, my name was sent to the Missionary Society, and I was sent to India.

"The days of waiting and suspense were ended; and with my appointment came a sense of responsibility. I felt so unworthy for the position! One incident in my home-life I must relate. At one time in my infancy my life was despaired of, all hope of recovery being given up. My dear father, who has wonderful faith in prayer, took the case to the Lord, asking him for my life, and dedicating me to missionary service if God saw fit to spare me. The answer came—my health was restored; but I knew nothing of the prayer or the promise during all those years of waiting. A short time before my appointment, in telling some of the wonderful answers to prayer he had received, he related this, adding, 'I hope Carrie will yet live to fulfill this vow.' Can you imagine my feelings? It came as a voice from heaven, confirming all the heart-yearnings I had felt for the mission work. I am glad to fall humbly in the dust, and say, 'It is not of self, but it is the hand of my loving heavenly Father, who watched and guided my wayward, faltering steps, in answer to the prayers of this chosen one, whose faith and trust have so often been honored.'

" After my appointment the time for preparation was short, and I was soon to say farewell to those whom I loved dearer than life. The youngest of a large family, petted, and made in every thing dependent, it was no easy task to break the ties that bound me to the home of my childhood, where, unfettered by care, I had spent my time amid the orchards, meadows, forests, and fields of my wildwood home. To part from my dear ones, and go *alone*, (for I knew no one in the mission, or of the company of missionaries then going out,) was a trying ordeal, yet I was not alone. I leaned on a strong Arm—the prayers of multitudes of friends who gathered around me were answered. 'My grace is sufcient for thee' was whispered to my inmost soul, and through this I triumphed.

"Pardon me, if I allude again to my dear father. During all the years of waiting, while he kept his trust secret, he never murmured or faltered; but with the last 'Good-bye' grief for awhile conquered—no relenting, but it was a struggle. After all was over, and I was on my way to New York, previous to sailing, he went alone to his room. After a time he came down, his face radiant, as was the face of Moses when he descended from the mount, and, extending his hand to my brother, he said: 'I have gained the victory! Glory, glory! I am glad she has gone, and glad she has such a message to deliver!'"

On the 15th, 16th, and 17th of October, 1871, three large and enthusiastic farewell meetings were held in Brooklyn and New York. The next morning, October 18, saw Miss M'Millan on board the steamer, with a large number of friends to say farewell. Those who watched the noble vessel as she moved from her moorings, spoke of the beaming faces of the departing missionaries, and of the last words spoken by one of them, 'It is all bright, not one spot on the brightness!'"

Miss M'Millan's first appointment after reaching India was in Moradabad. Here she rendered very efficient service, until she left it for another field of labor. In 1872 she was married to Rev. P. M. Buck, one of our most devoted and successful young missionaries, who had spent one year in India previous to her arrival, and with him she removed to Shahjehanpore, where they had charge of the Boys' Orphanage, village station work, and enough to fill their hands and hearts.

Miss M'Millan has proven herself to be a most self-sacrificing, zealous, and faithful missionary. Writing back she says: "Of my work in India I can only say, I LOVE IT. I love the people with a peculiar love. I am glad I have a place in this field. I am glad that prayer for India's redemption is being answered. We may not see it all, but the time is coming when the jubilant trump shall sound, and India's daughters, so long bound by the fetters of superstition, and dark and gross idolatry, shall hear it. The doors of the zenana shall swing back, and, redeemed in the light of God's countenance, they shall come forth. May God hasten the day, and help us who are engaged in this work to be very faithful!"

JENNIE M. TINSLEY.

JENNIE M. TINSLEY was the first missionary supported by the North-western Branch. A native of Ireland, she came with her parents to this country when eleven years of age. Her home was Mt. Auburn, Cincinnati. For a time she was a student in the Ladies' College, Indianapolis; then entered the Wesleyan College, Cincinnati, graduating with honor. After spending a few years in teaching and perfecting herself in drawing and painting, she laid aside her easel and turned her face eastward to the daughters of Asia. She possessed rare gifts as an artist. Her paintings are treasured, with merited fondness, in the homes of many of her friends.

Miss Tinsley was converted early in life, and with the knowledge of her sins forgiven came a burning desire to tell to those afar off Christ's wondrous power to save. She made her first appearance before the ladies of the Branch at their first annual meeting, which was held in the Centenary M. E. Church, Chicago. At the call of the president she arose, and in the presence of that large audience told of her love to God and his cause, and how thankful she was that the way was opened by which she might realize the one absorbing desire of her heart—to be a missionary. Those who saw and heard her that day were well assured of her eminent fitness for the work to which she was called.

From the " Heathen Woman's Friend " of October, 1871, we copy the following letter, written by the Corresponding Secretary of the Society, Mrs. Jennie F. Willing:

"The North-western Branch has sent its first missionary to India—Miss Jennie M. Tinsley, of Indianapolis, Indiana. She goes to England and Ireland to visit her relatives, intending to join the missionary party from New York in Liverpool. Miss Tinsley attended our Branch anniversary, last May, in Chicago. The ladies who were at the forenoon meeting will not soon forget the beautiful simplicity of her appeal for their sympathy and prayers for herself and her work. Our 'farewell meetings' in Indianapolis were most interesting. Monday afternoon a missionary prayer-meeting was held in Meridian-street Church. The burden of the petitions was for the baptism of the Holy Spirit upon Miss Tinsley, to help her through the severe ordeal of leaving her friends, and to lead her to the largest usefulness. Tuesday afternoon, a meeting in the interests of the higher Christian life was held in Asbury Church. The Lord answered prayer most graciously. The Comforter came to our missionary, filling her with the 'fullness of the blessing of the Gospel of Christ.' Tuesday evening a meeting was held in Roberts' Park Church. Dr. Andrus presided. Mrs. I. R. Hitt, of Chicago, Mrs. Dr. Seymour, of Jeffersonville, Indiana, Miss Tinsley, Mrs. Willing, and Dr. Holliday, spoke to the people. The meeting was most satisfactory and enthusiastic.

"Wednesday afternoon a similar meeting was held on the Acton Camp-ground, near the city. Wednesday evening the ladies of Meridian-street Church (of which Miss Tinsley is a member) gave her a 'farewell sociable.' A cheerful earnestness marked the hour. The 'good-byes' were full of hope.

"We need hardly request for our missionary the fervent and constant prayers of the women of the North-western Branch. We know you will remember her. She is well prepared, by natural endowment and by culture, for strong work; yet without the special help of the Holy Spirit she will be powerless. From the home of every western Methodist woman, be it in 'marble front' or prairie cabin, let prayer go to God daily for the unction of the Holy One to accompany her every effort to win lost souls."

Miss Tinsley's first missionary work was in the girls' school, Lucknow, India. She has since been engaged in zenana work. She has more than met the expectations of those who sent her out, having been eminently successful in her missionary work in all the departments in which she has served. One of the missionaries writes back: "Miss Tinsley is a grand success! Her characteristics are such that she cannot help succeeding. She is a cheerful Christian, always looking on the bright side. On every dark cloud she sees the bow of promise and hope. She is full of sparkle and wit; fun-loving but sympathetic, whole-souled, impulsive enthusiastic, energetic. She is very conscientious, and has a deep religious experience."

From the depths of social degradation, from cares and perplexities, she writes to her home friends; smiling at their suggestions of "sacrifice," she says: "I have just begun to live, and have but two regrets; firstly, that I did not come to India years ago, and secondly, that I have but one poor, little, short life to give to this work." After about five years of valuable service in the field, under the auspices of the Woman's Foreign Missionary Society, she was married to Rev. J. W. Waugh, one of India's most efficient missionaries; and with united effort they are still laboring for the salvation of the heathen.

ACTION OF THE GENERAL CONFERENCE.

THE third meeting of the General Executive Committee was held in New York, May, 1872. It was a meeting of peculiar interest, because during its session the Society received the approval of the General Conference. One year before, during the meeting held in Chicago, "it was voted to memorialize the approaching General Conference, asking for our Society the same recognition and sanction as are accorded the other benevolent organizations of the Church. The committee appointed for the purpose prepared the desired memorial, recounting the history of the rise and progress of the Society, its past and present relation to the General Missionary Society of the Church, and asking that it might be 'officially authorized to prosecute its work as a recognized agency of the Church, with no other than its present restrictions, its annual report having place in the annual report of the General Society.'"

After adoption by the General Executive Committee at the commencement of their session in New York, the document was duly presented to General Conference, when it received a most respectful consideration. It was referred, as desired, to the Committee on Missions, and ordered to be printed in the "Daily Advocate." Indeed, in anticipation of the possible desire of the ladies to communicate with the body, a committee had already been appointed to bear the greetings of the General Conference to the General Executive Committee, and to receive any papers which they might desire to present.

To give our committee an answer to the prayer of the memorial before their adjournment, the Committee on Missions reported as early as possible, and the General Conference suspended its order of business to consider and promptly adopt the following:

" Having earnestly considered the papers referred to us on the subject of the Woman's Foreign Missionary Society of the Methodist Episcopal Church, we recommend the following:

"*Resolved*, That we hereby recognize the Woman's Foreign Missionary Society as an efficient agency in the spread of the Gospel, and that we encourage our sisters to prosecute their work with no other restrictions than at present, and that they be permitted to publish their report in connection with the report of the Missionary Society of the Methodist Episcopal Church.

"*Resolved*, That we recommend that pastors report the amount raised in their several charges by the Woman's Foreign Missionary Society, and that such report be published in the General Minutes.

"*Resolved*, That we recommend that all real estate in foreign lands belonging to this Society be held for it by the Missionary Society of the Methodist Episcopal Church, as trustees in trust."

Not content with this hearty and complete authorization and "encouragement" of our work, the General Conference was pleased to allude most kindly and appreciatively to our Society in two other adopted papers. The following is from the "Report of the Committee on the State of the Church:"

"The Woman's Foreign Missionary Society was organized in March, 1869, by the ladies of our Church in Boston. This Society originated in the fact that in some of the mission fields women only can obtain access to the women of those countries, and that the condition of the latter is such as to appeal in the strongest possible form for the benign and elevating influences of Christianity.

"To the special and infinitely wise providence of God we believe the Church is indebted for the origin of this institution, which we regard as destined to be an agency of great power in spreading the Gospel throughout India and China. Although its origin is so recent, it already has six hundred auxiliaries and nine missionaries in the field. Its funds and resources are rapidly increasing. It eminently deserves the fostering care of the whole Church."

Not less appreciative and encouraging are the following expressions from the "Report of the Committee on Woman's Work in the Church:"

"Our women are already far on toward leading the advance in the actual work of the Sabbath-school, our home and city missions, in the distribution of tracts, and in the visitation of the poor and neglected masses.

"Recently God has directed their hearts toward their sisters of foreign countries, and a most successful organization has been effected for aiding in the evangelization of heathen lands. For these fields of labor they have peculiar capabilities, and we rejoice that the divine Spirit is leading their hearts earnestly into them.

"We commend to women, and, indeed, the whole Church, the 'Woman's Foreign Missionary Society' and the 'Ladies and Pastors' Christian Union,' as two organizations worthy of their highest gifts and noblest efforts. We exhort the women of our Church to still greater zeal in the Sunday-school, the class-room, the prayer-meetings and love-feasts, and in the evangelization of the masses.

"We exhort our preachers, also, to give all the wise, discreet encouragement they can to the exercise and development of the gifts which God has bestowed on our sisters for the furtherance of his kingdom on earth." *

Appropriations were made for sending two missionaries, Miss Howe and Miss Hoag, to Kiukiang, China, and two more, Misses Blackmar and Pultz, were sent to India.

* "Heathen Woman's Friend," August, 1872.

LUCY H. HOAG AND GERTRUDE HOWE.

THE call to China not only aroused the hearts of the women of the Eastern States, but from the West came also responses; and Miss Lucy H. Hoag and Miss Gertrude Howe, of Michigan, both signified their willingness to enter this field of labor. They were appointed by the Woman's Foreign Missionary Society to Kiukiang, to establish a girls' school. They sailed from San Francisco, October 1, 1872. Those who had the pleasure of hearing them speak at Evanston, and at the farewell meeting in Chicago, will never forget the impression made, and will not cease to cherish them in their hearts, and to sustain them by their prayers and sympathy.

Miss Hoag was left an orphan at an early age. Her brother, Rev. G. W. Hoag, of the Michigan Conference, early adopted her into his family, and Lucy ever regarded himself and wife with the tender devotion of a loving daughter. She graduated with honor from the College in Albion, Michigan, after which she spent a few years in teaching. She says, "I lost much of Christian joy by maintaining a controversy with my conscience and God's will on the question of missionary consecration;" but when she decided to give herself to the work of teaching in heathen lands she was happy. Her letters prove that she has never regretted her noble choice. Those who know her best speak of her "unselfishness, persistence, patience, and equanimity of disposition," and of her "wealth of affection;" all elements of character eminently qualifying her for her great work. A correspondent says, "She also makes good use of her musical talents, playing upon the organ while a wondering audience stand around to listen."

The home of Miss Gertrude Howe is in Lansing, Michigan. She is a graduate of the State Normal School, Ypsilanti, Michigan, and in an unusual degree possesses all the traits necessary for a missionary teacher. Of her early impressions Miss Howe says: "As soon as I knew about the heathen I wanted to teach them." When but a child she thought she must discipline herself preparatory to entering upon mission work, that she might the more easily endure its incidental privations and necessary self-denials. Among other things, she avoided cultivating a taste for tea, little dreaming, probably, that her mission-work would be in the midst of the tea-gardens of China. Her call to missionary labor was obeyed promptly and cheerfully, although, after weeks of suspense as to her field of labor, the summons and the departure were almost simultaneous. One short night for the good-bye, and the morning light found her hastening to join the outgoing party.

These young ladies reached China the last of November, and on the first of January they had established their school in good working order—a remarkable energy and perseverance that could accomplish so much in less than two months in a heathen land, confronted by an unknown tongue and deep-seated prejudice.*

The report of the official correspondent for the year 1879 says: "For nearly seven years the work of a female boarding-school has been carried on in Kiukiang with exceptional success. Our two faithful missionaries continued as heretofore until February, when Miss Howe was obliged to return to America to recruit her health. The school began, January 1, 1873, with seven pupils, and a poor man of the literary class as teacher. Much difficulty was experienced in finding a native matron who could read, but after a month or more had elapsed a woman, with the very small Chinese feet and ladylike manner, engaged to come for a month, studying and reading; she has continued in the school up to the present time. This was Mrs. Tong, of whom a recent letter says, 'She is as faithful as ever, self-possessed, dignified, gentle in her ways, with an unusual degree of tact in managing the school children.'

"The year began with thirty-one pupils and the five orphans who have been adopted into the family; it closed with forty-seven scholars, and four who were yet too young to commence study." Besides this, the school has proved an effectual door to many of the women of Kiukiang. Miss Howe writes, "Women come to our house to see the school in crowds. Within the last few weeks we have been compelled to lock the gate and refuse admittance.

* We are indebted for these facts to Mary H. B. Hitt's Sketch of Missionaries Supported by the North-western Branch.

The women are from all classes of the people, the larger proportion rude and boisterous, but some are ladies, attended by their servants. They all come in a rush, interrupt the exercises of the school, and wear out Mrs. Tong, who must stop to answer questions, or the guests begin to upbraid her in loud tones for her rudeness." Desirous of improving every opportunity for good, Miss Howe, (who expects soon to return to her work in China,) has secured the services of her sister, Miss Delia Howe, who will sail with her to take charge of the work among these women.

It was thought necessary to adjust the names of the missionaries to the sound of some Chinese "character," else they would not have a recognized written surname. Miss Howe's name was easily adjusted, as the natives decided it was a Chinese word, meaning, "the sun in the heavens." The address of Miss Gertrude Howe in China, is, therefore, Miss Gertrude "Sun in the heavens!" The Chinese have also conferred upon her a title which conveys in it the greatest compliment ever given to a lady of the highest rank in China.

In addition to the care and labor of founding the boarding-school, and teaching and superintending its general interests, they erected a new building for school and home. This was completed in 1876. Mrs. Keen, in reporting the Kiukiang work, says, "This was done at a marvelously small expenditure, and is, doubtless, owing to the ladies' knowledge of native character, and their personal supervision of the work."

LOU E. BLACKMAR.

> Our voluntary service He requires,
> Not our necessitated ; such with him
> Finds no acceptance, nor can find ; for how
> Can hearts, not free, be tried whether they serve
> Willing or no, who will but what they must
> By destiny, and can no other choose ?—MILTON.

LOU E. BLACKMAR was born in West Springfield, Erie County, Pennsylvania, March 21, 1841. Her father was a man of moral integrity and uprightness of character, reflecting in the ordinary walks of life the Gospel of Christ, and leading his children in the paths of wisdom and piety both by precept and example. Her mother was also deeply pious, and was possessed of more than ordinary mental capacity. Her maternal grandfather was a pioneer of Methodism in North-western Pennsylvania: three of his sons entered the Methodist ministry, and one daughter also shared in the toils and triumphs of the itinerancy. Coming from such an ancestral line, it is not surprising that missionary fire burned in her heart. Miss Blackmar says, "The constant and united aim of my parents has been to train up their children in the fear and love of God. They gave us good opportunities for securing an education, and early instilled into our minds the importance of being courageous and self-reliant, that we might be prepared to fill places of usefulness and honor, and that the world might be the better for our having lived in it. If any of us fail in this, *they* will be free from responsibility."

She was educated at the West Springfield Academy and Edinborough Normal School, Erie County, Pennsylvania. From her earliest recollections she says her ambition was to be what her mother had been — a teacher. When about seventeen years of age she commenced her first school, with a feeling that she had entered upon her life-work. Desiring a broader field for usefulness, she removed to Leavenworth, Kansas, where she became principal of one of the large city schools.

When about sixteen years of age she experienced the pardoning grace of God, and entered upon the activities of an earnest Christian life. She now felt that she was not only imparting instruction to fit her pupils for usefulness on earth, but was also sowing the seeds in their young hearts that should influence them for all eternity. Teaching was invested with new charms and new responsibilities, and the conviction that it was the work God had chosen for her deepened, until, she writes, " My heart is entirely filled with its blessedness."

Soon after her conversion she became desirous that her field of labor might be extended even unto the ends of the earth. She says, "I longed to be a missionary, and was impressed with the thought that whenever I could reach the height upon which this work stood it would be ready for me."

Again she says : " You ask me to write of the influences that led me to be a missionary. The books in my parents' library, which I read when a child, had a great influence on my mind. The life of Hester Ann Rogers, that of Mrs. Mary Fletcher, of her husband, and of the Wesleys, and also of Mary Lyons, made me desirous, like them, to do some real good in the world."

In 1871, in a conversation with her pastor, Rev. J. J. Thompson, she spoke freely of her convictions with regard to this work, and expressed a desire to serve under the auspices of the Woman's Foreign Missionary Society. He at once communicated the same to the parties interested. Among other things he said: "After a very earnest and close conversation with Miss Blackmar, touching her convictions concerning missionary work in India, I cannot doubt the Master has work for her in that or some other foreign field. Though we will feel her loss, yet, for the sake of the Master's cause, I will only rejoice if the way opens for her to enter upon what I esteem woman's highest opportunity for good."

The way *did* open, and she received her appointment to her chosen field in India joyfully; but prayerfully and conscientiously. In a letter to Mrs. Prescott, Corresponding Secretary of the Western Branch, written just as the question was pending, she says: "My desire to go to India is just as strong as when I first wrote you. As the society *must* have the very best returns for all funds expended, I dare not say, *I ought to go*. I know God has work for me to do somewhere, and I am in his hands. I purpose not to be idle."

Miss Isabella Leonard, Assistant Corresponding Secretary of the Branch, writing to a friend, said:

"I am so thankful for my visit with Miss Blackmar. She was present at the memorial service held in honor of the late Mrs. Waugh—sad, yet profitable and interesting. After the papers were read Miss Blackmar was introduced, and talked some minutes, touching all hearts with her sweet spirit of entire consecration to the work. I found she had surrendered herself wholly to Christ. In the Saturday night meeting she told her whole experience relating to the subject of full salvation; yet, after all her consecration, she did not dare claim the experience. Yesterday afternoon, during a visit to Mrs. Bishop Hamline, she yielded at this point, and stepped upon the promise, and goes forth now, I believe, to acknowledge that Christ saves her from indwelling sin. And now I must say, we are sending a noble woman to India. We may justly expect that God will use her in a peculiar manner."

Miss Blackmar sailed October 23, 1872, in the steamer Wyoming, for Moradabad, India. The farewell services were highly interesting, and were held in Bedford-street Church, New York city, on the 21st of October. The afternoon meeting was presided over by Mrs. Dr. Olin. Miss Blackmar was called, and addressed the meeting. As she spoke of her call to missionary work, her consecration to Christ, and her implicit trust in the promise, "Lo, I am with you alway," the audience was deeply moved, and many a prayer went up for the departing missionary.

Just before leaving she wrote to Mrs. Prescott, one of the Corresponding Secretaries:

"I am quite well, and my faith and courage are not in the least shaken as the time of leaving draws near. I think the hardest trial, after all, will be to leave my parents and my childhood home. I realize now, as I have not before, that it has cost me something, and I am thankful that I have a little to give up. All that it is, however, I give willingly. I shall not likely write again until I reach India. I know I have your prayers. 'O for a faith that will not shrink!'"

A few hours before she left New York, after she had parted from her parents, she wrote thus: "When you read this I shall have left the shores of my native land. God only knows whether I shall ever greet them again, but I do not feel any anxiety in regard to this. I hope my life will be long enough to witness some work for the Master, and that my health may be so firm that I may make the utmost use of my time. I realize, I think, that it will be just as short a way, and just as sweet, to enter rest in heaven from India as from my own dear home.

"I left my home with nature tried to the utmost, but without a regret. The trial was more than I had anticipated for my parents, especially my mother; yet they are not grieving that they gave me up; they know the greatness of the work, and that it is but a short separation."

Miss Blackmar reached India safely, and entered upon her work in Moradabad, January 1, 1873. The particular branch of labor assigned her was zenana work, visiting the homes of the native women, and endeavoring to win them to Christ. In this she has been very successful, and has been the instrument in God's hands of doing much to enlarge the borders of our Zion in India. During the terrible famine of 1878 Miss Blackmar was superintendent of the American Zenana Mission, in Lucknow. She was untiring in her efforts to relieve the panic-stricken and starving population.

November 21 the city magistrate, Major Newbery and lady, both of whom have taken the heartiest interest in the good work from the beginning to the end, and have most efficiently done all in their power to further it, waited upon Miss Blackmar and presented to her, with appropriate personal congratulations, the following letter, which we copy from the "Lucknow Witness:"

"From Sir George Cowper, Bart., C.B., K.C.S.I., Lieutenant-Governor N. W. Provinces, and Chief Commissioner for Oudh, to Miss Blackmar.

"CAMP LUCKNOW, *November* 14, 1878.

"MADAM: I beg to tender you my cordial thanks for the great and invaluable assistance you have rendered to the city magistrate and to the local committee of Lucknow in carrying out their measures for the relief of the distress caused by the recent scarcity. You kindly undertook to distribute the sum that was allotted for the relief of purdah-nashin ladies, and have discharged this duty faithfully and judiciously for a year. The labor it entailed was arduous, but you have grudged neither time nor trouble, and have given invaluable assistance, which the committee from time to time have brought to my notice, and which merits the grateful thanks which I venture to offer herewith for your acceptance.

"Your obedient servant, GEORGE COWPER,
"*Lieut.-Gov. N. W. Provinces, and Chief Commissioner for Oudh.*"

It is exceedingly gratifying to the Church at home that her missionaries abroad receive such testimonials to their fidelity and efficiency from the highest officers of the Government. It is one of the greatest stimulants to the workers at home to know these facts, and we shall continue to hope for Miss Blackmar long life, great usefulness, and the highest achievements in the missionary field.

LIZZIE M. PULTZ.

AMONG the honorable and heroic women whose hearts were enlisted in the cause of missions in the early history of the Society was Miss Lizzie M. Pultz, who went from her home in the peaceful vale of Windsor, Broome Co., N. Y., to far-off India.

Her earliest recollections, she tells us, are of a happy home in a quiet country village, with loving parents guarding and blessing her young life. While at a very tender age, one morning she noticed that those about her seemed sad. She missed her mother, and going to her father, and clasping her arms about his neck, she asked, "Where is my mamma?" He replied, with much emotion, "My dear child, your mother is in heaven." Young as she was, she realized most sensibly the loss she had sustained, and together they mingled their tears and sobs.

As we have heard this incident related we have been reminded of a similar one in the life of Rev. E. H. Stokes, now President of the Ocean Grove Camp-meeting Association. He had followed his wife to the grave, and was, one pleasant summer evening, walking in the garden with his motherless child, then two and a half years of age. Little Mary put her arms lovingly around her father's neck, and, bursting into tears, sobbed as if her heart would break, then exclaimed, in the fullness of her soul, "I have no mother!" Turning her eyes to the bright stars above, she said, "Is my mother *there?*" The fountain of grief in the father's heart was again unsealed, and, taking his pen, he wrote the following exquisite lines:

"I have no mother!" No! my dearest child;
 Though the bright, sunny spring-time is coming,
When birds fling out their music, richly mild,
 With brilliant plumes from milder skies returning:
But she returns not, like the passage-wing,
  Early in spring.

Yes! I have heard thee in sad autumn's day
 Calling thy mother, when the leaves were dying;
But with the leaves thy mother passed away,
 Leaving bare branches in the low wind sighing,
To make lone murmurs in its passing breath—
  The voice of death.

And I have heard thee in the winter time
 Sigh for thy mother when the snow was falling;
And yet I hear thee in the bright sunshine,
 In thy low sadness, for thy mother calling;
But, like the lonely sighing of some lovely bird,
  Thou art unheard.

Yet the warm sun will glow with summer's heat,
 And bright flowers up from the earth be springing;
Some little rose bloom by some other sweet,
 The tender vine around the parent clinging,
And nestling birds be by a mother fed:
  But thine is dead.

And yet not dead, but passed away from earth
 To a better, brighter land forever,
Where the sorrows of death, with joys of birth,
 Are never found mingling together;
Where the soul expands in immortal youth,
  Blooming in truth.

> And thou shalt be transplanted there, my love,
>   Where the autumnal winds are never blowing,
> To see thy mother, those bright stars above,
>   To which so oft thy little thoughts are flowing;
> And feel a kiss, sweeter than when she smiled
>   Last on her child.

Miss Pultz, at the age of fifteen, was called to mourn the loss of her father. This left her alone in the world. But He who has promised to be a father to the fatherless guided her footsteps, and she early consecrated herself to God and his service, and received the spirit of adoption, whereby she could cry, "Abba, Father." From that hour her sense of loneliness was gone; a joy unspeakable took possession of her heart; and with loving confidence she could look up and say, "My Father, thou shalt be the guide of my youth."

She became much interested in the cause of missions, and felt a burning desire to tell the story of redemption to those who had never heard it. The missionary spirit was fanned into a flame by a correspondence of some years with a lady friend who was a missionary in India, and she resolved to prepare herself to the best of her ability, and then offer herself to the Church for foreign work. With this object in view she entered the Wyoming Seminary, where she pursued her studies with untiring energy and industry, and closed not only with the honors of the institution, but with the esteem and confidence of the entire village. Rev. G. R. Hair, who was her pastor at the time, says: "She was a most conscientious, devoted, and useful member of the Church. Her life was deeply spiritual. The last prayer offered in the old church in Kingston, before it was destroyed by fire, was by Miss Pultz. I shall never forget it. It was uttered with a fervency and unction which will long be remembered by all who were present."

In 1872 she was accepted by the Society as a suitable person to be employed by them, and was appointed to Bareilly, India; and on the 23d of October she sailed in the steamer Wyoming from New York to her distant field of labor. Other missionaries were also going out at the same time. Interesting farewell services were held in the Bedford-street Church, New York city, on the 21st of October. The interest of the occasion was heightened by the presence of Babu Bannerji, a native of India, who made a short speech, and also by the appearance of two little sons of Brother Brown, (a returned missionary,) who sang a hymn in Hindustani, one of them being attired in Hindu costume. The thought of the sacrifice Brother and Sister Brown were about to make in leaving these precious boys behind while they returned to India, made the singing more touching, and many prayers went up for both parents and children. Miss Pultz was called, and addressed the meeting. While she was relating her experience the audience manifested intense sympathy, and seemed to realize that it was truly God's influence that had been leading her to this consecration. A friend who was present when she sailed wrote back to her Windsor friends as follows:

"I had the pleasure of attending the Monday

evening meeting. It was certainly very delightful, and I enjoyed it very much, all save the thought of the partings that were to follow. I carried the *large cake* for her which the ladies gave her to take to India. She showed me the beautiful watch and other presents which she had received. I am here this morning on the steamer Wyoming—came an hour ago, that I might have a little visit—but so many are here to bid the missionaries 'God speed,' that I cannot get a chance to talk much with Lizzie. I saw her state-room and met the other members of the company, and every thing betokens a pleasant voyage. But the bell sounds, and we must go ashore. We gather at the end of the dock, and as the steamer glides past us wave to the little band, who are gathered at the stern, our last good wishes. Some one starts that beautiful song, ' The Sweet By and By,' and the music floating out so sweetly upon the water carries to them the assurance of a meeting in the future with the friends they are leaving, if not again in this life. Near me stands Dr. Waugh, who came home from India last year, after a fourteen years' absence, on account of his wife's health. He was to have returned at this time, but the recent death of his noble wife, leaving five motherless children to be cared for, has prevented him. Mrs. Waugh was one of the most intelligent, cultured, and consecrated women that has ever gone as a missionary to the East, and was regarded by many of our missionaries as ' the pride and princess of the mission.' No wonder that Mrs. Bishop Thomson, when speaking of her, wrote :

> " 'Alas, for him who sheds
> The tear of loneliness;
> For those whose bright young heads
> Were pillowed on her breast,
> In infancy's soft rest
> By mother-love caressed;
> For each whose life she blessed,
> Who now in sorrow treads
> The path by grass-grown beds.'

"As he stands there wiping the tears from his eyes I can well imagine the thoughts that fill his heart as they sing:

> "'We shall meet on that beautiful shore,
> In the sweet by and by.'

"I wave my handkerchief again for you and Mrs. Colburn and Lizzie, and leave the pier, the whole scene leaving a very deep impression upon my mind. May God bless her richly as she goes forth so bravely, and make her the means of doing much good!"

After a pleasant voyage she reached India, and entered at once upon her work in Bareilly. Here she was associated with Miss Sparkes in the Girls' Orphanage, where she rendered efficient service. The next Conference assigned her a new field of labor among the native women in the zenanas. The Annual Report of the parent Society for the year 1875 says: "Miss Pultz has made an extensive acquaintance, and gained many friends by her zenana work in the city, and, with her assistants, is aiding much in extending our influence." From the "Fifth Annual Report of the Work of the Woman's Foreign Missionary Society in India," published at Lucknow, 1875, we make the following extract: "Our zenana work is steadily increasing in interest and importance as a means of reaching the women in the city, who can only be taught in their homes. Miss Pultz has had charge of this department."

Miss Pultz continued her missionary labors until 1875, when she was compelled by the failure of her health to return to America, where she hoped, after breathing for a short time her native air, to recuperate, and regain her health sufficiently for her to go back again to her chosen field in India. But in this she has been disappointed. Through continued ill health she is unable to resume her work in the mission. Her former pastor, Rev. G. R. Hair, says: "She feels keenly the trial she is compelled to endure in not being able to enter again upon that work that lies so near her heart. In a recent letter she speaks of her 'poor head' as still occasioning pain, the effect of the climate of India and her close application to study and work during the years of her residence in that country."

FOURTH ANNUAL MEETING OF THE GENERAL EXECUTIVE COMMITTEE.

THIS meeting convened in St. Paul's Church, Cincinnati, May 14, 1873. It was largely attended. The spirit of consecration and faith seemed to pervade all hearts. The reports from the various Branches showed an encouraging advance. Earnest applications were received requesting the extension of the work of the Society to Mexico and South America. The final report of the standing committee on extension of work, submitted and adopted, was as follows:

"*Mexico.*—Noting and accepting the openings of Providence, we are impressed with the expediency and necessity of commencing work in Mexico; yet not of investing in real estate at present—confining ourselves rather to personal missionary labor.

"*South America.*—We advise that the urgent plea of Brother Woods, of Rosario, for two female helpers, be heeded, and his hands thus strengthened.

"*Japan.*—We look forward with hope to the speedy entering and occupancy of Japan. Still, as our mission is not yet established there, we do not deem it needful to make arrangements for work during the coming year.

"*Africa.*—The time and place of entering Africa

not yet appearing, we also defer action with regard to work there."

Three new missionaries were appointed: Miss S. F. Leming and Miss N. Monelle, M.D., to India, and Miss L. L. Coombs, M.D., to China. The public anniversary was held in St. Paul's Church, Cincinnati, Mrs. Skidmore presiding. Mrs. Willing made the opening prayer, and Miss Coombs, under appointment as first medical missionary to China, addressed the audience, after which Miss Frances E. Willard, President of the Evanston College for Ladies, delivered an exceedingly graceful and effective address.

SALLIE F. LEMING.

SALLIE F. LEMING was sent to India as a representative of the Cincinnati Branch of the Woman's Foreign Missionary Society. She was born near the city of Cincinnati, November 12, 1845. Her father gave his heart to Christ and his hand to the Church when but fifteen years of age, and has ever since been one of the pillars in the house of God. Her mother was a granddaughter of Rev. Philip Gatch, one of the first Methodist preachers in the State of Ohio. He died when Sallie was but two years of age. Her childhood and early youth were spent in a quiet country home, surrounded with Christian influences.

She was always religiously inclined, and says: "I do not remember the time when I did not pray; and my convictions of sin date back to my earliest recollections. When about nineteen years of age God gave me the evidence of my acceptance, clear as the noon-day sun, and it has never since been clouded. The blessing that came to me that day was, Christ formed in me the hope of glory.

"About this time the work of holiness began to revive in the East. I read of the National Association and its work with interest, but felt no especial need of this experience. Some time after, while attending a revival in our own church, in which I worked with an earnestness, a joy, and a success such as I had never before known in bringing souls to Christ, I was led to seek earnestly for heart purity. I resolved that I would never stop short of being sanctified wholly. I read eagerly every thing that would give light on the subject, and endeavored to walk in the light as I received it.

"One day, after searching to see if I could find any thing more to bring to Jesus, for consecration had now become a joy, I found my heart asking, 'What shall I do that I may work the work of God?' and with a life-giving power came this answer: 'This is the work of God, that ye believe on him whom he hath sent.' Then came the witness to my soul that the work *was done*. The blood was applied to my perfect cleansing. O, the sweet consciousness of inward purity! The soul-rest into which I entered was wonderful. All glory to the cleansing blood!"

Up to this time her education was only such as could be obtained in a country school. After this baptism she coveted earnestly the best gifts, and resolved to seek an education that would fit her for the highest degree of usefulness. Accordingly she entered the Cincinnati Wesleyan College, from which she graduated with honor in 1873. After completing her education she offered herself to the Woman's Foreign Missionary Society for service in India. She was accepted and appointed to Bareilly. She sailed August 27, 1873.

Miss Leming reached India, and commenced her

work, but her health failed, and, after battling with disease, and hoping against hope for recovery, she was obliged to return home. So all-absorbing had been the one thought of preparing herself to the utmost for usefulness in her chosen field that she did not realize how rapidly her physical strength was giving way and yielding to the pressure.

Mrs. Bishop Clark, President of the Cincinnati Branch, writes: "It was remarkable how she developed spiritually and intellectually. Her father, a devoted Christian man of moderate means, sold a portion of his farm in order to meet her expenses for one year at college. During that year, the president told me her religious influence was widely felt. Her health failed on her outward-bound journey, and she was obliged to return. Her heart was almost broken, and she still feels the dull pain of past disappointment.

In a letter written to us Miss Leming says: "While at college the privileges I enjoyed seemed so rich that I was jealous of every moment of time. I studied and taxed my mind and strength to their utmost tension in spite of the remonstrances of teachers and friends. The result was that my health failed, and it was with difficulty that I finished the third year. I knew I was worn and weary; but thought, with my physician, that a little rest would restore me. I sailed very soon after graduating. Leaving home and friends caused a keen pain, but it was sweetened by the consciousness that I was going at the Lord's bidding. My health did not improve at sea, as was hoped it would, and by the time I reached

India I was almost unfit for any mental exertion. Miss Sparkes knows what a terrible disappointment it was to me, and how it almost broke my heart to be obliged to come home."

Though her stay was short in India, she was there long enough to endear herself to the hearts of all who came within the sphere of her influence, and to prove to them that, but for the failure of her health, she would have been a most successful and valuable missionary.

The following extract is from a private letter, written by Miss Sparkes, of the Bareilly Orphanage: "Miss Leming was in Bareilly the only year she was in India. She was bright, intelligent, unusually sweet-spirited and lovely in disposition, and she exerted a strong spiritual influence over all with whom she mingled. She was appointed to the zenána work in Bareilly, but was not strong enough to do much. She made frequent attempts to visit the women in their homes, but almost every time would come in looking so pale and exhausted, and sometimes so weak, she could scarcely walk across the room to her bed. She was soon obliged to give that up. In April, 1874, she went to the mountains (Nynee Tal) for the season. We all felt, and often said among ourselves, that she would never live to come down to us again. At the close of the season, however, she returned and soon began work again, but was too feeble to continue it. When so weak that she was unable to sit up, she would lie on the bed and study Hindustani hour after hour, or the greater part of the day. The latter part of the year she assisted a little in the Orphanage, but soon had to give that up also. Immediately after the next Conference, held in January, she was advised to leave for America. It was a terrible trial for her to give up the hope of laboring for the people of India. Only those who were with her constantly, and know how she struggled to be brave, and to say, 'Thy will be done,' can realize how severe the trial was."

Since her return to the United States, in May, 1874, Miss Leming has regained her health, and is now married, but still continues to give much of her time and energy to the promotion of the interests of our Society; often addressing missionary meetings, and presenting India's wants and woes so forcibly and clearly that her auditors cannot withhold their offerings from our treasury.

NANCIE MONELLE, M.D.

NANCIE MONELLE, M.D., is a native of New York, and was born in the year 1841. Her paternal ancestors belonged to the ancient family of Monellé, of the province of Tours, France. Her great-grandfather came to America with the young Marquis de Lafayette, and, admiring the country very much, did not return to France. Her father was an accomplished scholar, and a man of unusual literary attainments, but died while she was an infant.

Her mother was a devoted member of the Methodist Episcopal Church for more than thirty years. Miss Monelle says, "She did not *talk* much about her religious life, but she *lived* it continually; all who came under her influence knew that she walked and talked with God." Her mother's great desire was to have her children thoroughly educated, and prepared for lives of honor and usefulness. She was sent to school at an early age, and advanced rapidly in her studies. When about seventeen years of age she entered the Collegiate Institute of the City of Poughkeepsie, New York, from which she graduated in the year 1861. After this she pursued a course of teaching in academies, seminaries, and colleges. Sometimes she had a "night-class," composed of young men and women who were ambitious to become educated, but who were obliged to work all day in a shop or factory. These she invited to her house, and gave them free instruction three evenings in every week; thus commencing missionary work at home.

With regard to her conversion, she says, "While at Vassar College my mind became very much disturbed by the preaching and teaching of the Rev. John Raymond, President of the College. At this time the college was also visited by a dear elderly lady, named Bannister. She addressed the students twice on the subject of religion, urging them to give themselves to Christ. I listened attentively and pondered all her sayings. I obtained an interview with her in her own room. She perfectly comprehended my spiritual condition, encouraged me, and urged me to apply the remedy. I was 'almost persuaded,' but I hesitated, and my mind again became filled with doubts and fears, turmoil and darkness, and I was desperately miserable. This dreadful condition lasted several months, but gradually I came out of the darkness into the light, and my soul was filled with a sweet peace, and I was able to sing,

"'Fully persuaded—Lord, I believe!
Fully persuaded—thy Spirit give,
  I will obey thy call,
  Low at thy feet I fall,
  Now I surrender all
    Christ to receive.

"'Fully persuaded—no more oppressed!
Fully persuaded—now I am blest!
  Jesus is now my Guide,
  I will in Christ abide
  My Lord is satisfied,
    In him I rest.'

"While at Vassar College I formed the resolution to study medicine thoroughly, and strive to become a skillful practitioner, thus expecting to extend my sphere of influence and usefulness. This resolution formed, the question arose, 'Where will you practice it?' A still small voice replied, 'In India.'"

As soon as practicable she matriculated at the "Woman's Medical College of New York," founded by Doctors Elizabeth and Emily Blackwell. Here she remained four years, six months of the time being spent in a hospital attached to the college. In the spring of 1872 she graduated, receiving her diploma, and also a case of surgical instruments, as a reward for preparing and presenting the best written report of all the cases attending the surgical *clinique*. While she was a medical student in New York she joined the Forty-third-street Methodist Episcopal Church, of which the Rev. L. H. King, D.D., was pastor. He had known Miss Monelle and her family for many years.

During the summer of 1873, while at Round Lake camp-meeting, she says: "I was spiritually refreshed and greatly blessed. I returned to New York, and immediately presented myself before Dr. King as a candidate for India, as a *medical missionary*. He went with me to see Mrs. William B. Skidmore, Corresponding Secretary of the New York Branch of the Woman's Foreign Missionary Society. She received us in her usual courteous and sweet manner. I told her I was not good enough to go out as a missionary, but that as a physician I could go ahead as a pioneer, and open zenanas, and thus make a way for others who were more pious to follow, and teach and preach the glad tidings of salvation to the heathen. I felt greatly honored and very happy when I was appointed to go to India under the auspices of the Woman's Foreign Missionary Society. I wept for joy. I left New York with six other missionaries on the 20th day of August, 1873. As the steamer left the wharf I was filled with joy. It was the happiest moment of my life."

Miss Monelle landed in Bombay on October 20, 1873, and went to the beautiful city of Lucknow, where she remained just one year. Here she was admitted to several zenanas, and had a good medical work started. But Lucknow disagreed seriously with her health; she became disheartened, and began to think that she would be obliged to leave India. "I could not bear to yield to this thought," she writes. "I wanted to be an instrument for the Master's use, to be a torch-bearer in his service. I wanted to elevate and educate the poor, miserable women of India, and, therefore, the thought of leaving the mission field filled me with pain."

At length what seemed to her a great and effectual door was opened to her. She was summoned to Hyderabad to hold an important Government position. She was told that a lady physician would be welcomed with joy in the native State of Hyderabad—that she would be able to do great good in the zenanas belonging to the king and noblemen— that she could *talk* religion if she were judicious, but she would not be permitted to *teach* it. She accepted the proposition, and immediately forwarded her written resignation to the Woman's Foreign Missionary Society through Mrs. Skidmore.

Miss Monelle remained in Lucknow three months after this, hoping that a lady physician would be sent out to take her place. She says: " In leaving the mission it seemed as though Pharaoh and his hosts were behind me, and the Red Sea before me. To go away into a purely Mohammedan State, in an unknown region, a stranger in a strange land, *all alone*, seemed to me the most daring and dangerous enterprise of my life. But I resolved, God helping me, to undertake it. I was five days and nights in reaching my destination. Hyderabad is a purely Mohammedan city, without a single European inhabitant. It has a king, a court, a nobility, a gentry, and nearly a million of the common people, besides several regiments of Sepoys. It is a walled city, with several gates that are always shut and locked before midnight. One mile from the city the British Resident and his suite reside, and all the various government *employés*. Four miles from the city is a large cantonment of several European regiments, and at various points near Hyderabad are stationed European regiments. So that Hyderabad is the largest native city and also the largest military station in India. I was received and entertained by His Excellency Sir Charles Saunders, C.B., British Resident at the Court of Hyderabad, and by his kindness I was introduced to the officers and to the gentry of the station, and to the various lords and ladies of England who were visiting India. I was received in the native city by His Excellency Sir Salar Jung, Prime Minister and Co-Regent, who furnished elephants, a regiment of Sepoys, and a band of music to escort me through Hyderabad to the palaces of the various noblemen of the city. The British Resident, the Military Secretary, and the Surgeon-General of Madras accompanied me, and introduced me formally to the native gentlemen. The Government gave me *carte blanche*, and so I rented rooms in the busiest bazar in the city, furnished them properly, and put out the sign

'HIS HIGHNESS THE NIZANI'S HOSPITAL FOR WOMEN,'

in *four* languages. I sat and waited for patients. I prayed the Lord to send them to me, and he did. In a few weeks I had as many as I could attend to. I spent three hours every day in my hospital, except on Sabbath. I soon had a large private practice in the zenanas of the noblemen of the city. I was always received by the women with great interest and kindness, and, whenever I could, I talked to them of our God and our Redeemer and our religion. They would listen attentively, and often asked many intelligent questions. The women flocked to the hospital in such numbers that during the three years I was in Hyderabad I treated *forty thousand patients*."

It is due to Miss Monelle to say, that the money spent by the Woman's Foreign Missionary Society for her passage to India and her outfit was refunded when she left the service of the Society.

In November, 1877, she left her medical work in Hyderabad to be married to the Rev. Henry Mansell, M.A., of the North India Conference, a most faithful, devoted, and successful missionary. Mr. Mansell was returning to his work in India, after a brief visit to the United States for the restoration of health and recuperation, and was a fellow-voyager with Miss Monelle when she first went to India, in 1873. They were married in Bombay on the 3d of November, 1877.

Since then Mr. Mansell has been stationed in Gonda, Oude. We have this testimony by one of the missionaries of the parent board: " Mrs. Mansell is doing much good here, and is a precious help to her husband in all his work. I know she will not give herself due credit for her religious life and attainments. Her love and loyalty to Christ are supreme, notwithstanding she seldom speaks in prayer or class meeting; yet I do not know of any one who loves these meetings better, or who profits more by them. Her sainted mother's prayers are answered in her behalf. Five years ago, when she first reached India, I was telling her what rare opportunities she would have to preach the Gospel to those prisoners of the zenanas who never could have it in any other way. 'O,' said she, 'my brightest hope is to open the doors of the zenanas by my medical knowledge and skill, and those better and more worthy than I can carry the better medicine to the souls of these sin-sick ones.' It was principally her influence that brought to Jesus last year one who promises to be a most efficient preacher of the Gospel here. He is now our most impressive preacher to the heathen."

But whether in Afzulgunge Hospital or in the missionary station with her husband, we trust she will do what she can to carry forward the good work. John saw one casting out devils in Christ's name, and because he was not following the other disciples John forbade him; but Christ said, "Forbid him not: for he that is not against us is on our part." So we rejoice in the success of all missionaries sent out by us, whether they remain with our Society or not, if Christ is preached, the heathen elevated, souls saved, and the millennial glory hastened; for thus the object of the Gospel of Christ is accomplished.

LUCINDA L. COOMBS, M.D.

> "Every age
> Appears to souls who live in it most unheroic.
> Every age, through being held too close, is ill discerned
> By those who have not lived past it.
>   'Tis even thus
> With times we live in, evermore too great
> To be apprehended near."

THE history of the life we now present to our readers furnishes an illustration of the truth of the sentiment sung by Mrs. Browning. Heroes and heroines have lived in all ages, especially since the dawn of the Christian era. Of Christ it was tauntingly said, "He saved others, himself he cannot save!" "Looking unto Jesus, the author and finisher of our faith, who for the joy that was set before him endured the cross, despising the shame, and is set down at the right hand of the throne of God," it is not surprising that his followers should emulate his spirit, and should possess in an eminent degree the same self-sacrificing heroism, which is born of undying love for souls and uncompromising faith in God.

Of all the number sent out by our Society none have manifested more of this spirit than Miss Coombs. Left an orphan at an early age, she supported and educated herself. She consecrated her life to God, and the language of her heart was, "My Father, be thou the guide of my youth:" and in her case the promise was fulfilled, "When my father and my mother forsake me, then the Lord will take me up." After her conversion to Christ her constant thought was preparation for missionary work. Her attention was turned especially to India, and she resolved to prepare herself to the best of her ability for that field of labor. After teaching some time she entered Cazenovia Seminary, where, unaided, save by her own energy, tact, and industry, she kept at the head of her classes, and graduated with the highest honors.

During the vacations which intervened, while other students were resting and recuperating, Miss Coombs toiled on unremittingly, for she had set up her standard, and she was determined to reach it. With her to *resolve* was to *do*. When she made up her mind what was best to be done, the thing was half accomplished. Her motto was "Excelsior;" and her perseverance and indomitable will easily overcame what to many would have seemed insurmountable obstacles. What if she could not see the end from the beginning—was not He faithful who had called her, and could he not bring it to pass? She resolved to offer herself to the Woman's Foreign Missionary Society for service in India. Hearing much said about the value of a medical education for lady missionaries, she determined to secure such an education first, and to leave nothing undone which would aid in qualifying her to the utmost for usefulness in her future work. With the determination to do with her might what her hands found to do, and to trust in God for what she could not do herself, she entered a medical college in Philadelphia. If all the facts which have come to us concerning Miss Coombs' seminary and college life were given to our readers, they would prove her to be one of the greatest heroines of the present age.

The ladies of the Woman's Foreign Missionary Society, and Mrs. Annie Wittenmeyer, President of the Woman's National Christian Temperance Union, noticing her devotion to Christ, and her eager pursuit after knowledge, became intensely interested in her. They felt that God was in an especial manner calling and preparing her to fulfill a noble destiny. They extended to her their warmest sympathy and co-operation.

After completing her third course in college she sailed for Peking, China, June 5, 1873. Mrs. Wittenmeyer says: " The dream of her life had been the going to India as a missionary; yet when the Society decided that she must go to China, she made no objection or complaint. She simply said to me, 'I had hoped to go to India, but it is all the same. It is work for the Master, and the souls of the Chinese women are as dear to him as the souls of the women of India.' I was in San Francisco when she started on her mission, and had the privilege of talking with her before she left, and of seeing her safely settled in the stateroom of the ship, and of waving her a farewell from the wharf as the vessel steamed away. No more heroic soul has, in my opinion, ever left our shores for Christian work abroad."

Miss Coombs reached Peking the last of August, and entered at once upon her work. As was anticipated, she has been very successful, and has accomplished much for the cause of missions. After laboring as a single missionary for about five years, she was married to the Rev. A. Strittmater, of the parent Society, and together they are still toiling for the redemption of China.

FIFTH ANNUAL MEETING OF THE GENERAL EXECUTIVE COMMITTEE.

THE General Executive Committee opened its fifth annual session in Philadelphia, May 6, 1874. Two new Corresponding Secretaries were present at this meeting—Mrs. J. E. Latimer taking the place heretofore filled by Mrs. Warren, as Secretary of the New England Branch, and Mrs. W. B. Skidmore was appointed Corresponding Secretary of the New York Branch, in place of Mrs. Dr. Butler, who was called to engage in missionary work in Mexico.

Among the interesting incidents of the meeting was the reading of a letter from a converted Chinese woman, Wong Tingai, of Hung Moi, China, translated by Mrs. Baldwin. At the suggestion of the President, Mrs. Dr. Hibbard, the following stanzas were sung, amid deep feeling:

> "He breaks the power of canceled sin,
> He sets the prisoner free;
> His blood can make the foulest clean;
> His blood availed for me.
>
> "O that the world might taste and see
> The riches of his grace!
> The arms of love that compass me
> Would all mankind embrace."

Mrs. Bishop Simpson, having returned from Mexico, presented in a most interesting manner the result of her observations in that field. A number of missionary candidates were presented, the Corresponding Secretaries giving short verbal sketches of those accepted by the Society, and letters from some of the young ladies were read. Some minutes were spent in silent prayer for the new missionaries, accompanied with thanksgiving to God for his gracious gifts to them and to this Society, followed by prayer by Mrs. Skidmore. Before engaging in prayer, Mrs. Willing offered the following resolution:

"*Resolved*, That the Secretary is hereby instructed to write a letter of sympathy to the parents of Miss Josephine Copp, who, under appointment for India, has been transferred to the home above."

After prayer these words were sung,

> "His only righteousness I show,
> His saving truth proclaim:
> 'Tis all my business here below
> To cry, 'Behold the Lamb!'
>
> "Happy, if with my latest breath
> I may but gasp his name;
> Preach him to all, and cry in death,
> 'Behold, behold the Lamb!'"

On the morning of the 13th the regular business session was postponed in order to give time to complete the report of the Finance Committee.

"The morning was spent in prayer, followed by a love-feast. The meeting was opened by Mrs. Hibbard, by reading the third chapter of Ephesians. The hymn, 'Love divine, all love excelling,' was sung, and after the opening prayer the time was fully occupied in voluntary prayers and testimonies. A full record of this meeting cannot be given, for it is beyond the power of pen to describe the heavenly influence that filled the place. The secret springs of the power of the Woman's Foreign Missionary Society were revealed, and with the psalmist every heart adoringly exclaimed, ' All my springs are in Thee!'"

The following missionaries were appointed: Letitia Mason and Sigourney Trask, medical missionaries to China; Anna Julia Lore, medical missionary to India; Susan M. Warner and Mary Hastings, to Mexico; Jennie M. Chapin and Lou B. Denning, to South America; and Dora Schoonmaker, to Japan.

The anniversary was held in the Broad and Arch streets Church. A large audience was present, and manifested great interest in the exercises. Dr. Hatfield, pastor of the Church, presided. Addresses were delivered by Mrs. G. M. Steele, Mrs. F. G. Hibbard, Mrs. W. B. Skidmore, and Mrs. Johnson, returned missionary from India.

SIGOURNEY TRASK, M.D.

SIGOURNEY TRASK, M.D., was born June 14, 1849, in Youngsville, Warren County, Pennsylvania. Her mother, who was a very godly woman, died while Sigourney was a little child; and in the course of time she found a home with her paternal grandparents, who also resided in Youngsville. From early life she gave evidence of a superior mind and an eager thirst for knowledge.

At the age of fourteen she was converted, and joined the Methodist Episcopal Church. Two years afterward she attended a select school, taught by her pastor, Rev. C. M. Heard. Her studious habits, close application, and perfect recitations, placed her in the very front rank among her associates in school, and, in connection with her well-known fidelity and efficiency in her Church relations, impressed the mind of her teacher and pastor that Providence designed her for a more than ordinary sphere of usefulness, for which she would need more than an average education.

Knowing that she was without means to secure a higher education, this kind friend wrote a letter to the Rev. Dr. Pershing, President of the Female College, at Pittsburgh, giving him a brief history of Miss Trask, and a statement of his impressions with regard to her future work, in the hope that there might be in the hands of the president a fund for the education of young ladies who gave promise of great usefulness to the Church, and who had not the means to procure all the education they desired. The result was, that a wealthy Christian gentleman of the city of Pittsburgh, who withheld his name from the knowledge of all save Dr. Pershing, engaged to pay the expenses of Miss Trask's education at the College until she graduated. It was afterward discovered that this gentleman was the late S. M. Kier, whose memory is precious, being associated with many such deeds of disinterested benevolence. While this was pending her grandmother died, and in a few weeks after the funeral Sigourney was settled in her new college home. Here she more than justified all the expectations she had awakened in the hearts of her friends; and after a period of three years she graduated with honor, receiving two prizes — one for superiority in languages, the other for proficiency in mathematics.

Miss Lizzie K. Pershing, daughter of the President of Pittsburgh Female College, writes: "I first became acquainted with Miss Trask, when she entered our college in 1866. The purpose of entering the mission field was then the ruling motive, the inspiration, of her life. Your questions as to her call to the work, I think, first awakened me to the full realization of the fact that she did sometime have a call, and was not born with the purpose. I have been so accustomed to associate her with missionary labor, prospective or actual, that it is hard to separate her from it in my thought. I knew her as a student, (and a most earnest one she was,) but her studies were always understood to be simply preparatory to her chosen life-work. She was one of the few girls who stood in no doubt of their future. She walked in a path clearly marked out for her, and seemed never to look backward. Miss Trask was graduated from our college with high honor in 1870. She has a strong, keen intellect; an ardent, impulsive heart; and a deeply religious nature. To know her slightly, is to esteem her; to know her well, is to love her."

The following extract from a letter to her former pastor, Rev. C. M. Heard, dated October 9, 1869, written from the Pittsburgh College, gives an interesting statement from her own pen of her call to missionary work:

"The way the thought first came to my mind, and the subsequent unfoldings of Providence, have put it beyond my power to doubt God's will. I dare not do it. The thought was not always with me, that is, did not give fashion to my first ideas of life. One evening, nearly three years before you came to our place, I was sitting alone in my own little room, thinking. The question I was deliberating was, 'What shall I do?' It was not considered in the present tense, but looked altogether toward the future. No perplexing cross-roads presented themselves at that time. The connection which the present then had with the question was simply what it always sustains—the preparation time. Of this one thing I felt conscious, that every one whom God sends into the world he sends for some purpose. I wanted to know his purpose toward me. I had been reading the Bible. Closing it, and kneeling down, I prayed earnestly that God would teach me for what I should prepare myself. Looking in faith for divine guidance, I thought over every avocation that presented itself. Nothing was satisfactory. All were exhausted. Teaching school, the last and most favorably considered, possessed an indefinable something which made even it not fully satisfactory. I was on the point of rising with this thought in mind, almost involuntarily expressed, 'It must be that I am going to die young. There is nothing for me to do,' when a new thought struck me with almost electrifying force. 'The mission field!' I exclaimed, as if repeating the sound of an inner voice which had spoken the word, and clasped my hands in gratitude. The mental light which accompanied the conviction—rather, which forced the conviction—seemed to me to be something like that great light which changed the heart and life of Paul. I speak it reverently. The same God sent both. For several weeks, perhaps months, from that time it seemed as if I were in a new world. The *new life* had not come yet, but it was certainly a new phase in life to have something definite as an object. I did not tell any one for a long time. It seemed to me too sacred to talk about. I told my sister, and no one else till I told you. In the meantime I was not always strong-hearted; sometimes very weak and wavering, especially when soberly reasoning with facts before me, and looking at the probabilities and the improbabilities. At length, when in January of 1864 God made me his child, I felt anew the sacred obligation resting upon me."

After her graduation the question arose as to the field she should enter. The suggestion was made that she "study medicine, and go out as medical missionary." She entered a medical college at Cleveland, Ohio. At the end of one year she was transferred from the Cleveland college to Dr. Blackwell's College, in New York, from which she graduated in the spring of 1874. Shortly afterward she received her appointment to Foochow, China.

On board the steamer she wrote to friends as she was nearing the eastern shores of Asia: "The actual work of my life is to begin soon. I am *so* glad it is at hand! I do believe every feeling, faculty, and possibility of my nature is consecrated a living —I do not like to say sacrifice—a living energy to accomplish the mission God has given me among the Chinese. . . . 'Bound in spirit,' Paul said; under bonds of the Spirit I go. This bondage is my liberty; the bonds are my joy and my strength. I am grateful; but a *life*, not words, must show the gratitude that makes my spirit sing. Why God has given me so much—why one so perverse and unworthy should be so greatly blessed—remains a mystery. Nevertheless, it is of his mercy he saves us—

"'There's a wideness in God's mercy,
Like the wideness of the sea.'"

Miss Trask has been wonderfully successful in her work. As a Society, our most sanguine hopes with regard to the results of her labors have been more than realized.

Dr. Baldwin said, at the Shanghai Conference of missionaries, in 1877: "I am glad to bear witness to the great usefulness of female physicians. Miss Trask entered our mission only two years ago, but by having some one to interpret for her she began work at once, and has treated a large number of cases very successfully. At the outset she was asked to treat a case of dropsy that seemed so utterly hopeless that I went to the friends of the patient and told them that there was no hope of effecting a cure; that all we could hope to do was, to give some relief to the sufferer, who might possibly pass away in a few hours. They said they knew there was no hope of recovery, but would be grateful for any measure of relief that might be afforded. With this understanding Dr. Trask undertook the case, and treated it so successfully that the patient is still alive, and has come more than once to express her gratitude to the physician.

"One result of this is, that whereas we missionaries passed through the street where this woman lived for years without attracting any other attention than that of the dogs that came out to bark at us, when Miss Trask has gone to that neighborhood the people have *risen up* to show civility to her. She has a hospital capable of receiving forty patients, with all the necessary medicines and surgical appliances. Miss Trask has been called to attend the wives of mandarins, and to go a long distance into the country to attend poor women, and has responded to all such calls as far as possible. The whole work has a most excellent influence, and this branch of missionary service cannot be too strongly commended.

"Miss Trask is unwilling to write about her own part of the work, and her letters are full of the kindness and devotion of the ladies in the mission, who daily spend hours teaching the Gospel to those who come to her for medical help. Its success arises from the blessing of God upon the united efforts of all the Christian workers. Her success in treatment, with her kind, gentle manner, has won for her the respect and love of her patients and their friends. The hospital is a fine, commodious building, with wards for in-patients, nurses' room, drug room, and rooms for the resident physician and her assistants, and all other accommodations necessary for work. This was dedicated in May, 1877.

"As the inauguration of this hospital for Chinese women and children was a most important event, and the first of its kind, we give a condensed history of the enterprise. In January, 1874, the Methodist Episcopal Mission at Foochow asked for the appointment of a lady physician. The request was cordially responded to by the Woman's Foreign Missionary Society of the Methodist Episcopal Church, and in November of the same year Miss Sigourney Trask, M.D., arrived in Foochow. In 1875 the mission asked for an appropriation of $5,000 to buy a site and erect a hospital and residence for the physician. This request was also readily granted; $4,000 of the amount needed being assured by the

New York Branch, $500 by the Philadelphia Branch, and $500 by the Baltimore Branch. The first lot was purchased, and work begun upon the building in August, 1876. The building is ninety-eight feet by fifty-seven. It is a substantial two-storied house, in every way suitable for its destined purpose. It contains in the lower story drawing-room, library, and dining-room for the resident physician; drug-room, surgery, special ward-rooms, examining room, and waiting room for patients; with room for native assistants. The upper story contains three bed-rooms, connected with the physician's residence, two large ward-rooms, bath-rooms, rooms for nurses, etc. Upon the occasion of the dedication of this building a large number of prominent persons were present, both Europeans and natives. Mr. Delano, United States Consul, presided. His Excellency the Fantai, accompanied by several Commissioners of the Fohkien Province, were present. These remained throughout the whole of the opening ceremony, and manifested considerable interest in the details of the building, as also in its charitable object. Thus, under such favorable auspices, was the medical work of the Woman's Foreign Missionary Society inaugurated in Foochow. The dispensary is open daily for transient patients. These come in large numbers, so that the waiting-room is always filled with an audience ready to hear the words of the missionary and Bible reader. Dr. Trask never forgets that the chief object of her mission is to save souls. These women come from all directions; they are burdened with sorrows, sick in body, and almost hopeless. Mrs. Baldwin visits the hospital daily, and talks to the patients concerning their spiritual interests, while Miss Trask administers to their physical maladies."

We copy from the "Heathen Woman's Friend" the following extract from a letter giving an interesting account of one of Mrs. Baldwin's daily visits:

"After a little more kindly talk with her and the others, we go into the next ward. Some of these women have been here for some weeks, and greet me very kindly, and one (not sick, but who has a sick child) hastens to bring me a seat. On the first bed is a woman with a terribly ulcerated leg, that Dr. Trask first feared would have to be amputated; but now there is hope that this will not be necessary. She is a pretty, bright young woman, with bound feet. Two of the women are here with sick children. The mother of one is specially attractive and pretty. She also has bound feet. Another woman has had a large tumor removed from her back. She is now nearly well, and very comfortable and happy she looks, compared with what she did when she first came here. She can read some, and has heard a good deal of truth in these days at the hospital, and, I hope, not in vain. Her husband says he made offerings to many gods, but all to no good, for his wife. We sit down, and I tell them of our common parentage in Adam and Eve, of the entrance of sin into the world, and of the One who can alone save us from sin. They listen most quietly, and apparently with great interest. We fill up an hour with them, and then take our leave, inviting them to be seated, and they us to walk slowly—the Celestial good-bye. And thus our morning at the hospital ends.

"Recently Dr. Trask has been called to two very sad cases. One a woman who had attempted to commit suicide, because she had trouble with her husband. She had taken, probably, potash. She suffered greatly, and her mother-in-law scolded her for putting them all to so much trouble. 'And now,' said she, 'you are sick, and we shall all have to wait on you!' Dr. Trask gave her relief, but the effect of what she had taken on her stomach was very bad, and may cause her much suffering in the future. The second case was of a nice-looking young woman who had been terribly cut with a knife by her opium-smoking husband. There were great gashes on her head and back. When Dr. Trask went to her, at the call of one of the family, the others would not let her touch the wounds, and she was compelled to leave without doing any thing for the poor woman. The sorrows of the women of this land are indeed grievous, and they can only be lightened by the incoming of Christ himself, who has said to all suffering humanity, 'Come unto me, all ye that labor and are heavy laden, and I will give you rest.'"

This work has greatly interested many of the leading men of the Empire. A prominent Chinese merchant said to Miss Trask, "It would be a great blessing to the women of China if there was another hospital and many more ladies engaged in so good a work." A donation of two hundred dollars has recently been received by Dr. Trask for the Woman's Hospital, from high officials of the Fuhkien Province. This came to her through the United States Consul, and as it may be of interest, we give the letter:

> "CONSULATE OF THE UNITED STATES,
> FOOCHOW, *May* 21, 1878.

"MY DEAR MISS TRASK: I have much pleasure in handing you herewith a check for two hundred dollars, ($200,) which sum has been sent to me at the instance of His Excellency Pao Heng, Acting Governor of this Province, as a contribution made up by various high officials of the Province, in aid of the Hospital for Chinese Women, over which you so ably preside, with the request that I would forward it to you. It must be a source of gratification to you, as it is to myself, that the native authorities take so lively an interest in the good work in which you are engaged.

"Wishing you great success, believe me yours sincerely, M. M. DE LANO. *

"To DR. SIGOURNEY TRASK, *Foochow*."

Bishop Wiley, writing to Rev. C. M. Heard, says: "I wish I could see you and tell you what a fine lady Miss Trask is, and how grandly she is getting on in her work. I hope she may have long life and health in Foochow."

* Eighth Annual Report of the Woman's Foreign Missionary Society.

ANNA JULIA LORE, M.D.

ANNA JULIA LORE is a native of Buenos Ayres, South America, and was born in the year 1849. Her father, Dallas D. Lore, D.D., was by nature rarely endowed—physically, mentally, and morally; possessing a keen intellect, classical features, and a pure, gentle spirit. He joined the Philadelphia Conference of the Methodist Episcopal Church in 1837. From the time of his conversion he was thoroughly imbued with the missionary spirit, and in 1840 he was nominated as a missionary to Africa, but circumstances prevented his entering upon the work. In 1847 he went as a missionary to Buenos Ayres, where, two years after, the subject of this sketch was born.

Miss Lore's mother was a beautiful, refined, and accomplished Christian lady. She accompanied her husband to Buenos Ayres, and entered joyfully into all his plans for the spread of the Gospel and the salvation of the world. Here they remained seven years, during which time their daughter Anna Julia was born.

After founding the Methodist mission, Dr. Lore returned from Buenos Ayres, and was sent upon a tour of observation in New Mexico, with a view to the establishment of a mission in that Territory, after which he entered the pastorate, and in 1864 was elected editor of the "Northern Christian Advocate," which position he held until his death.

It was while in the city of Buffalo, and when about twelve years of age, that Julia was converted to Christ and joined "Grace Church," of which her father was pastor. The change was very thorough, and from that time her chief desire was to follow Jesus in all things, and fully to consecrate her life to him. Young as she was, she delighted in doing all she could to bring others to Christ, and was particularly interested in teaching a class of little girls in a German Mission School.

As she grew to maturity her interest in mission work increased. Says one who knew her well and intimately, "I cannot remember the time when she did not eagerly read all within her reach in regard to foreign missions." She began to have a burning desire to carry the glad tidings of salvation into the regions beyond—to those benighted souls sitting in darkness and in the shadow of death. Long before she mentioned the subject to her dearest earthly friends, (for she would not cause them unnecessary pain,) her heart was often stirred to its inmost depths by the thought of offering herself to the Woman's Foreign Missionary Society, for this work.

Those who saw her gliding through the house, singing a cheerful tune, or with skilled fingers sweeping the keys of the piano, filling her home with the radiance of her smile and the melody of her voice, had no idea that she was all this time painfully anxious to accomplish good in the world, and was so soon to relinquish home and all its endearments for this purpose. Few outside of the home circle knew of the depth of her piety. It was not obtrusive, but its genuineness impressed all who came under her influence. Those who knew her best, knew that she walked and talked with God.

> "Sweet promptings unto kindest deeds
>   Were in her very look ;
> They read her face, as one who reads
>   A true and holy book :
> The measure of a blessed hymn,
>   To which their hearts could move ;
> The breathing of an inward psalm ;
>   A canticle of love."

At last, after many severe heart struggles, in the summer of 1870, the day she completed her twenty-first year, the decision was made, and the Lord wonderfully blessed her in this consecration, and filled her with a joy unspeakable. One who knew much of her heart at this time writes us, " I fully believe if ever a minister was called to preach the Gospel, Julia was called to be a foreign missionary."

Desiring to prepare herself to the utmost for usefulness in her chosen field of labor, she commenced the study of medicine. After three years of close application, she was graduated at Ann Arbor, Michigan, and subsequently spent nine months in the Woman's Hospital, in Boston.

In 1874 she offered herself to the Woman's Foreign Missionary Society, was accepted, and appointed to Moradabad, India. At the great International Camp-meeting, held at Round Lake in 1874, Julia was present with her parents. One morning an unusually interesting love-feast was held before the stand. Bishops Kavanaugh and Doggett, of the Methodist Episcopal Church, South; and Bishops Janes and Foster, of the Methodist Episcopal Church, were present and spoke; also representatives from Canada, Europe, Asia, Australia, and other parts of the world. It was a glorious meeting. The power of God was manifested in a wonderful manner.

Toward the close a group of missionaries about to sail for their various fields of labor were called, and each spoke a few words. Among them were Mr. and Mrs. Thomas, of our India Mission; Mr. and Mrs. Banerjia, natives of India; Miss Trask, M.D., under appointment to China; and Rev. C. P. Hard and Miss A. J. Lore, under appointment to India. The meeting continued to grow in interest, and as these persons gave their testimonies it reached a climax. The power of the Most High overshadowed the audience. The people seemed electrified. The clergymen on the platform sprang to their feet, and, with tears in their eyes and halleluias on their lips, clasped each other by the hand, and pledged themselves to meet again on the heights of immortality. They sang

"Our souls by love together knit,
Cemented, mixed in one."

The benediction was pronounced, and the meeting declared closed; but of the thousands assembled there but few moved from their seats. They all with one accord began to sing the hymn ending with the chorus—

> "Pure robes, white robes,
> Washed in the blood of the Lamb,"

and the baptism of power fell upon the people. The scene was indescribable. There was no confusion —no noise save the singing—but there was a sound within a sound. A joy unutterable filled their hearts, and the light of heaven shone upon their faces as they sang over and over again the words of the chorus. As the singing ceased Dr. Deems, of the "Church of the Strangers," of New York City, attempted to describe his feelings as he drew near the altar and heard the singing, saying that he never expected to hear the like until he heard the songs of the redeemed in heaven. In his own inimitable style he added, "O paid choirs! O operas! O Jenny Linds! O all the rest of you! what is *your* singing compared with that of these, who sing with the Spirit of Christ burning within their souls, and the joy of the Lord welling up from the fountain of their hearts?" Others, turning to the missionaries, bade them go in the name of the Lord Jesus, and poured their benedictions and blessings upon them. One of our Bishops said he thought that the Church of Christ had never before received such a baptism of the Holy Ghost since the days of Pentecost.

During the days following Julia seemed to be "the observed of all observers." Noticing her youth and beauty, her intellectual and personal charms, it was no wonder that the lovers of Jesus were interested, and that they were ready to turn from others who were filling positions in the Church with ability and talent, to render honor to her who, laying on the altar of sacrifice whatever of genius or acquirement or loveliness she possessed, was going forth cheerfully on her errand of love to the heathen. A farewell meeting of great interest was held in Auburn, New York; and others, under the auspices of the Woman's Foreign Missionary Society, in Halsey-street Church, Newark, New Jersey, and in Saint Paul's Church, New York.

Miss Lore sailed from the port of New York October 20, 1874. It was a beautiful day. The sunlight came streaming down upon the water from the softest autumn sky, and seemed the visible expression of God's blessing upon the missionaries as the ship Minnesota faded in the distance from sight. A great many friends assembled on the ship to say good-bye. Among them were the Missionary Secretaries, Bishop Harris, and many clergymen of New York and vicinity.

One incident occurred at this time which, taken in connection with the death of her father so soon after,* made an impression upon our mind which we shall never forget. After the friends had left the steamer and she was about moving, we saw Miss Lore looking anxiously in all directions for something or somebody. Presently we saw her father coming with all possible speed. He had gone on an errand of love, to get something which he wished her to take with her, thinking he had plenty of time. But the steamer moved off sooner than

* Dr. Lore died soon after, suddenly.

he expected, and he only just reached it in time to say farewell! As he ran up the plank and reached the deck, Julia fastened her arms about his neck. They embraced each other most affectionately, but, though their hearts were full almost to bursting, they kept back the tears, and smiled upon each other, speaking only words of love and cheer. It was time for him to go, and as he turned to do so, Julia's loving arms once more encircled him; they kissed each other passionately, smiled, and parted. All eyes save theirs were moist. Friends standing at the pier began singing—

> "We shall meet on that beautiful shore,
> In the sweet by and by."

The missionaries stood waving their handkerchiefs, and joined in the singing, until the distance divided us so that we could no longer hear their voices. This was too much for Julia's father. He stepped behind the throng, with his beautiful daughter Bessie on his arm, and leaned against the building. He wore his accustomed smile upon his face, not a muscle moved, but the fountains of his heart were stirred. Nature would have her way; and the tears, like rain-drops, were trickling down his cheeks. We took his hand, but did not speak. We had passed through a similar experience, and we knew that at such a time

> "Words are so powerless, so vain to console,
> And the tears that we shed seem to lighten the soul."

Just at this moment Dr. Dashiell, our Missionary Secretary, came, and, taking his hand, said, "Dr.

Lore, your tears are as honorable as the gift you have made." "Yes," said the brave man, "I am not ashamed of them."

After a pleasant voyage Miss Lore reached India, and was stationed at Moradabad, where she entered heartily upon her work. All the reports we have seen concerning her and her work from its commencement until the present time prove her to be a most indefatigable and successful toiler in the mission field. She has also been eminently successful in her medical work.

In September, 1876, she was married to the Rev. G. H. M'Grew, whom she had met in America before leaving her native land; and who was afterward sent out as a missionary by the parent Board: a young gentleman of rare intellectual and moral endowments, and a most efficient worker in the cause of Christ in India. She has since continued her medical missionary work with unabated zeal. She is full of the spirit of her work, and her heart yearns with unutterable tenderness over those for whom she labors, as may be seen by the following account she gives of her visit to the Girls' Orphanage at Bareilly:

"I sat this morning in the really beautiful chapel of the Girls' Orphanage, which had been beautifully decorated for Christmas, in true American fashion. Before me, in orderly rows, sat Miss Sparkes' girls, on the floor; the favorite attitude is with the knees drawn up and the hands clasped under them. The little girls sat in front, proud of their brilliant new *chuddars*, pink, lined with yellow. They wear pink trowsers gathered around their waists—the string tied in front—and little jackets; their young faces looking out from their odd *chuddars* gives one unaccustomed to them an eerie feeling, not altogether comfortable. The older girls wear white, generally, and I have never seen a company of girls any where who looked one whit prettier or brighter. The lesson was the review of last month's study of the Berean Series. As I sat looking into those bright faces, my heart filled up until I, a doctor woman, had an ache in my throat and tears behind my glasses, just for love to them. My eyes rested on a 'Silent Comforter,' and they read, 'Thou shalt make them drink of the river of thy pleasures. For with thee is the fountain of life.' My heart has been enlarged since reaching India. I have loved people always, ever so many, but now it seems as if *I truly love souls.*"

During the time when the cholera was raging so fearfully in Bareilly, and many of the girls fell victims to the terrible scourge, Mrs. M'Grew was untiring in her efforts to relieve the sufferers. Leaving her own precious babe at the house of a government official—a friend of hers—she went to the Orphanage, and stayed night and day, looking after and nursing the patients with the tenderest care. Forgetting her own ease and comfort, constantly exposed to the contagion of the disease, she toiled on, not fearing the "pestilence that walketh in darkness, nor the destruction that wasteth at noonday," trusting in the promise, "There shall no evil befall thee, neither shall any plague come nigh thy dwelling." Mrs. M'Grew is very popular in India, not only among her fellow-laborers, but among the natives. She wins all hearts.

Speaking of one of her patients in Bareilly, she says: "I have an interesting patient in the city now—a Hindu lady, young and childless, but with a large supply of that self-satisfaction which I have come to regard as the unvarying factor in a prosperous heathen's character. She began yesterday to talk in a supercilious way of the custom of remarrying widows, as prevalent among us, adding, 'We people think it a very great sin.' In reply, I asked her if the widows she knew did not lead dreadful lives, and did not a great many people sin by making their lives so dreadful? She assented, and said, 'Yes, they are like dogs; death would be happier.' One thing led to another, until I had a good chance to tell her of Christ's love—God's love in sending Christ to die for us, and the constraining power of that love in us. Such opportunities make me very happy."

LETITIA MASON, M.D.

LETITIA MASON was the first medical missionary sent out by the Cincinnati Branch. She went from the city of Chicago, where, after completing her medical course, she received her diploma, and practiced during the following winter in the hospital. She was appointed to Kiukiang, China, and sailed from San Francisco, October 5, 1874.

Mrs. Bishop Clark says: "We looked upon Miss Mason as 'thoroughly furnished.' She attended one of our missionary meetings, held at Columbus. I shall never forget her as she stood by me on the platform, in the bloom of youthful health and beauty, her eyes full of tears, and her heart aglow with love and longing desire to help in bringing those nigh who were afar off. As she told of her experience, and how she was led to forsake all for this great work, many eyes in the audience were full also."

Full of life and strength, buoyant and enthusiastic, she went forth; and the Society never felt more hopeful in regard to the success and endurance of any of its candidates. The mystery of divine Providence is strikingly manifest in the events connected with her missionary career. She reached Kiukiang, and entered joyfully and successfully upon her work. The following year she was seized with fever, which so reduced her strength that she never rallied completely, but after battling heroically with disease and pain, determined, if possible, to continue in the missionary field, she was obliged at last to submit to the inevitable, and to return home to save her life. She sailed from Japan, June 25, and reached the United States in August, 1876.

The following letter, written by the Corresponding Secretary of the Cincinnati Branch, will be full of interest to our readers:

RETURN OF DR. LETITIA MASON.*

It is with deep sadness that we announce the entire failure of Miss Mason's health, and her sudden return to her home at Normal, Illinois. Letitia Mason, M.D., sailed from New York, in October, 1874, arriving at Kiukiang, China, the following month. In July of the next year she was seized with a fever peculiar to that climate, and was very ill for eight weeks. Her system was reduced and vitality so impaired, that, although we had hoped for her final recovery, it has been evident for a year past that she was declining. Hopeful and diligent, she labored on in weakness and pain, until last spring.

Under date of May 6, 1876, Miss Hoag wrote to us, as follows: "I am sorry to write to you of the possible return of Miss Mason to America. The winter has not restored her health and strength, as she sanguinely hoped, nor has it procured freedom

* "Heathen Woman's Friend."

from almost constant suffering. She is wonderfully enthusiastic in her work, and the idea of being obliged to leave, especially since it has opened so well this spring, is almost heart-breaking. We all, now, fear that she will never be well in China: also, that any treatment in this climate will be of no avail. We cannot endure the thought of losing her."

By the same mail Miss Mason writes: "After receiving treatment from one of the best physicians in Shanghai, and though much improved during the winter, nothing seems permanent. It nearly breaks my heart to have any word sent to America about my poor health. If I knew that possibly, in a few days, I should be laid within the little walled inclosure under the shade of yonder old vine-covered pagoda, I could not feel more utterly sad than at the thought of leaving work here."

Miss Mason grew alarmingly worse, and after urgent requests on the part of all the missionaries there, she set out from the home of her adoption, expecting to go to Peking to consult with Miss L. L. Combs, M.D.; but on arriving in Shanghai was so ill that her own physician said she could not live to take the trip to Peking, but that she must return home. She sailed from Japan, June 25, and was so ill then that her life was almost despaired of by two physicians who were called in consultation during her two-days' stay in Yokohama. They were Drs. Eldridge and Simmons, and gave as their opinion that she could not live a month longer in that climate, and that with a return to America at once the chances of life and death were about even. As soon as she landed in San Francisco she began to improve, and can now walk about a little with the aid of her mother's arm. She cannot speak or write of missionary work without the great tears gathering, and her return home is as bitter a disappointment to her as it can be to our Branch, who had hoped so much from our medical work in Kiukiang. These pioneers in this department in Asia seem to be laying down their lives for its sake. How often it is that some work even unto death, and others enter into their labors. Who will take up the great work laid down so sadly by our beloved Miss Mason?

One of the missionaries of the parent Board writes to Mrs. Ingham:

"By the time you receive this you will, doubtless, have heard of the utter failure of dear Miss Mason's health. She wrote me from Shanghai such a touching letter! She hoped for recovery while all around despaired, and she would not consent to quit the field. She goes with a heart almost breaking. Her failure is a greater trial to herself than it can possibly be to any one else. She loved the work dearly, and was planning for a great future; but a mysterious providence takes her out of it."

Under these circumstances resignation to the will of God becomes the imperative duty of all concerned.

SUSAN M. WARNER.

SUSAN M. WARNER went to Mexico from New Orleans, Louisiana, where she had been engaged in teaching school. She was converted in early life, and evinced an unquenchable desire to be useful. She was self-sacrificing to an unusual degree, and was always ready to relinquish her own ease or pleasure in order to prove a blessing to others. Few ladies possessed naturally a more keen, discriminating, intelligent mind. And these natural gifts had been cultivated to a high degree, until she was eminently fitted for the work to which she was called.

Of herself she says, with characteristic modesty: "There can be little of interest to the public in the details of the life of one who, after educating herself and spending several years in providing for her mother, was at last able to realize a long-cherished plan of engaging in missionary work." Mrs. Bishop Clark, President of the Cincinnati Branch, says: "Miss Warner was recommended to us by doctors of divinity and others who knew her well, as '*pure gold!*' Her views, both of teaching and government, as evinced by her well-written letters, were excellent."

Among the traits prominent in her character were courage and fidelity. She *dared to be right—dared to be true.* When convinced as to the *right* course to pursue, nothing could cause her to swerve in any degree. The voice of duty was imperative, and her only reply to those who questioned was, "Why is my liberty judged of another man's conscience?" She never would sacrifice her own individuality, nor consent to be the mere echo of another. For had not God called her, and given her a work to do? Notwithstanding, she was humble, teachable, affectionate, ever considerate of the feelings of others, and carrying out the spirit of the injunction, "In honor preferring one another."

She was appointed to Pachuca, Mexico, in 1874. She entered into her work heartily, and did with her might what her hands found to do, until, worn down by overwork, she was prostrated by fever, and, in 1877, was obliged to return for rest and recuperation. But her love for missionary work was not diminished by the fiery trial through which she passed; and as soon as practicable she returned again to her chosen work. Long may she live, to point the poor benighted and oppressed women of Mexico to Jesus, the light of the world!

MARY HASTINGS.

PAUL, the first Christian who ever went on a missionary tour, said, "Neither count I my life dear unto myself, so that I might finish my course with joy, and the ministry, which I have received of the Lord Jesus, to testify the gospel of the grace of God." There are many noble souls who emulate his spirit; who are so thoroughly consecrated to God and duty that they count all things but loss for the excellency of the knowledge of Christ Jesus, and cheerfully peril health, and even life, and suffer privation and severe hardships, for the sake of ministering to the suffering—of bearing the light of life to the homes of darkness and oppression. And in doing this, they never imagine for a moment that they have done any thing worthy of note, or that their lives can be of any interest to the public.

Of this class Miss Mary Hastings is a representative woman. Few have rendered more constant and valuable service to the Church, and few have ever been so wholly unconscious of merit. Accounting herself, with Paul, " less than the least of all saints," she regards it as her reasonable service to continue in her life of toil and sacrifice.

Miss Hastings was born in Blandford, Massachusetts, June 5, 1833. Her father was an earnest local preacher, powerful in prayer and exhortation. Her mother was a pious, devout, cultured woman, a sister of Miss Maria Hamilton, who was preceptress at Cazenovia Seminary in its first decade, and who was afterward the wife of Professor Johnson, of Wesleyan University, Middletown, Connecticut. Her maternal grandparents were members of the first class organized in Blandford; so that from her earliest recollections she was identified with the Methodist Episcopal Church and its work.

At a remarkably early age Miss Hastings manifested great love for books and study. She says: "A neighbor told me that at four years of age I used to read the newspapers to him, which, I suppose, was my first missionary work." At the same time her brother complained that she did not *recite* her geography lessons, but read them over the tops of the books. When but six years of age she was made the subject of the pardoning grace of God, and speaks of the great peace she received through faith in Christ.

"After this," she says, "while only a child, I listened to a sermon on holiness, and a meeting being appointed for those who desired to seek it, though the night was dark and unpleasant, I went all alone and consecrated myself to God the best I knew how; but it was not until some time later that I was able to say, 'Lord, I am thine, entirely thine.' The desire to prepare for usefulness became very strong as years passed on, and the conviction of my call to work for Jesus deepened. Standing by the bedside of my dying father, I heard him say, 'He will never leave nor forsake you.' Trusting that faithful word, I felt that I must take up the work that my father had laid down, and seek to win souls for Christ."

After the death of her father she entered the Wesleyan Academy, at Wilbraham, Massachusetts, and in 1858 graduated with high honors, being the valedictorian of her class, and most highly esteemed by teachers and students. She had an innate love for the beautiful, and for communion with nature, and was proficient in drawing and oil painting. After leaving Wilbraham, she accepted a call to Lawrence University, Appleton, Wisconsin, as preceptress, and teacher of the Art Department. Here she remained two years, during which time, she says, "There was some missionary work to be done, as among the interesting young people gathered in the University and its preparatory school there entered, from time to time, Indian youths of both sexes, mostly of the Oneida and Brotherton tribes."

Desiring to continue the study of art, and also of languages, she returned again to the East for that purpose. After some time spent in study, a call came for her to go as preceptress to a school in Canning, Cornwallis, Nova Scotia. She went, and while there a gracious outpouring of the Holy Spirit came upon the people. "The school," she writes, "was visited from on high in wonderful power."

As characteristic of her love of nature, we give the following extract from a letter written from this place to a former classmate:

"I have just returned from a ramble on the beach.

The tide being out, I went down a distance into the ocean-bed, and sat on a rock over which the wild waves dashed last night, and where they will soon be rolling again. It is delightful to sit thus on a rock of the sea and muse, while all around the waters foam and toss their spray, and rage in their rocky bed. Beyond the angry beating of the surf the waters lie calm and still beneath the summer sky, and thought glides swiftly across the bosom of the sea to my native land, and the friends who linger there. Involuntarily I pause and listen, half-expecting to hear familiar voices borne on the moaning breeze, and often my longing eyes seek the distant horizon, where sky and ocean meet, looking in vain for the green hills of dear New England."

After returning to her home a call came for missionary work among the freedmen. The field was Memphis. Miss Hastings accepted the call. Writing to a friend, she says: "I feel such a sweet sense of the divine protection, that could my eyes see the angels of the Lord encamping round me, I could feel no more certain than I now do that I am safe in His keeping. I am on the way to Memphis to do for Christ, in the person of his degraded and despised ones, whatever my hand finds to do."

After becoming somewhat established in her new field of labor, she writes again to the same friend: "Your kind letter was full of comfort to my weary, sorrowful heart. Only a day or two previous, news of my mother's death had come from my loved home; and here, among strangers, I bear this great sorrow; not, it is true, without sympathy, for I am surrounded with friends, Christian co-laborers. I feel, too, that for my dear mother I have no cause to mourn, for to her, as to the apostle, 'to die is gain.' She sweetly rests from all her toils and sufferings with all the blessed dead. I know that although I, her *only daughter*, was far away, loving hands ministered to every want, and gratified every wish; but it is sad to feel that no mother prays for the absent one, or looks for tidings from her wanderer. Still, the Saviour's precious promise—the last loving message from my dying father's lips—'I will never leave nor forsake you,' sustains my burdened spirit.

> "A little while! O, glorious word!
> Sweet solace of our sorrow;
> And then, forever with the Lord—
> The everlasting morrow."

Returning North, she was soon after appointed missionary to Mexico. She sailed from New York on the Cleopatra, Saturday, January 10, 1874. She went out under the auspices of the New York Branch, and was their first representative to Mexico. She was first stationed at Mexico City. We cannot give our readers a better glimpse into her character or her work than by giving her own words, written October, 1874, to Mrs. Nickerson, of Provincetown, Massachusetts:

"Our school increases; we number more than thirty now, and hope soon to have sixty girls. That will be a good family to feed, clothe, govern, and educate, wont it? Another little girl, Rafaelita, has just come; and as in my heart I said, 'Lord, may she be thine!' very sweetly came the promise, 'All thy children shall be taught of the Lord.' We will sow the seed as he gives opportunity, and 'tis his to make it fruitful. My life here is very unlike my notions of mission life; but if the Father's will is done, I am satisfied; and, as far as I am conscious, I am doing that, and that alone, and so, though often sorrowful, I am always rejoicing. O Beccie, darling, how I would like to see you, and fold you in my arms to-night! How I would love to have you here to help me tell the story of redemption, and help me sing for Jesus! Pray for us, that the word of the Lord may have free course, run, and be glorified. O the idols must fall in this land! 'Let thy kingdom come, and thy will be done,' is the cry of my heart day and night, and the dear Lord hears.

"A few days since an old man heard one of our Bible readers reading the commandments. As he listened and comprehended their meaning, he cried out in agony, 'They have left me to break God's commands! O what shall I do, what shall I do?' 'Believe on the Lord Jesus Christ, and thou shalt be saved,' was the reply. He stepped outside of the door, and in a few moments was *dead!* His grief and fear had been too much for him to bear, and his poor troubled heart was still.

"We often feel that we would like to do the work up in a hurry, and be able to tell you at once that all Mexico had turned from the Virgin of Guadaloupe and Remedios to Him who is the way, the truth, and the life; and that the thousands and tens of thousands who throng the Cathedral, the *Profesa*, and all the costly idol temples, are coming, through simple faith, to Christ. Well, it is almost two thousand years since the Gospel of salvation started on its errand, and notwithstanding the world has been so slow of heart to receive it, we must rejoice in the thousands on thousands who, through all these rolling years, have come, and still are coming, to find eternal life. And we will work on in faith, and hope, and love; sure that, in the multitudes gathered out of every nation and kindred and tongue, some shall come from Mexico to join the glad chorus, 'To Him who hath loved us, and washed us in his own blood.'"

In 1875 she removed from Mexico City to Pachuca, where she has since remained, laboring unceasingly for the evangelization of the poor, benighted, and much-neglected, women of that dark land.

We will let Miss Hastings close the sketch in her own words: " To-day (January 10, 1878) completes the period of five years since I sailed from New York. The Lord knows I have sown his truth with many tears; but when I hear my precious pupils confessing Jesus, giving thanks for the blessings that have come to them through the Gospel of Christ, praying for the salvation of their people, and asking that strength may still be given me to lead them heavenward, I know that our labor in the Lord has not been in vain. Some of the seed may perish by the wayside, but some shall bring forth fruit a hundredfold, unto eternal life."

JENNIE M. CHAPIN AND LOU B. DENNING.

THESE ladies are our first representatives in the South American work. Miss Jennie M. Chapin is a native of Chicopee, Hampden County, Massachusetts, and was born June 20, 1842. Her father was a farmer, and her childhood and early youth were spent amid the purest influences, in communion with nature, and in looking from nature up to nature's God. At fourteen years of age she was converted to Christ, and united with the Methodist Episcopal Church. Miss Chapin early evinced a great love for study, and, having availed herself of all the education the common schools afforded, she entered the Wilbraham Academy, where, after spending two years studying hard and doing extra work to pay expenses, she was prostrated, worn down, and obliged for two years to relinquish both study and teaching. As soon as health and strength would permit, she again entered the academy, after which she resumed her teaching. She also taught in a night-school in Lynn, Massachusetts, boarding in the family of Rev. E. A. Manning. She says: "I enjoyed this work very much, and look back to those as some of the happiest days in my life." Then affliction came. Her father died; her mother was prostrated by disease, but as

> "The sweetest scented plants that grow,
> When bruised their fragrance best bestow,"

so this young life began in a more marked manner to exhale its fragrance, and to devote its energies to the work of blessing others. Referring to her experience at this time, she writes: " The world lost all value. Heaven and Christ were more precious and near. I found the greatest pleasure in Christian society, and was in constant attendance at the missionary meetings held by our auxiliary of the Woman's Foreign Missionary Society. I was deeply interested in letters from South America asking that lady teachers should be sent there. Friends, thinking I had some of the characteristics that would fit me for the work, asked me if I would be willing to go. It seemed a call from God, and I permitted my name to be placed as a candidate, and was appointed to go to Rosario de Santa Fé, Argentine Republic, South America, in company with Miss Lou B. Denning, of Normal, Illinois."

January 20, 1874, a farewell meeting was held in Trinity Church, Springfield, Massachusetts, and January 23 Miss Chapin sailed from New York on the steamer Merrimac, reaching Rosario March 20, 1874. She has proved herself to be one of our most efficient and successful missionaries, and by her unselfish devotion to the interests of the Society has already won for herself many laurels. In a private letter she says: " My life, since coming here, is so intimately connected with that of Miss L. B. Denning, that the work of one has been that of the other. We have roomed together and been together in all our interests, and are like very dear sisters to each other."

LOU B. DENNING.

Miss Denning was born in Wayne County, Ohio, December 18, 1840. Her parents were rich in faith and heirs of the kingdom, and early inculcated in the minds of their children that which is of far greater value than a desire for earthly treasure. Their family consisted of eight children, two of whom are traveling preachers.

When she was about twelve years of age her father removed with his family to Minnesota, where they spent four years during its early settlement, experiencing all the privations as well as enjoyments of a pioneer life. Miss Denning says: " I have often thought the time spent there qualified me to better endure the privations of a missionary's life in South America." After this they removed to M'Lean County, Illinois, where her parents still reside. Among her earliest recollections is, that of her father's house being the home of the itinerant, and the pleasure her mother always took in providing and caring for his temporal wants. Brought up on a farm, her life was a retired one, yet full of happiness. In 1870 Miss Denning graduated from the 'State Normal School,' Normal, Illinois, after which she taught school until her appointment to South America.

With regard to her conversion and call to missionary work she says: " I was taught to love and attend, from infancy, all the means of grace connected with our Church. At the age of fourteen, during a protracted meeting held in Concord, Illinois, I listened to the entreaties of my mother and the wooings of the Holy Spirit, and presented myself as a seeker of religion. After several days of darkness, light broke into my soul full of resplendent beauty. Satan has thrust sore at me in many other points, but he never has made me doubt my conversion. In May, 1869, while attending school at Normal, Dr. and Mrs. Palmer held a series of meetings in Bloomington, two miles distant. Their special theme was "Holiness—Entire Consecration to God." I attended as much of the time as possible, having a great desire to enjoy this perfect salvation. On the 23d of the month, at six o'clock in the evening, after a severe conflict with the enemy, who seemed to use all his weapons against my believing that the blessing was for *me*, I was enabled to consecrate myself entirely to the Lord. The joy and peace that followed are beyond description —must be *felt* to be known. I then promised to do whatever the Lord might require of me, little thinking I should be called to go to a foreign field of labor. But when asked, by those interested in the cause, if I would be willing to be employed by the Woman's Foreign Missionary Society, though feeling my unworthiness and insufficiency, I could but reply, ' If the Lord wants me there, and the Society will accept me, I will go.'

"The announcement of the case to my parents and sister was a severe trial for me, and came with almost crushing weight to them. At first they felt it could not be; the thought of separation for five years seemed more than they could endure. But the love of God finally triumphed, and they said if I felt it to be my duty to go they would not dissuade me from it. My mother said; 'I gave my children all to the Lord in their infancy, and if he calls my daughter to a foreign land I will not oppose her going.' It was really harder for my dear sister, who still remained at home, to give her consent, having a very strong attachment for her friends. The fact that time and distance would so separate us seemed to tear her very heart-strings. One day, when talking with her about going, she wept as though she had already been to my burial. I, naturally enough, sympathized with her feelings. I left her, and, as I crossed the room, picked up a small piece of paper that lay on the floor. It was folded up so there seemed to be but little of it. I opened it and read, ' Trust in the Lord with all thine heart; and lean not unto thine own understanding. In all thy ways acknowledge him, and he shall direct thy paths.' If the Lord himself had spoken to me, the words could not have been more forcible. I felt they were just what I needed at that moment. After receiving my appointment to South America I began preparations, not knowing who my companion would be. But the Lord took care of that, and gave me one who, in health and sickness, has filled the place of a sister. I refer to Miss Jennie M. Chapin."

On Jan. 18, 1874, a "farewell" meeting was held in the Methodist Episcopal Church, at Normal, Illinois. The large audience listened to an eloquent address by Mrs. Jennie F. Willing, an essay prepared by Dr.

Richard Edwards, President of the Normal School, and remarks by the pastor, Rev. Mr. Millsap. The following day she bade farewell to home and loved ones, and was on her way to New York, where she was to meet Miss Chapin, and with whom, on the following Friday, she was to sail for South America.

These young ladies commenced work at once on board the steamer, and employed a part of each day (Sundays excepted) in studying and writing out Spanish lessons, reciting to a native Cuban, who offered to give them any assistance needed. Arriving at Rosario, their destination, they were warmly welcomed by Rev. T. B. Wood and wife, then stationed there. They have labored untiringly for the advancement of the cause in South America. Ever happy and successful in their work, the Society feels much satisfaction in having such worthy representatives in the field.

Of their work there Miss Denning says: "One month after our arrival we began teaching a few pupils in reading, arithmetic, and geography, we having to study quite as hard as the pupils in order to understand the lessons. We did not open our school to the public until the second year, devoting our time to study and such other work as fell into our hands. In September of 1875 we began a school with eight or ten pupils. As pioneers on the field we had to contend with all the prejudice of the people toward Protestants. We spent a part of the time in visiting the women in their homes, reading, singing, and talking with them as opportunity presented itself.

"Our school gradually increased, till it occupied all our time. We closed the school year with eighty pupils in November last. The priests have worked against us, both privately and publicly, but there is too strong a liberal element here for them to manifest any open persecution. We have some orphans from whom we hope much in the future. Many times our labors have been exceedingly fatiguing, yet we have been sustained through them all. God has been with us, shielding, protecting, and guiding us. Whatever of good has been accomplished is all of the Lord; to him be all the **glory.**"

DORA SCHOONMAKER.

DORA SCHOONMAKER was born in Ulster County, New York, in the year 1851. When five years of age her parents removed to Illinois, and made their home on the Kankakee River, near Wilmington. Dora possessed naturally a vigorous and inquiring mind, and developed at a very early age the great love for reading which has followed her through life. At eight years of age she first read the "Life of Harriet Newell." This made a deep impression upon her mind, and she said one day to her mother, "Mamma, when I grow up big I am going to be a missionary." But the thought which at first elated her childish heart began, with its development, to disclose more of the dark side of the missionary's life. She had naturally a very affectionate disposition, and was fondly attached to her friends. The thought of a separation which might be final, to her was appalling. She read the book over and over again; and as she grew older and looked more deeply into the matter, the thought that she must be a missionary deepened into a conviction, and she could not cast it off. With her keen intellect, she had the usual accompaniment—a strong will. The idea of being forced into any thing roused all her innate resolution, and she threw the "Life of Harriet Newell" into the river. But though the book was destroyed, she could not drown the impressions it had made. It had surely done its work in one heart, for Dora never lost the conviction that she must be a missionary.

At eleven years of age she was converted to God, and made a partaker of his saving grace. "But," she says, "this joyful experience was afterward lost, and was succeeded by several years of doubt and half skepticism." Again, at eighteen years of age, she consecrated her heart anew to God and his service.

She was uniformly a close student, and when eighteen years of age graduated with the highest honors from the high school of her town, being valedictorian of her class. After finishing her course of study, she accepted a situation in the public schools of Morris, Illinois. One year later she was appointed Principal of the High School, which position she held for three years, when she resigned this for work in Japan.

Mrs. H. H. C. Miller, of Evanston, Illinois, says: "Here she displayed, more than ever before, her wonderful tact and ability as a teacher. She excelled in *belles-lettres*, as well as in mathematics, and in giving up her teaching she sacrificed not alone this position, but others, far more remunerative, which were open to her. Her ability as a writer, too, is rare indeed. Her letters, dashed off in a few moments of time to her intimate friends, are often models of composition and rhetoric."

Dora was always a hard worker. In connection with her teaching she kept up the studies of German and French, and translated several volumes in each of these languages, besides following all the time a good course of reading. During her last year as a teacher she conducted a large class in German, aside from her school duties. About a year before leaving for Japan, Mrs. J. F. Willing suggested to her that a knowledge of music was quite essential to her success as a missionary. She had never given any attention to music; but she saw that the suggestion was a good one; *music was necessary*, and with characteristic promptness and indefatigable energy she began the arduous task. Nor did she relinquish her efforts until she had acquired sufficient knowledge in the science to enable her readily to sing and play the songs that were necessary to her work. Soon after she began teaching her girls in Japan, one of the Tokio missionaries said to her, "I never heard Japanese children sing in better time and tune."

A meeting of great interest was held in Evanston, Illinois, at the departure of Miss Schoonmaker. She sailed from San Francisco, October 5, 1874, and was our first representative to Tokio, Japan. She has been eminently successful in her missionary work. Miss T. A. Spencer, one of our missionaries in Japan, writes: "Your mental eyes have followed Miss Dora Schoonmaker, our brave pioneer in the field, for nearly five years, as she labored and toiled, often beyond her strength, to acquire the language and establish a school. She is a brunette, with fine, large, brown eyes, through which you can read the depths of the great soul beneath this slight exterior. She walks with a firm, quick tread, and has energy and ambition enough for two people. She is *very* fluent in speaking both English and Japanese, and wields a powerful pen. I love her dearly, and rejoice that her undaunted zeal and untiring labor have been so abundantly rewarded by Him whom she delights to honor."

March, 1878, she writes: "O you do not know what an amount of work there is to be done here! Tell the ladies that Tokio *must* have two more missionaries this year. With that addition to our working force, and with our new building, we shall, by God's blessing on our labors, be able to push forward the Lord's work here to a position of wide and powerful influence. Tell the people at home how it is—tell them the positive need; bid them remember that the Roman Catholic Church is established here, spreading its manifold errors among the people; and, because of its large force and unsparing use of funds, is said to have gathered into its fold no less than three hundred children in this one city of Tokio. Shall we, who profess to hold the truth in its purity, be less zealous than they? God forbid!"

SIXTH ANNUAL MEETING.

THE General Executive Committee held its sixth annual session in the city of Baltimore, in the First Methodist Episcopal Church, May 5, 1875. One change during the year had been made in its secretaries. Mrs. Dr. J. E. Lattimer, the accomplished and gifted Corresponding Secretary of the New England Branch, having resigned, Mrs. C. P. Taplin, another of New England's elect ladies, was appointed to fill the vacancy.

After the delegates had responded to the calling of the roll, Bishop Ames was introduced and addressed the meeting. He spoke of the gratification he felt in welcoming the ladies to Baltimore, and said the Missionary Society greatly needed just such workers as the women send into the foreign field, and referred to the obstruction Catholicism offers to evangelical Christianity. From all he had learned of this Society he was prepared to encourage and indorse it fully.

A committee of clergymen from the Baltimore Preachers' Association were introduced, and in fitting words tendered fraternal greetings and good wishes for the success of missions as conducted by the Woman's Foreign Missionary Society. Mrs. Willing responded in a graceful address, saying: "We cannot be very formal in replying to the kind words of Methodist ministers. These words of encouragement are especially grateful at this time, as they are needed. Never has the Committee come together with more firm reliance on God and a deeper sense of the need of his presence and help."

Business was resumed. The Annual Reports of the various Branches were presented and read by their respective Corresponding Secretaries. "Unabated interest, untiring zeal, and fervent love, upheld by faith in the God of all nations, characterized the reports given." The Corresponding Secretary of the Cincinnati Branch, detained at home by illness, was represented by Mrs. Davis, whose touching allusion to her friend, followed by tender messages conveyed by Mrs. Bishop Clark, awakened a profound sense of sorrow at the cause of her absence. On motion, a suspension of business was ordered, and a committee appointed to express the sentiments of the meeting toward their sister, Mrs. G. E. Doughty.

The following paper was adopted, and a copy ordered to be transmitted to Mrs. Doughty:

"The General Executive Committee hear with deep sorrow of the cause which detains at home the Corresponding Secretary of the Cincinnati Branch. We remember her thrilling words for Christ and his work at our last executive meeting —how they helped us to a deeper consecration of our own lives, and impressed us as coming from one who had been with Jesus; therefore

"*Resolved*, That we express to her our sympathy

and love, and that we bear her in our prayers, that, if it be the will of God, her life may be long spared to carry on his work on earth ; that we ask of our heavenly Father for her the constant consciousness of the love of our Lord Jesus Christ, that great Shepherd of the sheep, and that she be preserved blameless until his coming with all his saints to receive his own into his inheritance.

"MRS. S. L. KEEN, *Chairman*,
"MRS. H. SKIDMORE,
"MRS. J. F. WILLING."

The paper was scarcely read before the following was received from Mrs. Bishop Clark, of Cincinnati :

" Our dear Mrs. Doughty has gone to her home in heaven. . . . A little while before she died her pastor asked if, in the near approach of death, her faith faltered. She answered, ' No ; I don't know any thing about a *faltering* faith.' After long-continued coughing, she said, ' Come, Lord Jesus, come quickly. I am weary.' Soon after she became unconscious, and died at 6 : 30 A. M., 19th instant. . . . I feel to-day that I am personally bereaved. Dear Mrs. Doughty, may my life's record be like yours, and my last hours sustained by the same unfaltering faith ! How much has our Society, our Church, and the world lost by her death !"

" The anniversary was held in the First Methodist Church. Bishop Ames presided with his usual ability and dignity, adding much to the interest of the occasion. Mrs. Willing and Mrs. Taplin addressed the large and attentive audience."

One missionary, Miss L. A. Campbell, was appointed to China. After the business was completed the President, Mrs. Francis A. Crook, spoke a few earnest and well-directed words of congratulation upon the spirit of love to God and each other which pervaded the entire session, and invoked upon the whole executive board the blessing of the Most High, after which " The whole wide world for Jesus" was sung, and the meeting adjourned.

LETITIA A. CAMPBELL.

> "O safe at home, 'mid brightness all eternal,
>   When shall I breathe with thee the purer air—
> Air of a land whose clime is ever vernal,
>   A land without a serpent or a snare?
> Gone to begin a new and happier story,
>   Thy bitterer tale of earth now told and done;
> These outer shadows for that inner glory
>   Exchanged forever—O thrice blessed one!"

THUS the soul triumphantly sings as it looks upward and catches a glimpse of the ascending chariots of our translated victors. But coming down from "the verge of heaven"—the mount of transfiguration and glory—and seeing only the earth-view, the newly-made grave, the yearning, desolate hearts, the brimming eyes, the blasted hopes, and broken plans, the soul cries out, "O cruel Death, what hast thou done! Surely thou hast not made a fit selection for thy conquests here!"

> "Youth and the opening rose
> May look like things too glorious for decay,
>   And smile at thee; but thou art not of those
> That wait the ripened bloom to seize their prey."

Letitia A. Campbell was born in Liverpool, England, and died in Peking, China, May 18, 1878. In her childhood she emigrated with her parents to America, and settled in Cambridge, Massachusetts. At an early age she gave her heart to Christ and her hand to the Church, and was ever after one of its most zealous, active, and efficient members. Her parents were intelligent, devout, conscientious Christians. Her father, being an earnest worker in the mission field, impressed on her young heart, both by precept and example, the needs and importance of so great a cause. Consequently, as she grew in years she became more and more impressed that, should her life be spared, God would eventually call her to labor for him in foreign fields.

Her early education was received in Cambridge, but, desirous to prepare herself to perform successfully all the duties of a missionary, and to care for all the interests that should ever be committed to her charge, she graduated from one of the leading commercial colleges in the city of Boston. One who was intimately acquainted with her, says: "With each year her determination to be a missionary strengthened, and she resolved to leave nothing undone in the way of preparation which would in any measure aid her in being a successful laborer; and she pursued her studies amid what seemed sometimes to be almost insurmountable barriers; but, having a strong will and great powers of endurance, she overcame every obstacle."

After this she continued her studies at home with private tutors, also reading all the missionary literature within her reach, and histories of foreign countries, making herself as familiar as possible with the manners and customs of the people of the various parts of the world—all this with a view to their ultimate salvation. With a divine eloquence, which only the Holy Ghost imparts, her tongue was burning to tell the story of Jesus and his love to those who, afar off in heathen lands, had never heard it. She was one of the "sweet singers in Israel," and often led this part of the devotional exercises in the social meetings at home. One of her favorite verses, and one oftener sung by her than any other, was

> "O that the world might taste and see
> The riches of his grace ;
> The arms of love that compass me
> Would all mankind embrace."

At the sixth annual meeting of the General Executive Committee, convened in Baltimore, May, 1875, Miss Campbell presented her testimonials, and was accepted as a proper person to be employed by the Society ; and on the following September 20 she left Boston for her distant field of labor. A correspondent in "Zion's Herald," says : "The North Avenue Church, of Cambridge, has been called to part with one of its most efficient members in the person of Miss Letitia A. Campbell, who is soon to sail for Peking, China, under the auspices of the Woman's Foreign Missionary Society. She has been a member of this Church since its organization, and always a faithful laborer in the Sabbath-school, in the Ladies' Society, in the missionary cause. In all the social meetings she was our 'chief' singer. Seldom absent from class, the last class-meeting found her present, the last Sabbath was occupied by her in church as usual, and the last prayer-meeting found her in her place. Faithful unto the last, she goes out from us with her record well made up, and with the tenderest wishes for her happiness and the most earnest prayers for her prosperity and success in missionary work."

Several large and highly interesting farewell meetings were held in Boston and vicinity.

At the Epping Camp-ground, New Hampshire, Miss Campbell's presence was also an inspiration. The people were much gratified in being permitted to look upon and listen to one who was so soon to be their representative in China. Hearts were touched, and many a hearty "God bless you!" followed her as she left the ground. Referring to this meeting, a correspondent writes: "The only after-exercise, save the pleasantly interspersed singing, was the brief farewell to our new missionary for China. A tender good-bye was trembling upon the lips of many present, for Miss Campbell was no stranger in our midst. A resident of Cambridge, a member of the Branch Executive Board, an efficient laborer in every department of Christian activity, she occupied the place of a sister beloved in the hearts of many. To yield her to the foreign work was a sacrifice as well as a joy. Her own calm, quiet words on this occasion, full of faith in Him to whom she had long since consecrated herself, increased the confidence already felt in her fitness for the field upon which she was about to enter. We trembled as we thought of her, unaccustomed to travel, commencing her long journey alone; but she had no fear; it would all be well. She left Boston September 20," and reached Yokohama November 1. The passage thither was not as pleasant or as speedy as is usual at that season, the steamer being ten days later in reaching port than was expected. Miss Campbell, with characteristic fidelity to the cause, sent back the names of three new subscribers for the "Heathen Woman's Friend," obtained on shipboard. Leaving Yokohama three days later, she arrived safely in Peking, December 3, and entered at once upon her missionary labors.

Two months later she writes of a new auxiliary in the North China Mission:

"At our missionary prayer-meeting last Thursday it was proposed to form an auxiliary Society, to be composed of all the missionaries and as many of the native women as would join. The object of the Society should be, to encourage these natives to give the little they can spare, of money and time, to help others to a knowledge of the Christian doctrine. The proposition was received most heartily by Mr. and Mrs. Lowry, Mr. and Mrs. Walker, and Miss Coombs, also by Mr. Pyke, who came up from Tientsin during the week; he also assured us that Mrs. Pyke would gladly aid this enterprise. The ladies appointed the following Saturday as the time to take the matter into consideration. Accordingly, on the day specified the Society was organized, under the name of the North China Auxiliary of the Woman's Foreign Missionary Society. Mrs. Davis has consented to serve as President, Miss Porter, Mrs. Lowry, and Mrs. Pyke as Vice-presidents; Mrs. Walker as Treasurer, Miss Coombs as Recording Secretary, and I as Corresponding Secretary. Some of the poor native women will not be able to pay a dollar a year for membership, but what they are unable to give will be made up by others."

June 2 she writes of a growing interest in the young Society, and says: "I send you a sample of some of the work done by one of our school-girls, by which means she obtained the dollar necessary for her membership in our auxiliary Missionary Society." In the same letter she says: "After the close of our school prayer-meeting the other evening, two little six-year-old girls took me by the hand, and asked me if I did not think they were Jesus' little lambs. On being answered that I thought they were, they bade me good-night with a happy smile, showing plainly that no doubt troubled their hearts. Neither did I doubt, 'for of such is the kingdom of heaven.'"

Miss Campbell's life was a deeply spiritual one, as all her letters testify. In one of the last she ever wrote she gives the following experience, precious at any time, doubly so since we shall hear from her no more:

"Mission life does not consist in giving up friends and the comforts of home—it means all for Jesus. In no stage of my Christian life have I found it sweeter to trust in the leading and teaching of the Spirit than at this time. We have, O! so many things to discourage and depress us; but they keep us humble, and conscious that of 'ourselves we can do nothing.' So many times have I found it easy for the Lord to accomplish his purpose, when, to human understanding, the way has been altogether closed! My soul is calmly resting in the promise of Christ." Still later, "I have precious communion with God, and unwavering trust in him."

In a letter written to her sister, Mrs. Johnson, a short time before her death, she says: "I never so fully realized the great importance of the work as at this time. For truly the harvest is great and the laborers few, and each day this vast empire seems to be opening more and more to the spread of the Gospel."

With such qualifications for usefulness—with a heart all aglow with love for the perishing—in the very spring-time of life, amid the bloom of youth and health, with such prospects of an abundant harvest if permitted to sow the seed, it hardly seemed possible that her work on earth was to terminate so soon. But

> "God is his own interpreter,
> And he will make it plain."

She continued working on, cheerfully, hopefully, but, alas! too constantly, until her physical system, worn by her unceasing labors, gave way, and she was prostrated with that dreadful disease, typhus fever. She fell at her post; refusing to yield to the approaching enemy, until yielding was inevitable. The most satisfactory account of her illness and death we find in Miss Porter's letter to Mrs. Johnson, Miss Campbell's only sister, which appeared first in "Zion's Herald." We know it will be read with interest by the many friends of missions whose hearts have been touched by this afflictive dispensation of divine Providence.

"Dear Mrs. Johnson: You know how our Father puts his arms about his afflicted ones, and helps them to bear the sorrows which he himself sends. You have found Christ your refuge. Knowing that his presence will sustain you, I take up the sorrowful task, and write you what we think you would like to know of the illness and death of your dear sister.

"The first symptoms of fever appeared on Monday, May 5, but she did not finally take to her bed until the following Friday, one week and a day before she died. On Monday she gave me a few general directions as to the disposal of her effects in case she should not recover. On Tuesday her mind wandered, and after that her disease progressed rapidly. A few hours before dying she was trying to sing, 'The Cleansing Wave,' but she seemed troubled to recall the words, and repeated many times, 'Cleanseth me, it cleanseth me.' She called for me to sing it for her, and I found her saying over and over the words of the chorus. Soon after this she went into an unconscious state, in which she died. She died quietly and restfully, without return to consciousness.

"Arrangements were made at once for the funeral. A grave was prepared in the English burying-ground, where are already buried a number of missionaries and children of missionaries, besides many other foreigners.

"The services were held in our Mission Chapel, on the Sabbath morning following the day of her death. Mr. Davis and Mr. Walker conducted the services, which were partly in Chinese and partly in English. A sympathetic company of missionary and other friends, together with many Chinese, gathered to pay this last tribute to our sister. Mr. Seward, American Minister to the Chinese government, and the Secretary of Legation, with their wives, were present. Mr. Davis read the funeral service at the grave. The cemetery is quite out from the city, approached by a long avenue shaded by close-planted trees, and is shady and beautiful inside—a quiet resting-place, well kept and cared for. We always have an English service on Sabbath evening, after the day's work among the Chinese. On the Sabbath evening of the day of your sister's burial, Dr. Edkins, who conducted the exercises, made it a funeral service.

"Perhaps you would feel better to know that your sister was not exposed to the fever more than any are who breathe in this fever-laden air. She had not been visiting people sick with the fever. Several missionaries have had the fever, and two have died in Peking, two in Tientsin, and one in the south. The famine that has carried off so many thousands has filled the air with pestilence. We have had some rain and heavy wind, and the doctors think there is a decided change for the better.

"My sad task is completed. Our prayers for you and your family circle, so sorely bereft, follow this message, with love and sympathy.

"MARY Q. PORTER."

"PEKING, *May* 21, 1878."

Rev. Mr. Lowry writes: "Just as Brother Pilcher and myself are starting upon our tour, a special courier from Peking brings the sad news of Miss Campbell's death, on the 18th of this month, (May.) She was buried on Sunday, the 19th, in the English Cemetery, outside the west wall of Peking. In her we have lost one of our most earnest workers, and the entire Church a most devoted missionary. She was physically very much worn down when the fever laid hold on her. In addition to the skill of Miss Dr. Howard, she had the attendance of both Dr. Bushnell, of the British Legation, and Dr. Collins, of the Church Missionary Society, as well as the most constant and efficient nursing of several of the ladies. But all that medical skill and affectionate care of her companions could do was unavailing. The testimony of her pure life, her sincere friendship, and her devotion to the work, for which she was peculiarly adapted, will ever remain dear to us who for three years have shared her labors."

The following remarks of Dr. Edkins, of the London Mission, Peking, also testify to her worth: "To-night we are reminded that our ranks are again broken. A familiar form has left us. A voice we used to hear in the music of our worship is hushed in the silence of the tomb. A missionary sister, eminently diligent and laborious in the discharge of her duties, has suddenly been removed. Last Monday she made all preparations for the approach of the last enemy, and after having placed in friendly hands all requisite arrangements, and sent her last messages, she said, 'And now can I not trust all in the hands of Jesus?' That was the spirit with which she met death only yesterday.

"Miss Campbell had great vigor of determination, and great persistence in action. She had a quick sense of duty, and an unflinching energy in doing it. She was remarkably kind to the Chinese with whom she was brought in connection, and won their uniform testimony to her amiability. Two years and a half was a period too short for our hopes, but was enough to enable her friends to see that she was adapted by disposition and gifts for achieving much useful work for the Master.

"She labored energetically in the Girls' School of the Methodist Episcopal Mission. While she had its entire control for fourteen months, her zeal and devotion were such that the standard of attainment became considerably higher, and improvement was manifest in every department. With characteristic devotion she attended weekly meetings for women in the Chinese city. Of her we all feel that it may be said, 'She hath done what she could.' We recognize in her one of that noble band of sisters, who, having sat themselves at the feet of Jesus, willingly devote time and effort to lead others to listen to the same Teacher, whose instructions are so sweet and so winning, so salutary and so blessed.

"We need many more such missionaries as Miss Campbell, marked by her simplicity of purpose and earnest determination to carry through the various departments of Christian work among women and girls. But He who first said to her, 'Go work to-day in my vineyard,' has come again, and said quite early, without waiting for further proof of her devotion, 'Well done, good and faithful servant; enter thou into the joy of thy Lord.'"

A mournful interest attaches itself to Miss Campbell's death, from the fact that of all the noble band of laborers sent out by the Woman's Foreign Missionary Society during the first decade of its existence, she was the *first* whom death has claimed. Not the first *lost*, but *saved*—CROWNED; the first to exchange labor for reward—" these light afflictions" of earth for the " far more exceeding and eternal weight of glory."

Her life was brief, but in it there are thoughts of pleasure as well as pain.

> "If now in youth, or when the head be hoary,
>   Earth's ties are riven;
> I know that sudden death is sudden glory,
>   To heirs of heaven.
>
> The traveler's glad, when weary with his journey,
>   The end to see:
> If short thy way that leads to joys immortal,
>   'Tis gain to thee."

She went from us in the glory of her young womanhood. Her eye had not dimmed nor her natural strength abated. There was no decay in bodily organs or mental powers; her zeal was not quenched nor her ambition fettered. She went in the glory of her prime.

She enjoyed the time of budding, blossoming, and fruitage; then God, with timely hand, prevented the sad season of her withering. She will always be to us an honor and delight, a treasure of the memory, a joy unutterable. The summer's sun and winter's storm will never whiten her locks; time will not furrow her cheek, nor take the cheerful smile from her lips. She will always remain the same generous, self-sacrificing, loving soul that she has been, and will live forever in our memory in the beauty of her undimmed youth.

Miss Campbell's work is done; she has fulfilled her mission, served her generation, and is fallen asleep in Jesus. Who will fill her place? God has infinite resources. Our little mission in Peking will not suffer because Jesus has said to one whom he loved, "It is enough, come up higher." The flagstaff has fallen from the hands of one palsied in death. Forward, young ladies! Fill the breach. Lift up the standard, and cheer onward the hosts of God's elect until the world is won to Christ—until

> "Mightiest kings his power shall own;
> Heathen tribes his name adore;
> Satan and his host, o'erthrown,
> Bound in chains, shall hurt no more."

Miss Campbell died well. Though far from home and kindred, she was not alone; Jesus was with her in the misty valley in the place of those she loved; and she leaned her head upon his bosom, and sweetly breathed her life away.

Farewell, dear sister! Sweet be thy slumber! We may not visit thy grave to weep over it and plant with loving hands the flowers of affection upon it; but the beautiful shade trees, like faithful sentinels, shall guard it. Nature's own tear-drops will fall gently upon our loved one's dust, and the birds sing their *requiem* in that far-off land where thou art sleeping.

Toward thy resting-place will turn the hearts of thousands whose eyes never saw it. Around it will cluster the affections of the good. Upon it and into it the light of the Gospel shines with effulgent beam, and promises to reclaim thy sacred dust to a glorious resurrection life.

SEVENTH ANNUAL MEETING.

THE seventh Annual Meeting of the Executive Committee was held in the Metropolitan Church, Washington, D. C., May 10, 1876. The session was opened by reading of Scripture by Miss Hart, of Baltimore, and prayer by Jennie F. Willing, of Chicago. Mrs. Dr. Hibbard was chosen President, and Mrs. Dr. Warren, editor of the "Heathen Woman's Friend," Secretary, and Mrs. Gracey, returned missionary, Assistant Secretary. There was an unusually large number of elect ladies present from all parts of the country; and, looking upon that noble band of Christian workers—of cultured, consecrated women—it ceased to be a wonder that the once little Society had grown to such large proportions, and that its influence in the Church was beginning to be felt from center to circumference. After the organization a committee from the Washington Preachers' Meeting was introduced, which extended most kindly greetings from that body.

"The Corresponding Secretaries of the different Branches presented their reports. They were teeming with interest and encouragement, and, although during the past year pressure was felt in every direction, yet they were able to show advancement every-where, which called forth gratitude from every heart." Mrs. W. A. Ingham was present, as Corresponding Secretary of the Cincinnati Branch, in place of Mrs. Doughty, deceased. The meeting was characterized by deep religious feeling, entire consecration, while with united faith they claimed "the whole wide world for Jesus." There were representatives in person from China, Formosa, India, and Mexico. Drs. Thoburn and Gracey, and Miss Swain, our returned medical missionary, were also present.

Among other distinguished visitors, Bishop Carman, of Canada, was introduced to the ladies, and, in a brief but beautiful address, referred to the fact that he was a Briton. He was proud of his nativity, proud that his sovereign was a woman—a queen! They often sang in Canada "God save the Queen!" He then pronounced an eloquent eulogy upon the queenly women before him, and said that the queenliest of queenly women were those engaged in the blessed work of evangelizing the world, lifting up the fallen, and rescuing their own sex from superstition, darkness, and death.

The anniversary was held in the Metropolitan Church, and was thought to be one of the most interesting anniversaries ever held by the Society. Rev. Mr. Black, of Washington, presided, and made a comprehensive opening address. Addresses were delivered by Dr. Thoburn, of India, and Mrs. Dr. Hibbard, of Clifton Springs, New York. Four new missionaries were appointed: L. H. Green, M.D., and Mary F. Cary, to India; Nettie C. Ogden, to Mexico; and Olive Whiting, to Japan.

May 13, Mrs. Dr. Newman invited the ladies to an excursion to Arlington Heights, once the home of General Robert E. Lee. This delightful drive, together with the entertainment at Mrs. Somer's, of Mount Vernon Seminary, (sister of the late Dr. Eddy,) and at Mrs. General Gowan's, (Dr. Thoburn's sister,) will linger long in the memory of those who were so fortunate as to be in attendance.

May 15, Mrs. President Grant gave the ladies a reception at the White House. The ladies were presented by Mrs. Dr. Newman to Secretary Boutwell, and by him to the President and family. Mrs. Fred. Grant, Mrs. Senator Logan, Mrs. Governor Beveridge, and other distinguished ladies, were present. President Grant asked Mrs. Dr. Hibbard (our President) if this was her third term. She replied that it was only her second. He said he thought it about time for the agitation to begin with regard to the third term. Mrs. Grant said, she regarded the work in which the ladies were engaged as one of the noblest in the world, and should consider herself a member of our Society.

After an hour of delightful conversation refreshments were served, after which the President offered his arm to Mrs. Dr. Hibbard, and Ulysses Grant, Jun., proffered his to Miss Annie Luisun, of Shang Nui, China, who was dressed in full Chinese costume, both of which were accepted, and, the rest of the company following, they were conducted into the East Room and from thence to the Blue Room, where the ladies were invited to sing and pray. Mrs. Keen, of Phi'adelphia, led in singing " Rock of Ages" and "I Love to tell the Story," and Mrs. Dr. Hibbard made a most impressive and appropriate prayer. Thus ended this highly interesting occasion.

On Friday, the 19th, the ladies made an excursion to Mount Vernon.

We were unwilling on this, the centennial year of our nation, to return to our northern homes without visiting the tomb of him who laid the foundations of this great Republic, and who, though dead, yet speaketh, and is first in the hearts of his countrymen. The tomb is built of brick. Within the inclosure, in two lead coffins, each in a beautiful marble sarcophagus, rest the remains of George and Martha Washington. In the rear, just over the coffins, is a marble tablet with the words, "I am the resurrection and the life; whosoever believeth in me, though he were dead, yet shall he live, and whosoever liveth and believeth in me shall never die."

Leaving the tomb, we went directly to Washington's private room, the "chamber where the good man met his fate," and looked at the furniture, and a *fac simile* of the very bed on which he died; and as we gazed with indescribable emotions we realized more fully than ever before that—

> "Though we wade in wealth, or soar in fame,
> Earth's highest station ends in 'Here he lies,'
> And dust to dust concludes her noblest song."

LUCILLA H. GREEN, M.D.

AMONG the heroic, consecrated spirits who cheerfully gave up all for Christ, and laid down their lives for his cause, is Lucilla Holcomb Green. She was the daughter of Rev. Enoch and Martha A. Green, of the New Jersey Conference, and was born, July 15, 1853, at Lambertville, New Jersey, and died at Nynee Tal, India, September 30, 1878.

Her early childhood was marked by a power and grasp of mind, as well as a strength of judgment, unusual for one of her years. She seemed to take in knowledge almost as if by intuition and without effort, and hence her mind easily and rapidly developed. To this was added an acute tenderness of conscience and an understanding in religious things that was quite in keeping with her natural strength of mind. When not more than six years of age, often, after prayer had been offered in the family by visiting clergymen or others, who would pray especially for the children, she would go to her mother, and, laying her head in her lap, would say, with sobs and tears, " Mother, I do want to be good, I do want to be a better little girl."

Her education was received chiefly at home, where she studied the English branches and Latin, assisted by her father, who took great pleasure in watching her mind's development, and in rendering her the aid she needed. At the age of fifteen she entered Pennington Seminary, New Jersey. Here she was an earnest, ambitious, and successful student, and speedily became the leader in every thing good. Her teacher writes: "She was eminently religious, and took charge of all the religious meetings on the ladies' side. She had all the womanliness of years, and yet was so like a child in her frankness and simplicity and loving spirit." In July, 1870, she graduated, taking the highest honors of her class.

With a burning thirst for knowledge, and an ardent desire for self-improvement and usefulness, she then commenced the reading of medicine under private tutorship, and in the fall of 1871 entered the Woman's Medical College, where she graduated with the first honors of the class in March, 1875. She remained several months after in the hospital as an assistant physician, in order to perfect herself in her profession.

So early and so gradual was the development of her religious life that it is difficult to fix upon the exact time as to when she experienced converting grace. Her case reminds us of the words of Jesus, "So is the kingdom of God, as if a man should cast seed into the ground; and should sleep, and rise night and day, and the seed should spring and grow up, he knoweth not how." But the time came when her experience took on a more decidedly religious phase. In the fall of 1861, while her father was stationed at Long Branch, New Jersey, after a sermon, one Sabbath evening, by Rev. G. F. Brown, D.D., she immediately came forward and knelt at the altar, when she commenced crying and sobbing for mercy; and continued to do so until the close of the meeting, and for some time after she reached home, until she retired to rest, and her sobs were at last lost in sleep. "At this time," says her father, "she seemed to give every evidence of deep, sincere repentance for sin, though what the dear child had to repent of we scarcely knew, so thoroughly and tenderly conscientious had she always been." She was then about eight years of age. Though at so tender an age she manifested much concern as to the nature of faith, and, going with a younger sister (who was also at the time deeply affected) to the mother, she eagerly asked, "Mother, what is it to believe? we know what it is to repent, but what is faith?" After the explanation was given she seemed comforted and happy.

In regard to the expression of her religious feelings she was very quiet and undemonstrative, saying but little with regard to herself. She, however, soon showed such a strength of understanding and ripeness of experience in spiritual things, as to leave no doubt in the minds of those who knew her best as to the thoroughness of the change which had been wrought.

Soon after this she became anxious to partake of the sacrament, and expressed to her mother her desire to do so, but her mother soothingly replied that she was yet very young to go to the Lord's table, and that perhaps it might be better for her to wait awhile until she should get a little older. But she, looking up at her mother wistfully and with tears running down her face, said, "Why, mother, I *do* understand."

Prior to her being called to India by the ladies of the Woman's Foreign Missionary Society she had never expressed herself as feeling specially called to missionary work, but we have reason to believe that she had at times felt drawings in this direction, and had come to have a conviction that this would eventually be her destiny. In a diary kept by her while at Pennington Seminary she makes the following entry, after hearing a sermon by Rev. S. Parker, then stationed at Pennington: "Jan. 10, 1869—Mr. Parker's sermon was better than usual to-day—a missionary sermon. He made a strong appeal to the young to consecrate themselves to the missionary work. I wonder if I will ever feel it my duty to wander on the plains under an Indian sun, or mingle with China's strange inhabitants to teach of Jesus? If it is ever my lot, may I be willing and cheerful, remembering all Jesus has done for me!"

This, considering the prompt and cheerful manner in which she entered upon the particular mission to which she was afterward called, seems almost prophetic. She did not, however, enter upon the study of medicine with a view to this work. But she was, without doubt, providentially led thereto, as a prerequisite for the work which God was preparing for her.

At the annual meeting of the General Executive Committee, convened in Washington, D. C., May,

1876, reference was made to Miss Green's call to the missionary work, and, on invitation of the committee, Mrs. Taplin gave a most interesting account of the manner in which Miss Green was found. Miss Swain, whose health was suffering from overwork, must be relieved. Her place must be filled by a competent person, where or how to be obtained she could not tell. Many unsuccessful attempts had been made to secure a medical missionary. In her extremity she concluded to "take it to the Lord in prayer." Her attention was at once directed to Miss Green. She wrote to her. The first reply was a negative, but something in the letter convinced her that Miss Green *was* the help long sought for. She did not wish to urge her, but, selecting two quotations from missionaries in the field, one from a letter from Mrs. Parker, the other from a letter written by Miss Sparkes, without note or comment she sent them to her. After reading them, and consulting with her parents, Miss Green decided to accept the call as from the Lord, and wrote to Mrs. Taplin "I am willing to go, and do the best I can."

As Mrs. Taplin closed the narrative every heart seemed thrilled, and many eyes were moist with tears. In view of this special answer to prayer, the president asked the Committee to unite in singing the verse—

> "Depend on him; thou canst not fail;
> Make all thy wants and wishes known;
> Fear not; his merits must prevail:
> Ask but in faith, it shall be done."

After making the necessary arrangements she sailed from New York for India, January 1, 1876, and arrived at Bombay, after a safe and pleasant voyage, on the 25th of February following, having for her traveling companion the Rev. N. G. Cheney, who was also going out as a missionary to Nynee Tal, India, to take charge of an English congregation at that place, under the supervision of the parent Board. After a short rest she passed on to Bareilly, and entered at once upon the work to which she had been assigned. Her work here was one of grave responsibility, and especially so for one so young and inexperienced; yet she showed herself entirely adequate to the position, exhibiting, as all the missionaries who knew her testify, a skill and judgment quite beyond her years. Her time here was almost wholly taken up with the duties of her medical profession, she often having from forty to fifty patients in attendance at her morning clinics to examine and prescribe for.

On January 24, 1878, she was united in marriage to Rev. N. G. Cheney, in the Mission Chapel at Bareilly. She then removed from our special medical work in Bareilly to Nynee Tal.

Notwithstanding we, as a Society, felt a sense of loss, we have reason to believe that she was actuated by the purest of motives, and in this, as in all other important steps of her life, followed what she conceived to be the leadings of Providence, the all-absorbing desire of her heart being to glorify God and win souls to Christ. In a letter to her mother, written a short time before her marriage, she says: "Nor is this new love allowed to usurp the place of Christ in my heart; for, much as I love Mr. C.,

I could freely give up all for Christ's sake if duty required it at my hands." Again, shortly after, she says: " Our marriage means no seeking of any merely personal, selfish satisfaction within ourselves, but broader, deeper work for God."

At Nynee Tal she entered heartily into all her husband's plans, and became an earnest co-laborer with him in the work of saving souls. She was constant in her labors among rich and poor, administering to both soul and body. She was Mr. Cheney's constant companion in all his parish visiting, and oftentimes, after they returned home, she would go back again alone to visit some interesting cases, talking and praying with them, and weeping over them, to bring them to Christ.

In a letter to Mrs. Taplin, written September 2, 1878, the last month of her earthly life, she says: "The year has more than half gone, and the months as they have gone by have been filled with earnest, prayerful endeavor for God, and not without his manifest blessing. Some medical work opens up in this place. I have converted part of one of the closets in my home into a little dispensatory, and receive patients here, visiting them also at their own houses in the bazaar. The principal druggist of the place has made most liberal terms for furnishing medicine and for filling out receipts, and I find the patients very willing to procure their own medicines. One place where I visited as physician opened up to us a house where many women congregated gladly listening to the word. Sister Judd, whose health is very poor, has given over to me the charge of the zenana work here, and while we have only two Bible-women, yet I never knew more faithful and zealous ones than they. Our English work here is full of interest, and while often laborious, still we feel that it is a labor that God does not forget. This afternoon we have two meetings; one, our monthly missionary prayer-meeting with our workers; the other is a meeting for mothers and wives among the soldiers' wives of the place, than whom a more forsaken and forlorn class of people could scarcely be found. These days seem full of the presence of God to me, and I am very happy—happy in that he gives me work to do in his own needy vineyard."

But in the midst of her usefulness, with all her plans and bright hopes for the future, she was suddenly stricken down. On Saturday, September 28, 1878, she was seized with Asiatic cholera, and in forty-eight hours the struggle and suffering were over, and her pure disembodied spirit entered into the joy of her Lord. A few hours previous to her death she rallied, and the physician had strong hopes that the crisis was passed, and that she would get up again. But soon the disease seemed to assume a new and more dangerous phase, and she became unconscious, in which state she continued until she calmly and sweetly fell asleep in Jesus.

The peculiar nature of her disease did not allow of her leaving any special dying testimony; but we need none. "She was ever ready," is the universal testimony of all the missionaries who best knew her and her work. The expressions of popular regard shown for her memory and worth at her funeral, by both rich and poor, prove conclusively how deep was the hold she had upon their confidence and affection. Multitudes of poor natives, who were not in the habit of attending English funerals in India, came and begged the privilege of attending with the rest. When told they could do so, they came in crowds, bearing with them beautiful bouquets of flowers, with which they strewed her coffin and grave, their eyes streaming with tears, showing the strength and sincerity of their emotion.

"Such a funeral," says Mrs. M'Grew, "was never known in Nynee Tal, as the oldest inhabitants there testify." Twenty-five Englishmen were selected to bear her coffin on their shoulders, by turns, to its burial, and the English flag on the government buildings was lowered at half-mast as the funeral procession passed along to the grave.

She sleeps in the valley—the beautiful valley—of Nynee Tal, near the grave of the sainted Mrs. Thoburn, whose dust also hallows the soil: a spot she loved to visit, and where she often said, while living, she would like to be buried if she ever died in India.

The tidings of her death brought sadness to the hearts of all the friends of the mission, both in India and America; and the blow fell with crushing weight upon her devoted husband and parents. In a private letter written by her father to us, he says: "No words can express the anguish we feel in the thought that we shall see the face of our dear, dear Lucilla no more. She had been in India so long, and had enjoyed such uniformly good health, that we had begun to look forward to a happy reunion with her at no very distant day. But, alas! how precarious are all human hopes! In a moment all our cherished anticipations are swallowed up and lost in the deepest and most poignant sorrow. O, what an inexpressible satisfaction it would have been to have looked once more into that calm, quiet, loving face, and imprinted one more warm kiss upon that fair cheek glowing with life and health; yea, could we even have been permitted to look upon her dear form, though cold in death, and imprint a kiss upon her icy forehead—followed her to her burial—planted with our own hands some flowers, and watered them with our tears—it would have been a privilege—a mournful one, indeed—and yet a privilege not to be forgotten. But our heavenly Father has ordered that it should be otherwise, and we can only bow in silent, unmurmuring submission to his mysterious behests, and exclaim, 'How unsearchable are his judgments, and his ways past finding out.'"

Miss Isabel Hart, Corresponding Secretary of the Baltimore Branch, says: "Why a life so grounded on the truest principles, inspired by the noblest ambition, devoted to the holiest purpose, so full of love, of hope, of joy, of work, should, in its very spring-time, be taken, we cannot fathom. With bowed heads and stricken hearts, we can only reverently admire its beauty and earnestly ponder its lessons. Only we dare not call such a life loss, but rather highest gain and glory to the parents who gave it birth, to the love and friends with which it is in association, to the work that consecrated it; while for its own culmination and consummation and coronation we must look beyond the vale."

The India Conference, at its session held January 14, 1879, unanimously adopted the following beautiful, appreciative, and deserved memorial tribute:

" The beautiful life which found its earthly close in Nynee Tal, on the 30th of September last, still speaketh to us of better things, and leads us onward to yet higher attainments. In full and constantly increasing usefulness she went in and out among us, totally unconscious of the call which she was so soon to obey.

" Suddenly she was not, for God had taken her— taken her from a wide sphere of usefulness, for which she seemed to have every endowment of nature and of grace; and we can think of her now only as increasingly useful in the unknown and higher work to which God has translated her. Her complete consecration to him bore early fruit. Probation ended, she was taken to a higher place in the eternal activities of the kingdom of Christ.

" We pay this loving tribute to her memory, and with those on whom this bereavement falls with heaviest weight, we look up and away to the everlasting hills of peace."

Also, the Woman's Missionary Society of the North India Conference adopted the following resolutions:

"*Whereas*, During the past year death has entered our midst, and our circle has been broken by the removal of Mrs. Cheney from among us; therefore,

"*Resolved*, That we recognize in this our grief and loss the hand of an all-wise, unerring, and loving Father, whose right it is to do with his own as he knoweth to be best.

"*Resolved*, That we recognize in Lucilla Green Cheney's beautiful life and character, as also in her acquirements, both professional and otherwise, eminent fitness for the work of a missionary, in any of its varied departments; and that, while we know her loss cannot easily be repaired, nor her place in our hearts and in the hearts of those among whom she labored be taken by another, we feel to pray more earnestly than ever, that God will raise up others to aid in this great work, and enable us, who are already engaged in it, to labor with renewed consecration and faithfulness.

"*Resolved*, That we tender our deepest sympathies to the husband, parents, sister, and numerous home friends of our beloved sister, and that we assure them of our continued sympathy and prayers, in this our mutual bereavement.

"FANNIE J. SPARKES,
"MRS. M. A. BADLEY,
"MARY F. CARY."

We give a few extracts from a letter written by Mrs. Parker, of India, to the bereaved mother:

"PAORI, GURHWAL, INDIA, *October* 19, 1878.

"MY DEAR MRS. GREEN: Others have given you the sad news which did not come to you more suddenly than it did to us all here in the mission. You have heard all about the last days and hours of your dear daughter's life, but I felt that I must write to tell you how deeply I sympathize with you and your family in this affliction. The news came to us about three o'clock on Tuesday morning, when Mr. Badley and Mr. M'Mahon arrived at our house on their journey down from Nynee Tal. It was very hard for me to take in the full meaning of the terrible words, '*Sister Cheney is dead*—died of cholera, and was buried last evening.' The first shock over, I thought of the desolate husband, and in a moment I was with you in imagination, and very earnest were the petitions that went up to God from my heart that he might prepare you for the message, and sustain you when it should reach you.

"My thoughts are much with your angel daughter. How strange to think of her as being in the eternal world! I do not think that I had ever thought that she might die first. Her health seemed so perfect, and she was in such a good climate, that I did not feel anxious about her physical condition. Her dear ones so far away she loved with a very tender love, which time and distance only seemed to increase. We cannot mourn for her. She is at rest with Jesus. Her work, so well done, was quickly finished. 'That life is long which answers life's great end.' We cannot understand it. It is all so strange and mysterious to us here. One so young, so full of life and health, so ready to work, and so needed in the work, why should she be called from the midst of such usefulness? We only know that the Master called and bid her come to him, and it must be right. She was greatly loved by all who knew her, and in the mission and out of it are many sorrowing hearts, now that she has gone. She has told you herself of her happy home, and her loved work in Nynee Tal. She visited us with her husband just before they went there. I am very thankful now that we had that visit. One of the last things she said to me was, 'I expect to put in a full year's work in Nynee Tal.' From all I have heard from her, and from others, I am sure the time was filled up with work for the Lord. . . . The seed she has sown will bring forth fruit to God's glory. You have sacrificed much in giving her to this work, but you have been peculiarly blessed in having such a daughter to give. He who gave her to you has only claimed his own. You have the blessed hope of a happy reunion in a better world. She has gone on before, and will be there to welcome you and all her dear ones when God shall call. I know that no words of mine can comfort you in your affliction, for human words are of little worth under such circumstances; but my heart prompts me to write and tell you that we sympathize with you, and weep with you, and pray for you. Mr. Parker is writing to your husband.

"Yours, with much love and sympathy,
"LOIS S. PARKER."

Of her natural gifts, her quickness and clearness of apprehension and grasp of mind, we have already spoken. Her memory was remarkable, and the accuracy with which she could commit almost any thing she chose seemed incredible. Referring to this, her father said: "I was not at all surprised to hear of the readiness and ease with which she acquired the Hindustani, and her knowledge of the common language of the people."

She had also a habit of *close, keen observation*, and a quick, intuitive insight into the minds and feelings of others. This, with her characteristic coolness and maturity of judgment, enabled her always to be ready for any emergency.

With regard to her religious character, we will speak only of a few of its most salient points. From a child her *conscientiousness* was a marked feature, as seen in those frequent manifestations of penitential feeling already referred to. What she regarded as wrong she would most scrupulously and resolutely refrain from; while no duty, however formidable, or distasteful to flesh and blood, could cause her to falter in her fidelity to the task put upon her. Then her *unfeigned, undisguised charity* and goodness of heart seemed to flow out spontaneously toward all. Nor could any provocation she might suffer from others dampen it. She seemed to be incapable of cherishing any feeling of resentment or vindictiveness. If any one, through any misunderstanding, became cold or alienated in their feelings toward her, she would proceed to treat them with a more studied attention and kindness than ever, and would eventually make them her warmest friends. The thirteenth chapter of First Corinthians was, of all the chapters of the Bible, especially dear to her. It was her custom to read it over and over, making it a test chapter, carefully measuring her life and spirit by its teachings. "And," says her father, "I think all who knew her best will bear witness to this truth, when I say that there was not a single virtue or grace mentioned in the fourth, fifth, sixth, and seventh verses of that chapter which was not strikingly exemplified in her daily life. Her refined tenderness of spirit often manifested itself in little things. On one occasion, after church, a poor girl of weak mind, and not well instructed in the proprieties of life, took the liberty to rush up to her and kiss her, as well as some lady strangers who were visiting her. On returning to her home some of the ladies seemed disposed to make sport of the poor girl's awkwardness and ignorance; but she, with that calm, thoughtful, subdued look which was so peculiar to her, said, "Mother, I was thinking of that text of Scripture, 'Who maketh thee to differ?'"

This tenderness toward others did not forsake her even amid the intense suffering of her last hours. Through the terrible cramps and convulsions peculiar to the cholera, she retained her mental powers unimpaired, and showed a meekness and patience in suffering that was the wonder of all around her, speaking only in tones of the *sweetest subdued tenderness* to all whom she addressed.

Another of her prominent characteristics was her *strong, implicit, unquestioning faith in God and his overruling providence.* This was, we think, the foundation of that uniform cheerfulness and patience of temperament which seemed to possess her under all circumstances, even in the most trying ordeals of her life.

Every dark cloud that came over her sky her faith seemed to illumine with bright and cheering light. This feature of her religious character was also evinced at the time she sailed for India. On the night previous to her departure, when alone with her mother and sister in their room in New York, she said to her mother, "Why, mother, I am as glad as I can be that I am going to India." And then, opening a book of poems, she read to her in a most touching and beautiful manner the following lines, entitled:

GOD KNOWETH.

"I know not what will befall me,
    God hangs a mist o'er my eyes;
And o'er each step of my onward path
    He makes new scenes to rise:
And every joy he sends me comes
    As a sweet and glad surprise.

"I see not a step before me,
    As I tread the days of the year;
But the past is still in God's keeping
    The future his mercy shall clear;
And what looks dark in the distance
    May brighten as I draw near.

"For perhaps the dreaded future
    Has less bitterness than I think;
The Lord may sweeten the water
    Before I stoop to drink;
Or, if Marah must be Marah,
    He will stand beside its brink.

"It may be there is waiting,
  For the coming of my feet,
Some gift of such rare blessedness,
  Some joy so strangely sweet,
That my lips can only tremble
  With the thanks I cannot speak.

' O restful, blissful ignorance!
  'Tis blessed not to know;
It keeps me quiet in those arms
  Which will not let me go;
And hushes my soul to rest
  On the bosom which loves me so.

"So I go on, not knowing,
  I would not if I might;
I would rather walk out in the dark with God,
  Than go alone in the light;
I would rather walk with him by faith,
  Than walk alone by sight.

"My heart shrinks back from trials
  Which the future may disclose;
Yet I never had a sorrow
  But what the dear Lord chose;
So I send the coming tears back
  With the whispered word, 'He knows!'"

We do not wonder that she selected it, for it expresses so exactly the cheerful, submissive character of her faith, that it seems as if written almost expressly for her; and it was peculiarly adapted to express what were then her feelings with regard to that unknown, adventurous future upon which she was about to enter. How solemnly prophetic they seem now!

The next morning, in parting with her friends, she maintained the same calmness and serenity of spirit. A few hours after she sailed she sent back a note to her parents, with the pilot boat, concluding as follows:

"Now, dear ones, do not grieve after me at all. I am perfectly happy, for I am *sure* God will take care of me, and you too."

God *did* take care of her. He was with her during the voyage, with her in all her days of labor for him in India, and in the valley and shadow of death she feared no evil, for God was with her there. Mysterious as this dispensation of Providence may seem to us, we will not murmur that she is early crowned, that she has gained the bliss of heaven a little sooner than we expected. She has ceased from her labors, and her works do follow her; and, sounding back from the portals of her tomb, we hear the voice of Jesus saying, "Father, I will that they also, whom thou hast given me, be with me where I am; that they may behold my glory."

NETTIE C. OGDEN.

THIS lady is a native of Springfield, Ohio, and was born April 1, 1837. Her father was an English gentleman of wealth and refinement. Before coming to America he was licensed to exhort by the Wesleyan Methodists of his native country. His library was well stocked with choice literature and theological works, to which our young missionary, from her earliest recollection, had free access. Her mother was from Maryland, and was a devoted Christian lady. She consecrated all her children to the Lord in their infancy, and sought to train them for lives of usefulness. With regard to her religious experience Miss Ogden says:

"I cannot recall any time when I did not feel desirous of pleasing God, but in my eighth year I first expressed a desire to unite with the Church. At that time Rev. R. S. Foster, now Bishop, was our pastor. To him my mother expressed her fears that I was too young. In passing through the room I caught enough of the conversation to understand that I was the subject of it, and to hear the pastor's reply that it might not be safe to oppose me, as I might never again have the same desire, and might afterward reproach her. The tempter whispered, 'That is just the thing for you to do; give it up, and lay all the responsibility of your salvation upon your mother.' But instantly God's Spirit was with me, showing me that by so doing I would injure no one so much as myself. I never more clearly detected temptation than at that moment, and I turned upon the adversary, bidding him depart, at the same time promising the Lord that I would unite with his people as soon as I should be old enough. In my tenth year I was blessed with a sweet sense of God's presence in my heart, and was permitted to unite with the Church.

"Two years after, while reading a memoir of a beautifully consecrated life, God touched my heart, causing to spring up a most earnest desire for a like consecration. I was enabled to offer myself fully—body, soul, life and all its energies—to the Master's service. O, what a blessed baptism of love and light and power rested upon me! I knew God accepted me, but could not see how or where I should be called to labor. But I resolved to improve well my opportunities, and fit myself for work when it should be given.

"Thus I passed my school-days, sheltered from evil and nurtured in a Christian home-circle, educated with a private governess, our home being just out of the city, I enjoyed the most blessed privileges." But "whom the Lord loveth he chasteneth;" and there were days of trial in reserve for Miss Ogden.

Her father died, and with his death came financial reverses. Friends fondly cherished disappeared amid the mists of misfortune. But the Friend that sticketh closer than a brother revealed himself in all his glory and loveliness, and, joyful in tribulation, she was enabled to sing :

> "The dearest idol I have known,
>   Whate'er that idol be,
> Help me to tear it from thy throne,
> And worship only thee."

She now began to have a great desire to labor in the cause of Christ. With the help of a neighbor she organized a Sabbath-school in the district schoolhouse near her home, where she taught for some years, and had the pleasure of seeing her entire class—ten girls—happily converted to God. When the temperance wave swept over Ohio she enthusiastically enlisted in the crusade, and threw the whole energy of her soul into the work. She says: "The sweetness of complete and perfect consecration in active service in the Lord's vineyard had taken such a firm hold upon my heart that I was loth to give it up."

She was at this time serving as Corresponding Secretary of the High-street Auxiliary, Springfield, Ohio. Becoming in this way more familiar with the work and its needs, she could not help regretting keenly that the call for laborers did not come earlier, so that she might have had the privilege of carrying the tidings of salvation to those who are afar off. Expressing herself thus, she was asked to offer herself as a candidate, which she did, Mrs. Bishop Clark presenting her name to the General Executive Committee. She was accepted and appointed to Pachuca, Mexico, to labor with Miss Warner, who was already in the field. She immediately began to make preparations for instruction in the language, and entered the Wesleyan Female College, of Cincinnati, where she remained for one year. She sailed for Pachuca, Mexico, 1876. Miss Ogden was faithful and efficient in her missionary work, and greatly beloved by the pupils in her charge. She returned to the United States in 1878, to rest and recuperate. Her zeal for God and the missionary cause is unabated, and she is anxiously hoping for strength to return to her loved work.

MARY F. CARY.

MARY F. CARY is a native of Fishkill, Dutchess County, New York, and was born May 12, 1845. Her father, an affluent and influential farmer, has lived in the neighborhood of Fishkill all his life. With his children he was affectionate and indulgent; and being himself possessed of rare intelligence, he desired to have them thoroughly educated, and gave them superior advantages in this respect. In 1864 Miss Cary graduated from the New York Conference Seminary, at Charlotteville, New York, after which she entered the Musical Institute, at East Greenwich, Rhode Island, and spent some time in acquiring superior skill in this art. After teaching music for a short time, she resolved to strive to satisfy her thirst for knowledge by pursuing her studies. She prepared for college in the Genesee Wesleyan Seminary, at Lima, New York, and entered Genesee College in 1868. In 1871, when Genesee College closed and Syracuse University opened, she entered this institution, and remained a member of it till she graduated in the classical course, in 1874, receiving the degree of A. B. In 1877 she received the degree of A. M. in course. After leaving this institution she went to Europe and spent a year in Germany and Switzerland in a further acquirement of the German and French languages. Returning to America, she was next installed as teacher of German and French in the seminary at Amenia, Dutchess County, New York, which position she held until she left to prepare for her departure to India.

With regard to her religious experience she says: "I cannot remember when I did not have religious impressions, and desires to become a Christian." At the age of fourteen she experienced the pardoning love of God, and united with the Church on probation. The light which then dawned upon her pathway continued to shine more and more unto the perfect day. While at Lima she became convicted for a deeper work of grace, and had an ardent desire to be wholly saved from the power and dominion of sin. Rev. Daniel Steele, D.D., author of "Love Enthroned," writes us:

"My first acquaintance with Miss Cary was while I was a professor in Genesee College, at Lima, New York. She impressed her teachers as a young lady of unusual diffidence, self-distrust, and absence of self-assertion. But their acquaintance revealed other qualities, such as indomitable persistence and deep piety. After my own spiritual enlargement, which was so marked that it could not be hid from the students, she became very deeply convinced of her need of entire sanctification as a definite work to be wrought in her own consciousness. Her hunger for full salvation became intense and almost intolerable. At last, one Saturday, at Syracuse—for Genesee College had by this time, 1871, been merged in the Syracuse University—she came to me in the deepest distress of mind to find Jesus a complete Saviour. I told her that I would excuse her from Church the next day, and that she must go into her closet and make it her Peniel. At the same time I put into her hands that wonderful lyric, Charles Wesley's Wrestling Jacob, the unabridged hymn in fourteen verses, and told her to pray that hymn until she found deliverance. On the following Monday or Tuesday she came to me with her face radiant with a new, an unwonted joy, or rather heavenly glory. Her closet had been to her the bank of the Jabbok indeed. She had the clear assurance of full salvation. Every one observed a marvelous transfiguration in her character and life. I was not surprised when the intelligence reached me that she had received an appointment to foreign work in India. It may be an item of interest to some to know that she was at Lima a room-mate of Mrs. John T. M'Mahon, who preceded her to India, and is now doing excellent service at Roy Bareilly. Long may they live to prove to the heathen, by lip and life, that Jesus Christ is able to save unto the uttermost them that come unto God by him.

"Yours with the Abiding Comforter,
"DANIEL STEELE."

Miss Kate Hogoboom, who was in the same institution, says: "I remember distinctly of calling upon her one afternoon and listening to her glowing account of the great joy and peace she had recently obtained as a result of an entire consecration to Christ. It was certainly a real work with her, as it changed her conversation and aims so completely; and it was the development of this spirit, I believe, which led her to sacrifice home-happiness and friendships for the cause of Christ in other lands. The characteristic by which she was distinguished among her friends in college was *persistence*. She was always gentle and unobtrusive, but firm and persevering in what she considered right."

Miss Rena Michaels, of Utica, who was also an intimate friend, says: "From early childhood Miss Cary had cherished a desire to become a missionary. Every thing pertaining to missionary work or life was of deep interest to her. 'It is such a glorious work,' she would say, 'to lead immortal souls out of darkness into the perfect light.' She was corresponding with a lady then engaged in missionary work in India. Often she would read these letters to me—letters full of a sweet, spiritual radiance, which only those hearts can emit that live perpetually in God's sunlight. 'If that is the work God has appointed for me he will open the way, and give me the opportunity,' she would reply when urged to seek the work in which all her desires were centered. Her religious feelings and experience were, like her personal address, unostentatious, simple. Her religion was just as real and vital as the air she breathed. It flowed out in benevolence and good-will to all around her. But yesterday I passed the rude cottage where, five years ago, a poor German woman lived, a widow, whose children Miss Cary clothed from her own purse and wardrobe during her last year at the University. The house is unoccupied; the widow has gone; but wherever she may be, she will remember and tell many pleasant things of 'meine gute Fraulein Cary.'"

Her way to India was opened in this manner: Mrs. E. B. Stevens, of Wilmington, Delaware, one of the purest of the pure in heart, and a most efficient worker in the home field, was out on a three weeks' missionary tour, addressing public meetings, and trying to awaken greater interest in the cause. The Society was in need of re-enforcements, and Mrs. Stevens prayed earnestly that God would aid her in finding a missionary, and the assurance was given that her prayer should be answered. Everywhere, in public and in private, the need was stated, but no response came until after the close of nearly the last meeting, when Mrs. Stevens felt impressed that she had now reached the place where she should hear of her missionary. So sure was she that she should get tidings of her, that, after presenting the case and meeting with no response, she was sorely disappointed. "But," she writes, "noticing that my hostess was not present, I sent to her and told her what I wanted. She replied, 'The very person for you, if you can get her, is Mary F. Cary, Peekskill, Dutchess County, New York.' I took her address, and went on my way, praising God. As soon as I reached home I wrote to her. Her reply was to this effect: 'How strange! the only person living, so far as I am aware, that knows I have any drawing to missionary work is my father. I once asked for his consent, and he withheld it; I will speak to him again, and let you know the result.' In the next letter, she wrote: 'Father says, this is so evidently of the Lord that he dare not stand in my way. I am ready to go if needed.'"

Miss Cary went out as a representative of the Philadelphia Branch. She sailed for India, September, 1876. She reached her destination safely, and entered at once upon missionary work in Bareilly, assisting Miss Sparkes in the care of the Girls' Orphanage. Shortly after, Miss Sparkes returned to America, and Miss Cary was appointed superintendent in her absence. Her duties during the year following were most arduous. Disease entered the Orphanage; first, small-pox, then malignant dysentery, and, last of all, cholera came, and before the year closed *sixty-seven* had died. Many of them being in a starved and wretched condition when they entered the institution, the result of the preceding famine, they had not sufficient vitality remaining to repel disease, and fell ready victims to the destroyer. The year closed, leaving its record as one of the saddest in all the history of the Orphanage. This was a terrible strain on Miss Cary's mental and nervous system; but she was unceasing in her devotion to the sufferers, and faithfully performed her duty. During all her missionary labors in India she has manifested the same spirit of consecration to the one object, namely, the salvation of the heathen.

17

OLIVE WHITING.

OLIVE WHITING was born in Jasper, Steuben County, New York. Her parents were New England Presbyterians, and came—her father from New Hampshire and her mother from Vermont—to New York State when the wolves still howled around the settler's cabin, and bears and deer were often among the game brought down by the hunter's rifle. They built their little log-cabin in the wilds of North-western New York, and in that same home Olive, with her five brothers and a sister, was born. She says: "My early life was spent in such an ordinary way, that, though I may search never so untiringly over the green hills, and through the valleys and forests, and by the dear old streams of my Jasper home, I could find nothing that I might not share in common with all the other farmers' girls, my playmates."

Her first religious impressions were received so early as to be beyond her memory. She was always religiously inclined, and grew into favor with God so gradually that she never knew the exact moment of her conversion. Referring to it, she says: "There was never any sudden and wonderful change. It was rather a *growth* thereunto. Not always constant and steady and sure, as it should and would have been had He who nourishes our religious life been left uninterrupted in his gracious ministry. But I do know that Christ is my Saviour, and that he answers my prayers."

Miss Whiting was fond of study, and, after educating herself to the best of her ability in the common school, and in an academy in a neighboring town, she commenced teaching school. Afterward she went to Lima, and entered the Genesee Wesleyan Seminary, from which she graduated in 1872. After leaving the seminary she engaged again in teaching, until her departure for Japan.

While casting about to ascertain what she should do, and how she should spend her life to make it productive of the greatest good, the question was suggested, "Why not be a missionary?" She did not try to banish the thought, but cherished it. As she prayerfully considered the matter, she thought, " My parents are in heaven; my dear sister is dead; my brothers are married; God and his cause only have claims upon me. I will offer myself to the Society for service." She did so. She says: "From that time until my appointment was definitely made I left nothing undone that I could do to secure it, having resolved that no effort on my part should be lacking; and, should I fail to receive the appointment, I might reasonably conclude that I was not intended for that work."

She was accepted by the Society, and in May, 1876, was appointed to Tsukiji, Tokio, Japan, and shortly after sailed for her new field of labor.

When almost across the Pacific a terrible storm, a typhoon in fact, raged for a day and a night, threatening death and destruction to ship and passengers.

November 8, 1876, Miss Schoonmaker wrote: "Miss Whiting is here. Yes, she is here, and she is all I could desire in the way of a true, congenial companion, friend, and fellow-helper. I cannot thank God enough for his great goodness to me in this respect. We are admirably adapted to each other in tastes and habits, and are taking real comfort in working together. Doubtless you will have heard, ere receiving this, of the terrible storm which came in as a part of her experience in coming hither. She came very near finding a watery grave. It is fearful to hear her accounts of the horrors of that one night—when it seemed as if every hour might be her last. The sea, beating into her stateroom, swept away her waterproof cloak, her Bible, and many other prized possessions. She lost about a hundred dollars' worth of clothing, but was so thankful to escape with her life that she has never uttered a word of complaint, but endures the loss very cheerfully."

Miss Spencer also writes: "Miss Whiting is tall and fair, with hazel eyes, and an abundance of wavy golden hair. She came to Miss Schoonmaker's assistance in the summer of 1876. She is a grand worker, but is not very strong, having had a severe attack of illness about a year and a half ago, the result of overwork and severe study. She has progressed finely with the language, however, and will be a worthy successor to Miss Schoonmaker when she retires from the field. Miss Whiting is superintendent of our culinary department, and is an excellent manager."

The highest testimonials from missionaries on the field, together with written reports of her work, assure us that God has indeed chosen, and peculiarly qualified, her to aid in the great work of evangelizing and elevating the women of Japan.

EIGHTH ANNUAL MEETING.

THE General Executive Committee held its eighth session in the Centenary Church, Minneapolis, Minnesota, May 10, 1877. Mrs. L. E. Prescott, Corresponding Secretary of the Western Branch, opened the meeting. Mrs. Dr. Goodrich, of Minneapolis, was elected President, and Mrs. D. L. Williams, of Delaware, Ohio, Secretary. The Corresponding Secretaries were all present, and responded, with their respective Branch Delegates, to the calling of the roll.

The meeting was characterized by deep religious feeling, and was largely attended by ladies and clergymen from Minneapolis, St. Paul, Winona, and adjacent towns. The reports were very encouraging. The results in foreign fields were thus estimated:

"We have sent missionaries to all the countries occupied by the parent Board, except Europe and Africa, and at one station in each of these, Bulgaria and Bexley, we are employing native Bible-women. There have been sent to foreign fields thirty young ladies as missionaries. Seven of these have left our work; four to remain in the same calling as wives of missionaries, and one to take professional employment under the government in India, we trust still to be a teacher of the Gospel. Five ladies have returned on furlough. Those remaining in the field are working with rare efficiency and success. We have introduced medical work into Asia through five of our ladies. Under their direction one dispensary and three hospitals have been built. Besides the Orphanages already established, one in Paori, one in the city of Mexico, and six buildings for homes and boarding-schools, have been erected in the different stations occupied. We have supported the work carried on by the wives of missionaries, besides employing one hundred and forty Bible-women, native teachers, and other helpers, and are sustaining one hundred and thirty day-schools."

The following returned missionaries were present, and contributed much to the interest of the occasion: Rev. and Mrs. L. R. Hoskins, of Budaon; Miss Fannie J. Sparkes, of Bareilly, India; and Miss Mary Q. Porter, of Peking, China.

The anniversary was held in Centenary Church, Rev. Daniel Cobb, the pastor, presiding. Devotional exercises were conducted by Rev. Mr. Hoskins, of India, and, after reading the secretary's report, by Mrs. Williams, addresses were made by Revs. Cobb and Hoskins, Mrs. Ninde, and Misses Porter and Sparkes.

"An interesting feature of the anniversary was the reading of a note from a native African woman, as the result of a sermon preached by Bishop Haven, in Monrovia, Liberia, and sent by Rev. J. T. Gracey to Miss Isabel Hart, Corresponding Secretary of the Baltimore Branch, which has hitherto maintained our sole African interest."

The note was as follows: "I inclose these three

finger-rings; they are dear to me as keepsakes; but wont you please take them away with you, sell them, and give the proceeds somewhere for missionary purposes? I could not bear to see them worn by any one here; this makes it necessary to ask of you this favor. May God bless you!" The rings were well worn; inside of one was a casement for hair, showing it to be a token of some loved one. One hundred and two dollars were raised on these rings, to constitute the unknown donor an honorary manager in the Woman's Foreign Missionary Society.

In appropriating the work for the coming year, the Executive Committee decided to purchase the Cawnpore property, and make of it a Normal School for Eurasian young ladies, thus enabling them to become trained and efficient helpers for the mission fields now so grandly opening in the Orient: they took more work in Africa: and made a noble beginning in Rome and Venice. One new medical missionary, Leonora S. Howard, M. D., was appointed to Peking, China.

The Committee adjourned after a session of eleven days. The farewell prayer was offered by Mrs. Skidmore, and Mrs. Keen bade good-bye in God's name.

LEONORA S. HOWARD, M.D.

THE ladies of the North-western Branch are justly proud of the name of Leonora S. Howard, M.D., who so recently went out as their representative to Peking, China. This lady is a Canadian, having been born and reared in the County of Leeds, Ontario. She was educated at Ann Arbor, Michigan. A correspondent, in one of the Canadian papers, says: "By noble self-denial and perseverance she graduated as a physician in one of the United States' colleges, that she might the more successfully serve as a missionary in China."

Miss Howard left Chicago for Peking, China, on Friday, March 23, 1877. On the previous evening a "farewell meeting" was held in Langley Avenue Church. Her remarks were simple and direct, and those present carried away the impression that in her they were sending out one of our very best and strongest missionaries; and they were not mistaken. Rev. Dr. Parkhurst also gave an interesting address. A sociable followed, in which opportunity was given to make the acquaintance of Dr. Howard, and Dr. Letitia Mason Quinn, our returned China missionary.

The next afternoon the ladies of Michigan Avenue Church came together to meet Dr. Howard, where interesting addresses were made by several ladies, Dr. Williamson, and others. The meeting was most enthusiastic. Tears, prayers and songs of praise were mingled in that hour of consecration and Christian fellowship.

Miss Howard reached China in due time, and entered at once upon her work. She has succeeded in winning her way into the highest social circles of Peking, and by her professional skill has unlocked the social citadel which for ages has withstood the efforts of foreigners to enter; and having thus found access to the homes of those high in official position by the aid she could give the suffering body, she may find access to the hearts of the inmates, and in them sow the seeds of life; and from the palace of the great, light may go down to the dwellings of the poor, and the missionaries' influence be felt through all grades of society.

The following Associated Press dispatch appeared in the secular papers, under the heading, "Immense Practice of English Physicians:"

"WASHINGTON, *October* 21, 1879.

"The United States' Consul at Tientsin, China, in a dispatch to the Department of State, reports that two English physicians have had remarkable success in their practice in the royal family, leading to an immense practice among the common people.

"The viceroy has established a free dispensary, and placed one of the doctors at its head. The expense is borne by the viceroy. He has also noticed favorably Miss Howard, M. D., an American lady, who holds a high rank among the physicians of Peking. This liberal and humane course by the foremost man in the empire will do much to break down the prejudices of the people. This is only one illustration of the enterprise and progressive spirit of the viceroy."

The correspondent of the "North China Herald" writes: "After residing, as physician and guest, for a month at the viceroy's *yamen*, Miss Howard, M.D., of the American Methodist Episcopal Mission, has completed her present treatment of Lady Li, and has departed on her return to Peking. She bore with her copious presents of silks, satins, and rare china ware, and was honored with the rare courtesy of having the viceroy's dispatch-boat to tug her house-boat as far on the way to Tung-chow as the water (now high) will allow. Before her departure she was led to accept, for the winter, the pressing invitation to join in the dispensary work so generously established and fostered by the viceroy. She treats the female patients, while Dr. Mackenzie, of the London Mission, treats the males. It is hoped this may lead to the establishment here of a hospital for women under her direction, while one for men is likewise to be established under the direction of Dr. Mackenzie."

NINTH ANNUAL MEETING.

THE ninth Annual Session of the General Executive Committee was opened in the Tremont-street Church, Boston, Massachusetts, May 9, 1878. This meeting was one of the most memorable and interesting in the history of our Society. Mrs. Taplin, Corresponding Secretary of the New England Branch, opened the meeting and conducted the devotional exercises, by reading the Scriptures and announcing the hymn, "Jesus, lover of my soul." Mrs. Skidmore led in prayer. Mrs. Warren, President of the New England Branch, extended to the delegates and visitors a most hearty address of welcome, to which Mrs. Willing, of the Northwestern Branch, responded, referring to the organization of the Society, nine years before, in that very church, when only nine ladies were present. Mrs. B. R. Cowan, sister of Dr. Thoburn, appeared as Corresponding Secretary of the Cincinnati Branch, in place of Mrs. Ingham, resigned.

A committee from the Boston Preachers' Meeting was introduced. They welcomed the ladies with words full of sympathy and appreciation for the work of the Society, and an earnest "Godspeed" was extended to the workers. Mrs. Skidmore replied, thanking the brethren on behalf of the ladies for their kind words, and saying that without the assistance and support of the pastors it would be impossible successfully to carry on the work.

The devotional meetings, held every afternoon, "were characterized by great earnestness and faith in prayer, broadening outlines of spiritual sight, and increasing realization of the need of immediate, unwearied work for Christ's perishing little ones. The presence of an unusual number of returned missionaries, and their thrilling words of experience and hope, were an inspiration to all."

Provision had been made for, and a partial organization effected of, the Atlanta Branch early in the history of the Society, but no advance was made until January, 1878, when a reorganization was effected, and the Atlanta Branch formally entered the ranks. Mrs. E. Q. Fuller was appointed Corresponding Secretary.

In an official letter from Mrs. Parker, of India, reference was made to Miss Gorham, as one of the expected missionaries to that land, and Mrs. Taplin announced that her papers had been received and approved, and the time appointed for sailing, when she was taken ill, and suddenly translated from labor to reward. Some touching incidents were related in regard to her death, after which, with subdued spirits, all united in singing, "Jesus, lover of my soul." The following resolutions were then passed:

"*Whereas*, Miss Frances A. Gorham, under appointment for Cawnpore, India, has been called to her eternal reward; therefore,

"*Resolved*, 1. That the General Executive Committee desire to express their appreciation of the beautiful Christian character of Miss Gorham, and her eminent qualifications for the work to which she had consecrated herself.

"*Resolved*, 2. That, while we mourn the loss of one so greatly needed in that land of darkness, we recognize in her removal to the land of light the hand of Him who will provide for his work below, while he calls his beloved to the home above.

"*Resolved*, 3. That the warmest sympathy of this Committee be extended to the friends of Miss Gorham, and to the circle of wearied workers in India, anxiously waiting for help at her hand."

Several public meetings of great interest were held during the week. On Thursday, May 9, a reception was given the General Executive Committee in the spacious chapel of Tremont-street Church. A large number of returned missionaries and prominent home-workers were in attendance, among whom were Bishops Haven and Foster. After some time spent in social converse the company adjourned to the audience room of the church, where a public meeting was held. Bishop Foster presided, and addresses were delivered by Dr. Murdock, of the American Baptist Union; and Rev. Dr. Clarke, of the American Board; Dr. Humphrey, of the India Mission; and Dr. Dashiell, our Missionary Secretary.

On Monday following a large number of delegates visited the beautiful and classic city of Lynn. They were warmly welcomed, and invited to a bountiful supper prepared for them in the vestry of the First Methodist Episcopal Church, after which a public meeting was held in the audience room. The audience was large and enthusiastic. Rev. Mr. Hills, the pastor, in his opening remarks alluded to the fact that they were standing on historic ground, and spoke of the different reception which had been accorded to them from that given to Jesse Lee when he came to Lynn. Mrs. Lathrop, of Michigan, was introduced, and in eloquent language spoke of the emotions she experienced as she looked down the vista of the past, and in imagination beheld Lee and Asbury standing on this hallowed spot, preaching Christ and him crucified. She loved New England, although a Western woman, and was happy to know that they could work together in sending the Gospel to a heathen land. Mrs. Emily Huntington Miller read an original poem of great beauty and appropriateness, after which Mrs. Ninde, of Minnesota, and Rev. Mr. Humphrey, addressed the meeting.

The anniversary, held in Bromfield-street Church, May 15, was an occasion of great interest. Mrs. Skidmore presided. Mrs. Willing, of Chicago, led the devotional exercises. Mrs. J. T. Gracey, the Secretary, read the report, and addresses were delivered by Mrs. Chandler, of Baltimore; Miss Sparkes, of Bareilly, India; and Mrs. Keen, of Philadelphia. The presence at the meetings of Mrs. Flanders and Mrs. Rich, who were among the early workers and originators of the Society, greatly enhanced the interest of the occasion.

Twelve new missionaries were appointed, namely, Mary F. Swaney and Clara Mulliner, to Mexico;

Julia A. Sparr and Clara A. Cushman, to China; Henrietta B. Woolston, S. A. Easton, Eugenia Gibson, and M. E. Layton, to India; and Susan B. Higgins, Matilda A. Spencer, M. A. Holbrook, and M. A. Priest, to Japan.

All the exercises, together with the large number of missionaries newly appointed to the work in foreign fields, inspired the ladies with courage and enthusiasm, and they returned to their homes filled with gratitude to God for the work already accomplished, and determined to labor with renewed earnestness for the extension of his kingdom.

MARY F. SWANEY.

MARY F. SWANEY is the daughter of J. A. Swaney, who was appointed by the American Bible Society to superintend Bible-work in South America. She was converted, when about twelve years of age, at a camp-meeting in Pennsylvania. Soon after, she became a Sabbath-school teacher, and has ever since been actively engaged in this work. In the Bethel Sunday-school, Cleveland, Ohio, she had marked success in this capacity, and exerted a powerful influence for good.

One who is intimately acquainted with her, says: " Her Christian course has been marked by conscientiousness, prudence, and a strict adherence to duty. She is naturally modest and diffident, and never thought she could do any thing in public till circumstances compelled her to try. When convinced of duty, no consideration ever kept her from attempting to perform it."

Miss Swaney spent about eight years in South America, going with her parents to Callao, Peru, in 1859, when nine years of age. She returned with them three years afterward, when they were recalled during the war in this country. She began the study of Spanish in Callao, with a native teacher, but her studies were mostly in English. She subsequently studied, first at the Beaver College, Beaver, Pennsylvania, and then at the Pittsburgh Female College.

In 1868 she returned with her parents to Chili, South America, where she remained five years. She taught Spanish-speaking Talcahuans during this time. The impression made by her school may be inferred from the fact that the Bishop of Concepcion thought it necessary to denounce it from the pulpit in Talcahuana. This occasioned the loss of one scholar. While in this place she was engaged in Sunday-school work also, and conducted the music for Church services.

Returning from Chili, she again entered the Beaver College, from which she graduated. In 1878 she was appointed missionary to the city of Mexico, Mexico. All her previous life has been peculiarly calculated to qualify her for her present work.

In a private letter to the writer, Miss Belle Hart, of Baltimore, says: "I know of nothing wanting in her to make her a most successful missionary teacher. She has enthusiasm, warm social qualities, but so chastened, so controlled, so imbued with common sense, that one that does not know her well might not know their power. Indeed, the simplicity and steadfastness of her faith, her patience, the clearness of her judgment, her guilelessness and sweetness of spirit, her calm courage, her unwavering devotion to duty, unmoved by outward circumstances, have been to me a most fruitful, even wonderful lesson. I think her a model missionary, and my association with her, before leaving and since, has been most intimate, and of a kind that would fully reveal all that is in her. Her appointment to Mexico, her waiting, her hasty departure, have all been under peculiarly trying circumstances, and they have only shown pure gold."

After reaching Mexico, Miss Swaney writes: "All goes well. The girls are in good health, bright and happy. My native teacher has left me, for unavoidable reasons. What I am to do I cannot tell, but expect to have a way shown me. My health is given me from day to day. Nothing annoys, nothing wears on me now. The next month promises to be very trying, with lack of teachers, and with the quarterly reports on my hands. How all is to be accomplished I do not see, and I do not ask. Each day brings sufficient grace and strength. I want to beg you to pray especially for the outpouring of the Spirit on our work in Mexico. It is the felt need of the hour. I need it, the children need it, the women need it, the Church, the preachers, the land need it. I long for it as for nothing else. Do ask Mrs. ——, and ——, and other blessed women, to pray for the Spirit's baptism on Mexico. God is with us. We realize his presence, especially in our class-meetings for our girls, but we need more."

JULIA A. SPARR, M.D.

JULIA A. SPARR is a native of Selina, Delaware County, Indiana, and was born July 17, 1853. Her father is a Methodist clergyman, and her mother an earnest and faithful Christian worker. Miss Sparr pays them the following tribute: "All the good of my present and future life is due to the careful and prayerful teaching of my parents, whose pure faith and spotless lives were an example and an inspiration to me." When about ten years of age she was converted, and united with the Methodist Episcopal Church. As she presented herself for prayers, during a season of revival, she said to her mother, "They say I am so young I have no sins to be forgiven; but Brother S. said we would know it when we were converted, and I do not know it yet."

From the time of her conversion she began to have a desire to be a missionary. She says, "The purpose became stronger as I came to girlhood. I put other bright dreams aside, and, although this was but a dream also, yet it seemed more precious than any of the others." In 1872 she graduated from the Academy at Muncie, Indiana, and for two years after she was engaged in teaching school. She then offered herself to the "Woman's Foreign Missionary Society" for service in a foreign field. She was accepted, and advised to study medicine, in order to enlarge the sphere of her usefulness. She commenced the study in 1873. In the spring of 1875 she entered the hospital in Ypsilanti, Michigan, where she remained until September, when she removed to the medical department of the University of Michigan, at Ann Arbor. In October, 1877, she received her degree from this institution.

In July of the same year she went to the Woman's Hospital, of Philadelphia, where she served for several months. In May, 1878, she received her appointment to Foochow, China. Though devotedly attached to her home friends, she joyfully forsook all to follow Christ, saying, as she left them, "This is the happiest day of my life."

Our Society has much to hope from the services of Miss Sparr. She is intelligent, bright, cultured, conscientious, self-sacrificing, and affectionate in disposition, and will be sure to *win souls*.

Mrs. Baldwin, of Foochow, China, writes: "Dr. Sparr is with us at Sharp Peak. I can assure you we have two of the nicest doctors your Society has sent out. Dr. Sparr is just the associate for Dr. Trask, and they live together like sisters. They are as good girls and good workers as I want to see."

The Ninth Annual Report of the Woman's Foreign Missionary Society says: "The medical work in Foochow has been most ably re-enforced during the year by the arrival of Miss Julia A. Sparr, M. D. By the presence of two physicians one will be able to give herself chiefly to hospital practice, the other to meet the demand in the city and adjacent country for medical treatment. Miss Sparr has already given abundant proof of her devotion and success in the treatment of patients, and of great heroism and self-sacrifice in the care of small-pox patients under quarantine in a pest-ship."

Miss Sparr also wields a graceful pen, as is shown by the many beautiful articles written by her before her appointment to China, and published in the home papers.

SUSAN B. HIGGINS.

SUSAN B. HIGGINS is a native of Georgetown, Maine, and was born August 10, 1842. She is the daughter of Rev. Josiah and Sarah Higgins, and, like the children of other itinerant Methodist preachers, in her early childhood she had no "continuing city," no local habitation; but, with her parents, at different times resided in the different villages within the bounds of the Maine Conference, of which her father was an influential and prominent member. Mingling with the purest and best of her father's flock, the influences brought to bear upon her young life were of the most healthful character. Of her home life she says: "My mother— now in glory—walked as a saint before her household. She led the way to heaven by the blessedness of a gentle, consecrated life. Guided by such a one, can you wonder that I distinctly remember gentle knockings from a pierced hand when only eleven years of age?"

In 1855 her father was stationed at Chelsea, Mass., in the suburbs of Boston. Here Susan remained to complete her education, graduating with honors from the Chelsea High School, and immediately after commenced teaching in the same city. She remained there teaching in the various grades, and being constantly promoted until she reached the highest post of honor, which she relinquished only after her appointment to a wider and more distinctive field of labor in Japan.

In relation to this she says: "I was converted in the year 1858, and early in my Christian experience became greatly interested in the cause of missions, and after my graduation from school, cherished the thought that some day God *might* call *me*. I felt so utterly unfit for any such service, that I dared not mention it. Many a time, when our yearly offerings were solicited, it was in my mind to write, I give myself.'

"While perplexed and pondering these questions came the Annual Meeting of the Board in Boston. At the very opening Dr. Dashiell's remarks as to the needs of the work in Mexico made me linger at the close of the service questioning with my heart as to whether I had better offer myself. The same battle had to be fought after listening to Miss Sparkes's tender words: 'It did seem as if in all Christian America some one would be found willing to go.' On my way home from the meeting I was told by several persons that *it was thought that I ought to go*, but I felt so unworthy I did not let my heart be known.

"O, how dear my native land and friends became as I tried to relinquish them! Surely they were the idols that bound me! Nothing but the peremptory command of God himself can satisfy the soul in that hour when a woman, alone, solemnly resolves to put half the world between herself and her kindred in the flesh, for the sake of those who are to be made kindred through the blood of Christ. No 'romance of missions' will satisfy in the hours when she is battling with a new tongue among a strange people, seeming bound on the right hand and on the left by new and untoward circumstances. In these hours nothing will sustain like the recollection of God's sure voice *having called*, and the certainty that one is under *his* appointment. So through those days of meditation I came to the decision, 'Here I am, Lord! Only let me be sure of thy call, and I will follow thee.' The meeting of the Board closed without my offering myself. Then came our quarterly meeting, on the 12th of June, 1878, a day long to be remembered in my history. I had been anticipating much from the meeting, feeling an unusual interest in it; but just as I was about going, a sudden and severe shower arose, so that I deemed it imprudent to venture out, and I began laying other plans for my time, in the midst of which I felt strangely moved to ask God's decision about even this seemingly unimportant event. I sought him, and implored his aid and guidance, asking that he would show me from the word just the duty of that hour. Opening my Bible my eyes immediately fell on this passage, 'And I said, What shall I do, Lord? And the Lord said unto me, Arise, and go into Damascus; and there it shall be told thee of all things which are appointed for thee to do.' Acts xxii, 10. Like Paul, I immediately went into the city, finding the meeting in session, but no message for me, but feeling sure that God's will concerning me would, somehow, there be revealed.

"At the close of the meeting, as Mrs. Daggett passed, she remarked to me, 'I think we will send you as a missionary some time.' '*Any time,*' I replied. She passed on a little, but returned, and, taking my hand, while her eyes looked into my very soul, she said, 'Apply, then ; apply.' God had met me on the very ground where I had been hesitating. I went to my room pondering the question as from God, and feeling that now the question must be fairly met and decided. The first salutation that met me, yet undecided, was from my room-mate, 'Susan, are you going to be a missionary?' and with it came the decision and answer, '*I am going to apply.*'

"I went to Mrs. Daggett, telling her that I had followed her instruction. She said, 'Why could you not have decided at the annual meeting ; our work is all planned for another year, and there may be no vacancy; but,' she added, 'God never calls one without a place for her.' Within two weeks there is to be a meeting of the New England Branch for other business, and I will send for you to come and meet the ladies.' In less than a week I was summoned from my school-room to meet them. When I told them my reasons for my coming were, that the responsibility of the matter, as far as my efforts were concerned, might hereafter cease, Mrs. Warren, the President, said to me, 'We consider this a very providential thing, for our Secretary to-day has brought the resignation of the lady appointed by the Annual Meeting to Yokohama, and we appoint you in her place.' On the 6th of August I received notification of my acceptance by the Board, and on the 14th was informed that I must be ready to start by the middle of September."

From a September number of " Zion's Herald," published in Boston, 1878, we copy the following, written by Rev. Mark Trafton, D.D.: " But I see another and familiar name—the name of one who is soon to sail as a missionary—Miss Susan B. Higgins, daughter of my old friend and class-leader, Rev. Josiah Higgins, for many years a popular member of the Maine Annual Conference. When I first knew him he was a theological student in the Bangor Seminary, and a local preacher in the Methodist Episcopal Church. He was zealous, active, and influential, and had a large share in the planting of the first Methodist Episcopal Church in Bangor. He was at the first Methodist inquiry meeting I attended, and when I joined the class he was present. His words of counsel and earnest exhortations were a blessing to me in my early Christian life. I recall those labors with gratitude, and from my quiet home, at this midnight hour, I send my congratulations for the honor put upon him by this cheerful offering of a daughter to the cause of Christ.

" Her sainted mother—I see her now, not in her bridal robes, as I saw her once, but in the radiant glory of the redeemed—will look down upon her with a mother's tenderness, and watch her in her labors. I give you joy, my old friend! Give her one of your old-time smiles, and send her off in gladness. She is only going to Japan, no farther. The distance is comparatively no greater than from your father's house, in Bucksport, to your first circuit. You can hear from her every hour, if need be. Science and art have annihilated space, and brought the nations to be next-door neighbors.

"And blessings upon you, daughter of my old friend and companion in labor! May the good God and Father guide, sustain, and bless you, filling your crown with stars which shall shine for ever and ever! Soon you and the loved ones you leave, for a Saviour, shall be reunited to part no more."

> "Hark, how the gentle echo from her cell
> Sighs through the cliffs, and murmuring o'er the stream,
> Repeats the sentence, We shall part no more."

After a pleasant voyage she reached Yokohama, and entered upon her work November 1, 1878. Writing back, she says: "On account of the illness of Mrs. C., a change of locality, etc., the school had nearly lost its existence, when, on November 1, I entered it as English teacher. Weekly the Lord has blessed us and enlarged our borders. We unite with another school for Sunday-school services, as we are too far removed from the church for them to attend the regular Sunday-school held under its auspices. Once in three months we hold union services there, where are shown the results of a healthy rivalry in learning the things taught in the respective schools.

"On Tuesdays I hold a Bible-class for students who can read in Japanese. We are taking the Gospel of Matthew in course. It gives me an opportunity, by help of my personal teacher as an interpreter, not only to teach them the Bible truth, but to examine them on the work of the Japanese teacher, who is a member of the Church, and is instructed to teach Christianity with his daily lessons.

"My mornings I devote faithfully to the study of the language, longing that communication may speedily be given me with all who are ready to hear the truth. There are numerous suburban villages which we could enter for school purposes, could it be found possible to meet the expense of teacher and rent. My hope and plan for the future, is somewhat like this: to watch carefully among the girls for those who might become desirable Biblewomen, and, after I am sufficiently familiar with the language, and they are sufficiently educated, to take them under daily instruction, and send them to the homes of those who come not to inquire the way. There are three girls now that I am consecrating to this work, if the Lord will; two of them are reading in easy English, of which four months since they knew nothing. My one desire is to be led of the Lord in my work for him among this people."

To the writer she says: "We commenced here in November with four scholars, and now have sixty-seven. We are encouraged by the interest the mothers of some of our children take in the school and in the hymns taught there. Seed is being sown that one day shall bring forth fruit for the garner of the Master.

"There is not much to be said by a new-comer, but I hope before another six months shall have fled to have something of interest to tell. There is little to show in the foundation of a house that is interesting except to a builder. The Book up yonder will show the true record, and whether we have put into our building precious stones, or 'wood, hay, and stubble.' God grant it may stand in the day of the Lord!"

She closes her interesting letter with the following beautiful lines from Horatius Bonar:

" Needs there the praise of the love-written record—
   The name and the epitaph graved on the stone?
The things we have lived for, let *them* be our story,
   We ourselves but remembered by what we have done.

'I need not be missed, if another succeed me
   To reap down those fields which in spring I have sown,
He who plowed and who sowed is not missed by the reaper,
   He is only remembered by what he has done.

" Not myself, but the truth that in life I have spoken,
   Not myself, but the seed that in life I have sown,
Shall pass on to ages—all about me forgotten
   Save the truth I have uttered, the things I have done.

" So let my living be, so let my dying;
   So let my name be unblazoned, unknown,
Unpraised and unmissed, I shall yet be remembered,
   Yes, but remembered by what I have done.

We leave our sister in her school in Yokohama. Our hearts are beating high with hopes for the future of our mission there, and we believe that when life's labor is ended and the records proclaimed before an assembled universe, she will be " remembered by what she has done," and from the lips of the supreme Judge shall hear the welcome words,

"Inasmuch as ye did it unto one of the least of these, my brethren, ye did it unto me."

NOTE.—Scarcely had we finished writing the above sketch ere the tidings flashed over the wires, "Miss Higgins is dead!" Being taken suddenly ill she consulted a physician, who said, "You may get well, but it is very doubtful." She calmly replied, "I am in the Lord's hands. Living or dying, I am his." She lived but a few weeks after. During her last hours she was filled with unutterable joy. She requested singing.

> "Jesus can make a dying bed
> Feel soft as downy pillows are,"

was sung, and before the sound of the last line had died away, she herself took up the verse,

> "O would my Lord his servant meet,
> My soul would stretch her wings in haste,
> Fly fearless through death's iron gate,
> Nor feel the terror as she passed."

Thus triumphantly she passed into the heavens. She was buried in Tokio, July 4, 1879.

HENRIETTA B. WOOLSTON, M.D.

HENRIETTA B. WOOLSTON is a cousin of the two ladies of that name, who have so long and faithfully served the cause of missions in China. She was born at Mount Holly, New Jersey. After pursuing her education at home, she entered a school in Newark, and from thence she went to the Philadelphia Medical College. Subsequently she removed to Vincenttown, New Jersey. She sailed from New York, November 9, 1878, in company with Misses Gibson and Sparkes. She reached Moradabad, India, and entered at once upon her medical work, in which she is still engaged at the present writing.

SALINA ALCESTA EASTON.

SALINA A. EASTON was born in Middlesex, Yates County, N. Y. When about eighteen years of age she entered the Female Wesleyan Seminary, at Lima, remaining there two years. From thence she went to the Wesleyan Female College, in Cincinnati, from which she graduated in 1854, after which she taught in the same institution, and also in an academy in Perry, Wyoming County, N. Y. She next taught mathematics and English literature, in the Wesleyan Female College, in Wilmington, Del. Here she remained for about seventeen years, being also preceptress in the institution for several years of the time.

The last teaching she did before her departure for India was in connection with Mrs. Somers' Ladies' College, in the City of Washington, D. C. Here she remained two years, at the expiration of which she received her appointment to Cawnpore, India, and sailed in the autumn of 1878.

Miss Easton is a lady of large capabilities—intellectually, socially, and spiritually. She has a classical education, a keen, discriminating mind, can readily read character, is unselfish, unremitting in her efforts to advance the interests of the pupils committed to her care. Eternity alone can reveal the good she has already accomplished by the influence of her pure life, as it has come in contact with, and left its impress upon, the youth who have been under her instruction. She was converted to Christ when about sixteen years of age, and has ever since been a most conscientious, devoted Christian. She was appointed by the Woman's Foreign Missionary Society to superintend and teach among the English-speaking people of Cawnpore. We know, if her life is spared, great good will be sure to result from her efforts to enlighten and elevate the women of India.

MATILDA A. SPENCER.

MATILDA A. SPENCER was born in Philadelphia, January 16, 1848. Subsequently she removed with her parents to Germantown, now incorporated in the city limits, where she resided until her departure for Japan. Her parents were intelligent and deeply pious. Miss Spencer says: "To them I owe all my early religious impressions. They were untiring in their efforts to set before me a true Christian example, and they led me in the paths of righteousness."

From her earliest childhood she longed to be a Christian, and greatly admired holy, devoted followers of Christ. She joined the Church when about fourteen years of age. But she says: "I had not as yet experienced the removal of my burden of sin, and while conscientiously striving to do duty, and serve the Lord aright, I had no comfort or peace of mind. I did not love the class-meetings. I had not the joyful experience which other Christians enjoyed, and which I knew it was my privilege to have, and when communion Sabbath came I felt that I was too unworthy to have a place at the Lord's table, and constantly grieved that I could not understand the way of salvation.

"Thus matters stood for several years, until, through the labor of one of God's chosen handmaids,

I was brought to see the simplicity of the plan to save mankind, when, casting away all self-laid plans and purposes, I trusted Jesus and *was saved*. At the Executive Meeting held in Minneapolis, in May, 1877, I was led to make a full consecration of myself to Christ; and ever since that time I have felt a sacred nearness to him, a blessed *abiding* of the Holy Spirit, satisfying my longing for peace and rest, and giving me implicit confidence in the promises of his word."

Of her call to foreign work she says: "It came unexpectedly to myself one evening while alone. It was as if a voice said to me, 'You must be a missionary, and carry the Gospel to heathen lands.' I said nothing for several weeks, praying and seeking guidance from above. But when I became assured that it was of God's appointing, I offered myself to the Society."

Miss Spencer was educated in private schools, in the vicinity of Philadelphia. When she offered herself to the Ladies' Society for foreign work, she expected to be sent to the English-speaking people in Cawnpore; but when it was decided that she was to go to Tokio, Japan, she made no objection. "Anywhere for Jesus!" she replied, and accepted the field with gratitude.

Miss Spencer is a graceful and ready writer. She has but just entered her field of labor, but the Church has much to expect from her pure life and consecrated talents.

MARY A. HOLBROOK.

THE subject of this sketch was born in England, on Christmas-day, 1852. Her father was a local preacher, but, emigrating with his family to America, joined the Wyoming Conference, of which he has continued an honored member. He is a man of marked ability, sterling integrity, and deep piety.

She was also blessed with a mother whose unobtrusive piety and gentle, loving spirit have done much to mold the character of her children, and give the right course to the current of their lives. Mary was the eldest daughter, and while very young evinced a great love for learning. In her childhood she began to write poems for the press, some of which have appeared in our Church periodicals.

At the age of thirteen she had mastered all that was then taught in the common schools. Her thirst for knowledge was always encouraged by her parents, and they cheerfully made every possible sacrifice on their part to enable them to render her all the assistance in their power. Accordingly she was placed in the Wyoming Seminary, where, with an almost incredible amount of self-denial, untiring energy, and persistent labor, she assisted in defraying her expenses, and graduated at the end of three years with the highest honors. The late lamented Dr. R. Nelson was then principal of the institution. He was much interested in his young pupil, and, desiring to see her persevering industry rewarded, kindly opened the way for her.

Having secured her own education, her next ambition was, that her sisters should be educated in the same school; but, fearing for their health, she would never consent for them to undertake the extra labor she had performed. Self-forgetting, she resolved to devote her time to securing funds to assist them.

After her two sisters had graduated, she felt that her work in this direction was done, and that she was now free to entertain the hope deferred, but still cherished within her inmost soul, of devoting her life to missionary teaching and labor.

Miss Ellen R. Martin, A.M., the lady Principal of Wyoming Seminary, thus speaks of Miss Holbrook:

"I take great pleasure in giving you any facts concerning my friend, but I feel that I know more of her history since we parted as pupil and teacher than I knew of it while she was a student. I came to Wyoming Seminary in the fall of 1868, and that was Miss Holbrook's last school year. Among a bevy of merry school girls might have been selected one as full of glee as the most joyous, yet one with a degree of earnestness and thoughtfulness that hinted she was cherishing noble purposes, though, as yet, they might not be clearly defined. It did not take me long to discover that this young girl of fifteen was a ruling spirit among her mates; yet so gently did she win the girls over to her opinions, and sway them by her influence, that, I think, they scarcely knew that she was leader; she certainly did not recognize her own power in this respect.

"Desirous to establish a young ladies' prayer-meeting in the seminary, I felt that to her I must look for its chief support. At first she seemed to think the effort would be futile; but after several conversations she expressed a willingness to undertake the work. I assured her there could be no failure if she would promise to be faithful, and often on the Sabbath afternoons of that fall term there were only the two to claim the promise, but Miss Holbrook was always there.

"During the glorious revival in the winter she saw her faith rewarded, for many of the girls were won into the meetings, and not only the Sabbath, but the every-day prayer-meetings became an established fact. Not only was her steadfastness of purpose manifested in this, but in her society she proved herself an indefatigable toiler. The young ladies of Wyoming Seminary who to-day enjoy the beautifully furnished room of the Adelphian Society, do not realize how many of her recreation hours were sacrificed to obtain the time to labor for it; nor did her zeal for her society die out when she said 'Good-bye' to her school life. Her letters were always asking, 'What are the girls doing for the Adelphian?'

"I think hers was an evenly-balanced mind, perhaps showing a little more aptness for *belles-lettres* and languages; in composition she was particularly felicitous. The society leaned upon her for its best work, and on public occasions the audience was disappointed if she had no part. Many speak of her anniversary effort, 'Tarrying in the Vestibule,' as a production of exceeding merit; yet she was unsatisfied with it, fearing her father would be disappointed. Only a few knew the hard struggle she had to undergo while obtaining her education. It was no flowery path of knowledge she was traveling, but the sharp thorns of sacrifice and toil were in every step of the way.

"After her graduation, through the kindness of Dr. Nelson, her beloved teacher and willing counselor, she secured a position as teacher. There were no idle vacations in her life, and she must not tarry for rest. She soon left this field of teaching to take the important position of preceptress at Ingleside, near Baltimore. This position was also obtained for her by Dr. Nelson, and she proved herself worthy the important trust, being loved and esteemed by her Southern girls. I have no doubt a nobler womanhood has been built up through the inspiration of her daily example. After leaving Ingleside she spent her last year in teaching near Baltimore, and it was from this place that she first unburdened her heart to me on the subject of foreign missionary work. She says: 'I have long felt a desire to be a missionary teacher. In my early years I used to think much upon the subject, but the door has always seemed closed until now. My sisters have now received their education, and I feel I am free to go; but what am I to do? I do not feel that I am sufficiently consecrated to do the work of a missionary; can I not secure a place as teacher? and to whom shall I look for assistance?'

"Though silence was imposed upon me, you know, Mrs. Wheeler, that I brought the case before you for your larger experience in missionary matters, and I feel that it is greatly due to your exertion that my once student-girl and now dear friend, Miss Holbrook, is a worker in Japan.

"The letters lately received from her are full of enthusiasm for her work, though she realizes the barrier, in the strange language, between her pupils and herself, and prays for patience while she is acquiring. I believe she brings to her work a strong faith, a cheerful hope, a consecrated love, and a sanctified zeal, that will, in time, win souls for the Master. Her seminary life was but the 'vestibule' to the great active world that was calling to her for assistance; and her missionary life, that she is endeavoring to fill up with holy toiling, is but the vestibule to that heavenly life in the Beyond. May she tarry long in this vestibule, and labor until she hears a voice from the excellent glory of the inner temple saying, 'Enter into my rest; thou hast finished the work that I gave thee to do.'"

With regard to her conversion and Christian experience her father says: "Mary was almost a Christian at home, but became decided when she went to the seminary. She united with the Church, and I heard of her activity in Christian work."

Speaking of herself, she says: "My life has been

quite uneventful thus far. I have been happy in teaching, happy in helping the younger members of my family; but my influence has told but little outside of a narrow circle. I have never had the positive revelations of duty some people have, nor the glowing experiences others seem to enjoy; but I do find now a settled peace, a quiet satisfaction in God's service, and I am coming to feel more and more that I can adopt the language of the hymn, 'Thou, O Christ, art all I want.' I cannot tell when I was converted. I commenced the life of a professing Christian while at the seminary, and was greatly helped by the blessed influences there; but, if I know my heart at all, I was not converted until long after. With me the work of conversion has been the work of years. It has been a gradual growth." The illuminating rays of the Sun of Righteousness dawned upon her young heart as the morning; almost imperceptible at first, but gradually shining more and more unto the perfect day.

At the ninth session of the General Executive Committee, convened in Boston, May, 1878, she was formally accepted, and appointed to Tokio, Japan. She received the appointment with pleasure, and at once set about making preparations for the journey. A farewell missionary meeting was held on Dimock Camp Ground, Susquehanna County, Pennsylvania, September 3, and one of great interest was also held by the faculty and students of Wyoming Seminary. After an eloquent address by Dr. Copeland, President of the institution, Miss Holbrook spoke briefly but impressively. As she reached the conclusion, and repeated with tearful and uplifted eyes the following lines of consecration, the audience were deeply moved:

> "O God, I would not dare to offer thee
> Gifts which have nothing cost to me,
> But, looking deep into my heart,
> Whatever treasure I would strive to keep,
> Whatever talent I have hidden deep,
> These, these to thee I bring.
>
> "I would not dare to come to thee,
>   All worldly prospects blighted,
> And lay upon the altar of the Crucified
>   A life the world had slighted;
> But in life's dewy hours,
>   With bright hopes on the wing,
> My life, my love, my all,
>   To thee I bring."

She sailed from San Francisco, October 1, 1878. Her work in Japan thus far has been eminently successful in every respect, and her friends have more than realized their fondest hopes with regard to her.

The following is from the pen of Miss T. A. Spencer, of Japan:

"Miss Mary J. Holbrook, my companion in travel, and sharer of my joys and sorrows, is a sweet girl, rather petite, with fair skin, large blue eyes, and light hair. Together we are threading the intricate mazes of this very difficult Japanese language, day by day comparing notes and condoling with each other that our progress is so slow. She is wonderfully persevering, is very gifted with her pen, is a great favorite with the scholars, and, if she can be toned into willingness to study in moderation, will be a brilliant success. I am so thankful to the dear heavenly Father that we were allowed to come here together, to labor side by side in the interests of the cause we love. You will pray, dear sisters, will you not, that our years of service here in Japan may be crowned with success; that we may be the instruments, in God's hands, of persuading many precious souls to turn from darkness to light?"

EUGENIA GIBSON.

EUGENIA GIBSON is the daughter of Rev. David Gibson, of the New York Conference. She pursued her studies in the schools located in the different towns and villages where her father was appointed pastor. Afterward she entered a school in Albany, also the State Normal School in that city, from which she graduated. She was converted very early in life, and is an earnest, devout Christian. The story of her call to missionary work was related in a forcible manner by herself at the "farewell meeting" held in New York, November 7, 1878.

A telegram was read by Dr. Newman from Trinity Methodist Episcopal Sunday-school, Albany, New York, through its superintendent, Mr. Kelly, as follows: "Trinity Sunday-school sends greeting and good-bye to Miss Eugenia Gibson. Num. vi, 24-26: 'The Lord bless thee, and keep thee: the Lord make his face shine upon thee, and be gracious unto thee: the Lord lift up his countenance upon thee, and give thee peace.'"

Dr. Newman then introduced Miss Gibson, who said she came to speak "only a few words of experience." But what a precious experience! Many a Christian who has traveled much farther in the Christian path has failed to gather half as many sweet and precious things as she has found in her short but intimate walk with the Lord Jesus. She said all her life, since she gave herself to God, she had desired to be a missionary, but she had found her joy in doing the little things next to her. In listening to an address by Miss Sparkes, about a year ago, she felt the time had come for her to offer herself for foreign work. She placed her letters in the hands of the General Executive Committee at Boston, feeling that in so doing she was committing her way to the Lord. When the news came that she was accepted, and would go this year to India, her whole heart went out in a song of thanksgiving to God. Then followed a deep sense of responsibility and questioning as to her fitness to meet the great demands of missionary life. First came the thought as to physical strength, "Have I sufficient to meet the trial of climate?" And with peculiar emphasis this promise was breathed into her soul, "My God shall supply all your need." Then came the question, "Have I mental power to acquire a difficult language? shall I not fail here?" and swift the answer of the Spirit came, "My God shall supply all your need." Higher and deeper and beyond all other needs came the thought of spiritual strength, and again the questioning heart asked, "Have I sufficient spiritual power to win those to whom I am sent, to my Saviour?" and with threefold meaning and closer personal application came the blessed promise, "exceeding broad," "My God shall supply all your need." Not according to the sense of need, nor according to the human conception of how that need could be supplied, but "according to his riches in glory by Christ Jesus." No one who heard this testimony, and looked into the youthful face of the speaker, will ever forget the spiritual impressions of the hour. Miss Gibson closed by saying, it was a great comfort to believe that she had not chosen this responsible work, but God had chosen it for her, and she went to it trusting in his immutable promise, which cannot fail.

The following, written by Rev. C. H. Fowler, D.D., we take from the "Christian Advocate." After speaking of the general meeting and the other outgoing missionaries, he says:

"The marked feature of the evening was the experience of Miss Gibson, daughter of Rev. Brother Gibson, of the New York Conference. She is a lady, twenty-two years of age, with a peculiarly attractive face. Nature, culture, and grace have combined to do a perfect work. Her narration of the steps by which she came to this great work were simple, compact, classical, sublime. She stood before us beautiful, radiant, inspired; and as she told the wonderful dealings of God with her, from the earliest longings of her childhood for this mission work up through her conversion and call, and to the opening of the way for her departure, she seemed the only calm one in the great audience. When the Church can bring such offerings as these for the redemption of India, there can be no doubt of what she thinks of the work. These women in India will show to that sorrowing land of sorrowing women what sort of women Christianity can produce, and what Christianity will do for them. Angels from heaven could not serve the cause more efficiently.

" While the Woman's Foreign Missionary Society sends out such representatives, and can convene such audiences to bestow their benediction upon the messengers, there will be no need of other defense."

Miss Gibson was appointed to Lucknow, India.

MAGGIE ELLISON LAYTON.

MAGGIE E. LAYTON, who was appointed to the English work in Calcutta, India, was born in Newcastle County, Delaware. She was educated in the Bordentown Female College. She graduated, at the end of a three years' course, with the highest honors, being the valedictorian of her class. She afterward taught in the same institution, and still later in the Wesleyan Female College, Wilmington, Delaware.

She was converted in her early youth, while in attendance at the Bordentown College. Her conviction for sin was deep, and her conversion clear and marked. Referring to it she says: " Never, until reason forsakes her throne, will that memorable night be forgotten. It was a beautiful Sabbath evening, and while the worshipers of Jehovah had repaired to his holy temple to offer their accustomed oblations, I, in the bitterness of my heart, was deeply mourning my sinful nature. So long had the conflict continued, and so great had become my distress, that the evil one seemed about to gain the victory, when Omnipotent power interposed and saved a soul from ruin. So easily was the weight removed I was almost unconscious of the change. All was joy and peace, and I could only praise and adore the blessed Redeemer, who had heard the cry of one of his most unworthy creatures. And in the stillness of that hour I promised to devote myself to the service of God the remainder of my life."

From this time her all-absorbing desire seemed to be to lead other youths who came within the sphere of her influence into the same blessed relationship with Christ. She exerted a wonderful influence among the students in the institution, many of whom she led to the Saviour. Not only in college, but in the Church and Sabbath-school, she was fruitful in good works, actively engaged in instilling into youthful minds the pure principles of Christianity.

From the time of her conversion she was thoroughly imbued with the missionary spirit, and in the first letter written to her sister after her conversion, she speaks of her determination to follow Christ, even though he leads her into foreign lands. Soon after this she wrote again: "This has been a week of great peace and comfort. Have consecrated myself entirely to God. Recently, while reading the lives of the fallen missionaries of China, my whole soul went out after the heathen."

The circumstances connected with her going to India she has told so pleasantly, that we give the account to our readers in her own words:

"My Dear Miss Hart: Although personally unknown to the ladies of the Baltimore Branch of the Woman's Foreign Missionary Society, your warm letter of welcome in admitting me to their charge, and the short but memorable interview with you at Wilmington, have entirely taken away the feeling of being a stranger. Then, too, we have common interests, as co-workers in establishing the Master's kingdom upon the earth.

"Before beginning that journey which takes me to far-away India—the land that has cost so much of life and suffering in the past, yet promises so much for God in the future—I feel very desirous of sending a word of greeting to these new-found friends, and pleading for their prayers, that the good work already begun among the English people may be ably sustained and greatly advanced by the teacher whom they are sending.

"Dear Christian sisters, I go to the same work, but in a new field, and bear away the same spirit that came to me when the grace of God first took hold of my heart and life. Every one of the sixteen years spent in teaching has been one of precious privilege in training young ladies for holy living. I do not go to India with any different feeling, excepting that which the greater responsibility of being in a strange land brings. I was so fully committed to the home work that, when Mrs. Keen asked me to consider the call for teachers in Calcutta, I was slow to perceive it was a call to me; but when the discipline of the past two years came before me, the light began to dawn. More than two years since I was laid aside from school duties by overwork. While resting, my mind was drawn to a closer study of the Bible, and to the reading of missionary labor in foreign lands, particularly in India, among the natives. My spirit was so constantly stirred by this reading, and my desire to do more for God than I had ever done became so intense, that the conviction forced itself upon me, Perhaps the Lord is going to use me for some peculiar work. Unusual church work, which came in various forms, tended to increase this conviction. Being sent to the Philadelphia Branch as a delegate from Columbia, Pennsylvania, I went to Harrisburgh, praying most earnestly that the Lord would there reveal his will to me. Then it was that Mrs. Keen spoke to me of teaching in Calcutta. Since that time the all-wise Father has led me so gently and patiently to a decision in this matter that my heart is full of gratitude for his forbearance in my lack of faith. My struggles have not been so much to give up home and friends, and to prepare for self-sacrifice among strangers, as to believe these leadings of Providence to be a call to India. I have at last come to such a spirit of trust that fears and doubts have passed away, and I am making preparations for my departure, feeling it the highest privilege of my life to carry the old work into this new part of the vineyard.

"I cannot doubt that you, who have so readily given your means to send the laborer, will follow her with your prayers and sympathies. While you are sowing the good seed, supported by the presence and counsel of friends, you will remember the difficulties of doing this among strangers, where so much that is new must first become familiar to insure success.

"I shall take pleasure in sending you word from

time to time, respecting the progress of the school, and now say farewell, confident that the blessing of the Lord will rest upon every effort you make for the good of humanity.

"Yours in Christian fellowship,
"M. E. LAYTON."

A "farewell" meeting of great interest was held in Columbia, Pa., (Miss Layton's late home,) July 28, 1878. After the opening exercises, Miss Layton made a beautiful and effective address. The crowded house, the close attention of the auditors, and the many moist eyes, all told of the high estimation in which the out-going missionary was held.

Miss Layton has for a long time been associated with the Church in this place, and has been one of its most faithful laborers.

She possesses, in an eminent degree, all the elements of a successful missionary. With her rare intelligence, culture, and piety, her untiring energy and love for souls, she cannot fail in accomplishing much for the cause of missions in India.

MARY ADELAIDE PRIEST.

MARY A. PRIEST was born in the city of Auburn, Cayuga County, N. Y., February 3, 1854. While she was young her parents moved to the southern part of the State, where, among the hills, in the beautiful village of Bath, Steuben County, she spent a happy childhood. She was early taught to pray, and was trained up in the Methodist Episcopal Church by a devoted Christian mother.

When a little girl, she saw in her pastor's cabinet an idol that had been presented to him by a relative who was a missionary in some heathen land. It made a deep impression on her young heart. Referring to this she says: "I shall never forget my feelings on seeing the hideous image, and being told that there were people who knew no other god than such as this. My heart yearned over them, and I then resolved to be a missionary."

She says: "I thought myself a Christian until I was twelve years of age. I was very conscientious; I prayed much, but sinned so frequently that I became discouraged, and began to realize that I was trying to serve God with the natural heart; that I needed to be converted, and to have a more definite religious experience before I could be a successful missionary."

Accordingly, when the invitation was given by her pastor for those desiring salvation to present themselves at the altar she came, and earnestly sought the pardon of her sins, but did not receive peace. She became disheartened, because, though she was persistent in her efforts to obtain the favor of God, she did not receive a word of encouragement from pastor or Church member. They doubtless thought her too young to understand the matter.

Concluding that she must wait until she was older, she deferred the further seeking of salvation until she reached her eighteenth year, when, in answer to prayer, the Holy Spirit

> Assured her conscience of her part
> In the Redeemer's blood,
> And bore the witness with her heart
> That she was born of God.

Some years after her conversion she became convinced that it was her privilege to abide in Christ more fully—to be saved from inbred sin. She sought earnestly for a *pure* heart. The cleansing blood was applied, and she was saved to the uttermost, and was thus better prepared to tell the story of redemption to those afar off.

She was always eager for missionary intelligence, and used to steal away alone to read, lest her friends should suspect how deeply she was interested. Returning with her parents to her native city, she entered the High School, from which she graduated in 1875.

In reference to the missionary work she says: "I

was a member of the Wall-street Auxiliary of the Woman's Foreign Missionary Society, and held the office of Secretary till I left home for Japan. I coveted the privilege of going to a foreign field to labor. In August, 1877, while attending a camp-meeting at Auburndale, I heard Miss Fannie Sparkes deliver an address. She was fresh from her chosen field in India. Mrs. Lore, our Conference Secretary, introduced me to her, saying that she thought I would be a missionary some time. I was surprised at that statement, for she was only slightly acquainted with me at that time. I had been extremely careful that none should know how I felt with regard to the subject; only told my heavenly Father that I would gladly go if he would give me the fitness; and it seemed to me that he must have revealed it to Mrs. Lore." Soon after this Miss Priest received her appointment as missionary to Japan.

Mrs. D. E. Green, wife of her former pastor, writes us: "She was a missionary at home, in the Church, and every-where seemed ever possessed with a consuming desire to save souls. She started a meeting at the Church for young people, commencing with eight. It increased in interest until the class-room was too small, and they went into a larger room; and many have been converted in these meetings, *now* carried on by the boys she led to Jesus. Her home-life was always beautiful. Her mother says: " It seems to me she was always a Christian. She prayed from her cradle, and as a child had the grace of God."

"I had the pleasure of being with her for a few days before her departure last fall, and I noticed such a quiet exultation in the prospect of her being on the threshold of her coveted work. I wish you could have seen her as she went from one to another of the many friends who had assembled at the depot to see her off. I shall never forget that mother's look as her trunks were taken out of the house. It meant something to give that beautiful daughter to Japan! In a letter received from her mother a short time since she says: 'I have given Mary to the Lord, to the Church, to Japan, and God only knows what it has cost me. It has been the struggle of my soul for years.'"

Miss Priest sailed from San Francisco, Cal., October 1, 1878. From the steamer she writes: "Yesterday we went on board our steamer, City of Peking. We expect a safe and pleasant voyage. Our Father will take care of his children and his freight, I think; though it does not matter much whether I land at the city of Yokohama or the City of the New Jerusalem—whether I reach my home with Mrs. Harris or my home in the palace of the King."

After reaching her destination and entering upon her work, she says: "My work here is, of necessity, only preparatory at present, but I am contented and happy in it."

CLARA LOUISA MULLINER.

CLARA L. MULLINER was born in the city of Camden, New Jersey, October 29, 1855. She received a liberal education, first attending school in Camden and afterward in Philadelphia. After completing her education she taught in the public schools in her native city. She was converted when about thirteen years of age, and united with the Methodist Episcopal Church, of which she has ever been an active and influential member.

With a heart full of love to Christ and sympathy for souls, she yearned for the redemption of the whole world; and as often as she prayed, " Thy kingdom come," she felt a great desire to do what she could to advance the interests of this kingdom, until

> " Jesus shall reign where'er the sun
> Does his successive journeys run ;
> His kingdom spread from shore to shore,
> Till moons shall wax and wane no more."

For years she entertained a desire to be a missionary, and in the spring of 1878 she offered her services to the Woman's Foreign Missionary Society. She was accepted and sent to the city of Mexico. She sailed from New York for Mexico, October 19, 1878, reaching her destination in thirteen days.

Her work in the Girls' Orphanage has been arduous, but each day has found her at her post, laboring faithfully and efficiently; and already she is winning the hearts of the waifs who have there found refuge. Miss Mulliner is full of faith and hope for the future, and promises much for the Society, the Church, and the world.

CLARA M. CUSHMAN.

CLARA M. CUSHMAN is the daughter of Rev. Mr. Cushman, formerly of the New Hampshire, and now of the Texas, Conference. She was born in Walden, Vermont, May 23, 1851. In her early childhood she was noted for her conscientiousness and loveliness of disposition and character. When only nine years of age she sought and obtained the forgiveness of her sins, and was consciously saved through the blood of the Lamb. All her life has been characterized by purity, virtue, integrity, and devotion to Christ, as she has followed the injunction, "Whatsoever things are true, whatsoever things are honest, whatsoever things are just, whatsoever things are pure, whatsoever things are lovely, whatsoever things are of good report; if there be any virtue, and if there be any praise, think on these things." She was fond of study, and graduated with honor from the New Hampshire Conference Seminary and the Female College in Tilton. In 1878 she was appointed to Peking, China.

Miss Cushman has been very successful in her work. Miss Porter writes: "You could not wish any thing better for me than to have Miss Cushman as an assistant in school and home work. She is tall, bright, and affectionate. I cannot feel that she is a stranger; she seems like a dear friend whom I have known for a long time."

MARY A. SHARP.

MARY A. SHARP, our first representative to Africa, was sent out by the Parent Society, April, 1879, and was soon after transferred to the Woman's Foreign Missionary Society. She has for many years been actively engaged in missionary work among the freedmen of John's Island, and is in deep sympathy with the oppressed and benighted sons and daughters of Africa.

Miss Sharp has a deep religious experience, making no compromise with sin in any form. She not only believes that God has power on earth to forgive sins, but that the blood of Jesus Christ his Son *cleanseth* us from all sin. Plain and unpretending in her appearance, she possesses, nevertheless, a brilliant mind, well-stored with valuable information. She has broad views, and looks out over the world, and watches with peculiar interest the events that are transpiring among the nations, considering their probable relation with regard to the coming of Christ's kingdom.

She is full of life and energy, witty and eloquent. We have heard her represent the cause of the freedmen at camp-meeting and conference occasions, when the entire audience seemed thrilled by her words, and would not be restrained from giving their offerings for the promotion of the cause, though no collection was asked.

Bishop Gilbert Haven, who was the chief instrument in sending her to Africa, was a firm friend. He regarded her as a most remarkable woman. We heard him say on one occasion: "Second to none in ability to organize and carry on mission work successfully—not even Ann Wilkins."

Upon leaving New York Miss Sharp received from the hands of a lady friend a beautiful bouquet of flowers, which she preserved during the voyage. Shortly after reaching Monrovia, on a set day she proceeded to the Mission Cemetery, and had the graves of the heroic missionaries sleeping there cleaned of weeds and grass, and mounded up anew, after which she planted upon them the flowers she had taken with such care from America. Thousands of hearts will thank her for this beautiful tribute to the memory of our heroic and sainted missionaries, who died at their posts, victims to the malarial poison peculiar to that climate.

Miss Sharp has been in good health since her arrival, and is busily at work among the people of Liberia. We are glad that our Society is ready to preach the Gospel to those that are in Africa also; and that the people of that land, so long in darkness, are now "rising to greet the light of Bethlehem's Star."

TENTH ANNUAL MEETING.

THE tenth Annual Meeting of the General Executive Committee convened in Centenary Church, Chicago, May 23, 1879. An admirable address of welcome was delivered by Mrs. I. N. Danforth, to which Mrs. Alderman, of the New England Branch, replied in fitting words. Mrs. Dr. Steele was chosen President, and Mrs. L. H. Daggett, Secretary. One change in corresponding secretaries had been made during the year, and Mrs. M. P. Alderman appeared as Corresponding Secretary of the New England Branch, in place of Mrs. Taplin, who, in consequence of failing health, had tendered her resignation.

The reports from foreign fields were highly interesting and encouraging. Several returned missionaries were present—the Misses Woolston, who had spent twenty years in Foochow, China; Miss Gertrude Howe, recently returned from Kiukiang; and Miss Warner, from Mexico. These were simply on furlough, expecting soon to return to their foreign fields.

Miss M. A. Sharp, who was sent to Africa the year previous by the parent Board, was transferred to our Society, and her support assumed by the ladies. The following resolutions were passed:

"*Resolved*, That, as Miss Sharp is doing the legitimate work of our Society in Africa, we will gladly undertake her support if the parent Board is willing.

"*Resolved*, That we appropriate $1,500 to be used for work in Africa when there is an opening that meets the approval of the parent Board and the Committee of Reference."

Memorial services were held for the missionaries who had recently died at their posts: Miss Campbell, of China, and Mrs. Cheney, of Nynee Tal. Also for Mrs. Dr. Olin, of New York, late President of the New York Branch.

The anniversary exercises were highly interesting. Miss Gertrude Howe gave some of her experiences in China, and Bishop Peck spoke weighty and kindly words. This meeting had special interest, from the fact of its being our decennial celebration; and a brief history of the decade by Mrs. Cowen, of the Cincinnati Branch, was read, from which we make the following comprehensive and beautiful extract:

"Ten years have passed since the first organization of the Society, and what is the result? To-day it numbers over two thousand auxiliary societies, and has more than fifty thousand members. In the costly city church, in the settlement on the frontier, in town and in country places, all over our land, we find the watch-fires burning, the thoughtful, praying women enlisting under this banner. This has required work, courage, and faith, and the 'good women and true,' who all over our land have carried the burdens and borne the heat of the day, have not toiled for naught, neither have their labors been in vain. For them the blessed recognition waits: 'Inasmuch as ye have done it unto one of the least of these, ye have done it unto me.' While the objective point of this 'woman's work for women' has been the conversion of their heathen sisters, the reflex influence on the women of the Church has been a most marked and blessed one.

"This being a co-worker with God has a wonderful uplifting power, and every woman bearing this relation has felt its influence, and in being brought nearer to Christ has also been quickened and made a more earnest worker in every department of his vineyard. Since the organization of the Society the amount of money contributed is $514,850 54—over half a million of dollars. When we remember that almost all of this comes as an extra offering, withdrawing nothing from other Church enterprises, we can have some idea of the magnitude of the field in our Church hitherto untilled.

But let us follow our contributions across the seas, and see whether, in the dark night of heathenism, there is a promise of the coming day. We have sent to the foreign field forty-three missionaries: twenty-five are actively carrying on the work under our Society, six have transferred their names to the parent Society, but are still, to the best of their ability, carrying forward the missionary work to which they have pledged their lives. Failing health compelled the return of three, and six are at home for a season of rest, expecting to return to their appointed fields during the coming year. Two have heard the Master's voice, 'It is enough; come up higher:' Miss Campbell, of Peking, China, and Mrs. Cheney, of Nynee Tal, India. The first shadow of death has fallen on our Society, but those who were taken from us in the midst of usefulness and labors for the Church militant have joined the Church triumphant, where 'they shall see his face, and his name shall be on their foreheads.'

"Nine of the missionaries sent out were medical graduates, who have inaugurated and carried on most successfully medical work. The first female medical missionary ever sent to Asia was Miss Swain, our pioneer in that field; and this agency is one of the most effective for reaching the women of heathendom, and has opened new doors for the entrance of the light. Even caste gives way before it. Not only in our hospitals and dispensaries has the work been done, but large classes of native women have been taught the principles of medical science, the art of healing, as well as the art of nursing, and these in turn are teaching and helping others.

"One hundred and forty day-schools are supported by our Society, four orphanages, nine boarding-schools, and one hundred and fifty native teachers and assistants. Most generously has the missionary spirit been shown, as well as faith in the future history of our Society, by the answers to appeals for school buildings, hospitals, homes for our missionaries, etc. In the large centers of our mission fields we find them every year increasing in numbers and value, and showing clearly the purpose to go in and possess the land in the name of our King. It is no longer necessary to coax or hire pupils to come to the school; they gladly come, and our boarding-schools have not capacity to hold the numbers desiring admittance. In addition to this, it must be remembered that in connection with every one of these schools there is a Sunday-school, where the Bible is taught exclusively. In some places, the desire for such teaching being greater than the supply of teachers, it has been necessary to hold a Bible-school on Saturday as well as on the Sabbath. New doors are opening, more laborers are urgently asked for. How many encouragements have been ours! Our missionaries have been 'chosen of the Lord,' and his presence has gone with them. Our schools have been promising, our teachers and Bible-women faithful and untiring. Little children have been cared for and taught the way to heaven. From our hospitals have gone out numbers capable of healing the sick body and comforting the sick soul, besides the thousands who owe life and health to the missionary physician. As our boarding-schools and orphanages have sent out trained teachers and Bible-readers, their places in the schools have been filled with new recruits, who, in time, will go forth sowing the same seed. Into many a darkened soul a great light has shone, and the 'signs of promise' multiply on every hand; and so we sum up the whole matter. Has our work been in vain, and our labor that which profiteth not? Shall we lay down our sickles when the fields are white unto the harvest? Rest in inglorious ease when victories are to be won for our King? A thousand times, *No!* While redeemed souls are perishing for the bread of eternal life, our mission remains. 'The world for Christ' is our watch-word, and victory is sure."

A TRIBUTE TO THE WOMAN'S FOREIGN MISSIONARY SOCIETY.

BY REV. BISHOP E. G. ANDREWS, D.D.

THE following, in regard to the importance and necessity of the organization of the Woman's Foreign Missionary Society of the Methodist Episcopal Church, is kindly furnished for this work by Rev. Bishop Edward G. Andrews, D.D. Such a high estimate of the *personnel* and efficiency of our noble corps of missionaries, formed upon the spot after personal visitation and inspection, by so distinguished an authority, is most gratifying to the workers, both at home and abroad.

"Admirable as is the work of the Woman's Foreign Missionary Society, it would be a serious injustice to speak of its organization as the beginning of woman's toil, patience, and suffering for the redemption of her heathen sisters. On the contrary, many missionary societies had previously commissioned women to their foreign fields. The names of Mrs. Wilkins and Miss Farrington are memorable among those who thus laid foundations in Africa. But even more notable is the spirit with which, from the beginning of modern missions, the wives of missionaries have shared the labors as well as the sacrifices and perils of their husbands. Every continent and island has witnessed their devotion, skill, and success. The first Mrs. Judson, eminent though she was in the morning of missionary effort, has had her peers on every mission field. The Church has never fully known the value of these unobtrusive workers.

"But a new and better missionary organization of Christian women was needed. It was needed, first, at home, and, second, abroad.

"AT HOME:

1. As a distinct and grateful recognition, by Christian women, of their indebtedness to that Redeemer by whose grace they differ so widely from their heathen sisters, both in worldly condition and in eternal hope. 2. As an explicit acknowledgment of the degree in which religious responsibility had accrued with the increase of intellectual opportunities, social power, and Church freedom. 3. As a means of enlisting in the service of missions the women of the Church; that is to say, the large numerical majority of the Church—the best possible guarantee, under God, of the final success of missions.

"ABROAD:

"1. Because the magnitude of the work in every considerable mission field far overpassed the resources of the societies already in occupancy. 2. Because a large and indispensable part of the work to be done is among women and children; and for this work women alone are fitted, both by original constitution, and by the peculiar conditions of domestic life which exist in the East, the great mission field.

"How perfectly the results have justified the new societies their annual reports fully set forth. Probably the Church never before saw so large and quick a result from small beginnings; and if Christian wisdom and zeal shall continue to guide as heretofore, these societies will bring at length vast reenforcements to the feeble missionary bands that struggle against such immense odds.

"It was my privilege, in the winter of 1876-77, to see the work of the Woman's Foreign Missionary Society in India. I remarked—

"1. The hearty co-operation of its agents with those of the parent Board. One heart beat through all. There was no division of interest, no distrust, no lack of sympathy. The wives of missionaries assist in planning and carrying out the work. One of them is Treasurer for the Woman's Foreign Missionary Society, doing her work with great labor and care; others supervise Bible-readers, schools, and medical dispensaries which are supported by the Woman's Foreign Missionary Society. In a word, all laborers, whether sent out by the parent Board or the woman's Board, are fused into one grand body of Christians. Keenly would they regret any division or alienation at home.

"2. The eminent character of the ladies sent out. It would be invidious, perhaps, to discriminate in the midst of so much intellectual and moral worth. Yet all who know will consent, that in Miss Thoburn, the first teacher, Miss Swain, the first physician, and Miss Sparkes, the first directress of the orphanage, the Society had agents of the very first class; eminent illustrations of what women may be, may do, may endure. Other ladies might be properly named with these, all worthy the high confidence which made them pioneers in the Indian empire.

"3. The variety of work done. (1.) The orphanage work, chiefly at Bareilly, provided not only homes, but also a plain domestic training and Christian instruction for about two hundred orphan girls. Already many wives of native pastors and teachers, and many Bible-readers, have gone out to do their part in the great work of evangelizing India. (2.) The school work is done by boarding schools, chiefly at Lucknow, Cawnpore, and Moradabad, and by a large number of elementary schools scattered throughout the missions. Gradually the opposition to the education of girls is being overcome, and the agents are being prepared by which wider good shall be accomplished. (3.) The medical work is carried on chiefly at the dispensaries at Bareilly and Moradabad, and is not only conveying great good to suffering women and children, but winning for the benevolent missionaries the good-will and the confidence of the people. (4.) The zenana and Bible-reading work, in which not only a number of missionary ladies are engaged, but also a large number of native Christian women, finding from year to year entrance into new homes, and a more ready attention to the message of salvation conveyed by song, or conversation, or readings.

"In all these forms of work it was easy to note innumerable striking incidents, illustrating the needs of India women, the devotion, faith, and skill of the missionary laborers, the adaptation of the Gospel to the human soul, and the certainty of its final triumph—but there is not space to detail them.

"4. The meagerness of the supply, and the greatness of the demand. Eighteen millions of people are in *our* peculiar mission field in India. For their evangelization the Methodist Episcopal Church is above all others responsible. Shall twenty missionaries, with their wives, sent out by the parent Board, and eight or ten ladies, sent out by the Woman's Foreign Missionary Society, fulfill the obligations which the Church has assumed? Ought not the Woman's Foreign Missionary Society speedily to double and quadruple its India agencies? Has it not access for this purpose to unmeasured treasures now withheld from Him to whom they belong, and used by His stewards for needless self-indulgence?

"May God, who gave his Son, give also to his redeemed daughters in America the spirit of sacrifice which brought our Lord from heaven to Calvary!"

CONSTITUTION

OF THE

WOMAN'S FOREIGN MISSIONARY SOCIETY OF THE METHODIST EPISCOPAL CHURCH.

ARTICLE I.
NAME.

This Association shall be called "THE WOMAN'S FOREIGN MISSIONARY SOCIETY OF THE METHODIST EPISCOPAL CHURCH."

ARTICLE II.
PURPOSE.

The purpose of this Society is to engage and unite the efforts of Christian women in sending female missionaries to women in the foreign mission fields of the Methodist Episcopal Church, and in supporting them and native Christian teachers and Bible-readers in those fields.

ARTICLE III.
MEMBERSHIP.

The payment of one dollar annually shall constitute membership, and twenty dollars life membership. Any person paying one hundred dollars shall become an Honorary Manager for life, and the contribution of three hundred dollars shall constitute the donor an Honorary Patron for life.

ARTICLE IV.

ORGANIZATION.

The organization of this Society shall consist of a General Executive Committee, Co-ordinate Branches and Auxiliary Societies, to be constituted and limited as laid down in subsequent articles.

ARTICLE V.

GENERAL EXECUTIVE COMMITTEE.

SEC. 1. The management and general administration of the affairs of the Society shall be vested in a General Executive Committee, consisting of the Corresponding Secretary and two delegates from each Branch, which delegates, together with two reserves, shall be elected at the Branch annual meetings, said meetings to be held within two months before the meeting of the General Executive Committee. Said Committee shall meet at Boston the third Wednesday in April, 1870, and annually or oftener thereafter, at such time and place as the General Executive Committee shall annually determine.

SEC. 2. The duties of the General Executive Committee shall be:

(1.) To take into consideration the interests and demands of the entire work of the Society, as presented in the reports of Branch Corresponding Secretaries, and in the estimates of the needs of mission fields; to ascertain the financial condition of the Society; to appropriate its money in accordance with the purposes and methods herein indicated; to devise means for carrying forward the work of the Society; fixing the amounts to be raised; employing new missionaries; designating their fields of labor; examining the reports of those already employed; and arranging with the several Branches the work to be undertaken by each.

(2.) To appoint a committee, consisting of one from each Branch, to have charge of the missionary paper of the Society, and to arrange for the publication of an annual report of the work of the Society.

(3.) To transact any other business that the interests of the Society may demand, provided all the plans and directions of the Committee shall be in harmony with the provisions of the Constitution.

ARTICLE VI.
BRANCHES.

SEC. 1. The organizations already formed at Boston, New York, Philadelphia, Chicago, and Cincinnati shall be regarded as co-ordinate branches of this Society on their acceptance of this relationship under the provisions of the present Constitution.

SEC. 2. Other Branches may be organized in accordance with the following general plan for districting the territory of the Church:

Constitution.

Districts.	States.	Head-quarters.
I.	New England States	Boston.
II.	New York and New Jersey	New York.
III	Pennsylvania and Delaware	Philadelphia.
IV.	Maryland, District of Columbia, and Virginia	Baltimore.
V.	Ohio, West Virginia, and Kentucky	Cincinnati.
VI.	Illinois, Indiana, Michigan, and Wisconsin	Chicago.
VII.	Iowa, Missouri, Kansas, Minnesota, Nebraska, Colorado, and Wyoming Territory	Des Moines.
VIII.	Arkansas, Mississippi, Louisiana, and Texas.	New Orleans.
IX.	Tennessee, North Carolina, South Carolina, Alabama, Georgia, and Florida	Atlanta.
X.	Pacific Coast	San Francisco.

This plan, however, may be changed by an affirmative vote of three fourths of the members of the General Executive Committee present at any annual meeting of the same.

SEC. 3. The officers of each Branch Society shall consist of a President, not less than ten Vice-Presidents, a Recording Secretary, a Corresponding Secretary, a Treasurer, an Auditor, and not less than ten Managers. These, with the exception of Auditor, shall constitute an Executive Committee for the administration of the affairs of the Branch, nine of whom shall be a quorum for the transaction of business. These officers shall be elected at the annual meeting of the Branch, and shall continue in office until others are chosen in their stead.

SEC. 4. The President, or one of the Vice-Presidents, shall preside at all meetings of the Branch and of its Executive Committee. The Recording Secretary shall notify all meetings of the Branch and of the Executive Committee, and shall keep a full record of the proceedings.

The Corresponding Secretary shall, under the direction of the Executive Committee, conduct the correspondence of the Society with foreign missionaries, with the other Branches, and with its auxiliary Societies, (hereinafter mentioned,) and shall endeavor, by all practicable means, to form auxiliary Societies within the prescribed territory of the Branch. It shall also be her duty to present to the annual meeting of the General Executive Committee a report of the work of the Branch during the year, for publication in their Annual Report.

The Treasurer shall receive all contributions to the Branch, keeping proper books of accounts, and shall make such disposition of the funds as the Executive Committee may direct, each order of the Committee being duly signed by the Corresponding Secretary.

SEC. 5. The Executive Committee shall have full supervision of all the work assigned to the Branch by the General Executive Committee, and may order the disbursement of the funds required for that work, provide for all the wants and receive all the reports of the missionaries, Bible-women, and teachers, who, by the plan of the General Executive Committee, are to be supported by their Branch.

SEC. 6. No Branch shall project new work or undertake the support of new missionaries, except by the direction or with the approval of the General Executive Committee.

SEC. 7. Each Branch may make its own by-laws regulating its meetings and those of its Executive Committee, also any others which may be deemed necessary to its efficiency, not inconsistent with this Constitution.

ARTICLE VII.
AUXILIARY SOCIETIES.

Any number of women who shall contribute not less than $10 annually, may form a society auxiliary to that Branch of the Woman's Foreign Missionary Society of the Methodist Episcopal Church within whose prescribed territorial limits they may reside, by appointing a President, three or more Vice-Presidents, or Managers, a Recording Secretary, Corresponding Secretary, and Treasurer, who together shall constitute a local Executive Committee.

ARTICLE VIII.
RELATION TO THE MISSIONARY AUTHORITIES OF THE CHURCH.

SEC. 1. This Society will work in harmony with, and under the supervision of, the authorities of the Missionary Society of the Methodist Episcopal Church, and be subject to their approval in the employment and remuneration of missionaries, the designation of their fields of labor, and in the general plans and designs of its work.

SEC. 2. All missionaries supported by the Society shall be approved by the constituted missionary authorities of the Methodist Episcopal Church, and shall labor under the direction of the authorities of the Missionary Society of the Methodist Episcopal Church, and of the particular missions of the Society in which they may be severally employed; and they shall be subject to the same rules and regulations that govern the other missionaries in those particular missions.

Sec. 3. The funds of the Society shall not be raised by collections or subscriptions taken during any Church services or in any promiscuous public meetings, but shall be raised by securing members, life members, honorary managers, and patrons, and by such other methods as will not interfere with the ordinary collections or contributions for the treasury of the Missionary Society of the Methodist Episcopal Church.

ARTICLE IX.
CHANGE OF CONSTITUTION.

This Constitution may be changed at any annual meeting of the General Executive Committee, by a two-thirds vote of each Branch delegation, notice of the proposed change having been given at the previous annual meeting; but Article VIII shall not be changed except with the concurrence of the Board of Managers of the Missionary Society of the Methodist Episcopal Church.

BRANCH LIMITS AND HEAD-QUARTERS.

NEW ENGLAND BRANCH

Includes Maine, New Hampshire, Vermont, Massachusetts, Rhode Island, and Connecticut, with head-quarters at Boston.

NEW YORK BRANCH

Includes New York and New Jersey, with head-quarters at New York.

PHILADELPHIA BRANCH

Includes Pennsylvania and Delaware, with head-quarters at Philadelphia.

BALTIMORE BRANCH

Includes Maryland, District of Columbia, and Eastern Virginia, with head-quarters at Baltimore.

CINCINNATI BRANCH

Includes Ohio, Western Virginia, and Kentucky, with head-quarters at Cincinnati.

NORTH-WESTERN BRANCH

Includes Illinois, Indiana, Michigan, and Wisconsin, with head-quarters at Chicago.

WESTERN BRANCH

Includes Iowa, Missouri, Kansas, Minnesota, Nebraska, Colorado, and Wyoming Territory, with head-quarters at Des Moines.

ATLANTA BRANCH

Includes Tennessee, North Carolina, South Carolina, Alabama, Georgia, and Florida, with head-quarters at Atlanta.

RECEIPTS OF W. F. M. SOCIETY, AS REPORTED IN "HEATHEN WOMAN'S FRIEND."

March 22, 1869, to June, 1870, receipts are as follows:

Massachusetts, $2,071 85; New York, $1,078 17; Illinois, $771 16; Vermont, $193 70; Ohio, $128 50; New Jersey, $126; Wisconsin, $85 48; Iowa, $35; West Virginia, $23; Indiana, $20; Maine, $7; Pennsylvania, $5; New Hampshire, $2. Total, $4,546 86.

Receipts by Branches from	N. E. Br.	N. Y. Br.	Phila. Br.	Balt. Br.	Cinn. Br.	N. W. Br.	Western Br.	Totals.
June, 1870, to June, 1871.								$4,546 86
" 1871, " 1872.	$3,691 23	$12,029 15	$1,855 22	....	$2,844 08	$3,069 56	$995 80	24,485 04
" 1872, " 1873.	6,729 53	10,226 32	2,238 26	$3,201 65	8,423 29	10,495 59	2,729 93	44,044 57
" 1873, " 1874.	10,667 77*	11,580 12	5,716 68	3,644 06	10,290 33	11,796 71	4,160 85	56,856 52
" 1874, " 1875.	10,928 83	12,713 71	5,065 35	4,253 40	9,647 64	12,456 00	3,943 07	59,008 00
" 1875, " 1876.	10,178 75	13,957 07	6,371 08	4,541 76	10,446 54	12,279 50	5,900 44	63,675 14
" 1876, " 1877.	11,927 04	17,094 33	6,930 28	6,158 88	10,797 18	14,547 09	7,272 37	74,727 17
" 1877, " 1878.	11,521 96	12,681 83	6,583 14	3,900 52	9,881 03	14,080 35	8,033 18	66,682 01
" 1878, " 1879.	10,979 96	11,303 08	6,685 10	4,470 63	10,174 80	13,287 12	7,032 05	63,932 74
" "	10,685 53	12,848 14	6,512 19	3,937 64	6,160 98	13,232 97	7,560 56	60,938 01
Totals............	$87,310 60	$114,433 75	$46,957 30	$34,108 54	$78,665 87	$105,244 89	$47,628 25	$518,896 06

* 2,000 of this not reported in Heathen Woman's Friend.

PAYMENTS TO WOMAN'S FOREIGN MISSIONARY SOCIETY.

The payment of $1 constitutes a member for one year.

The payment of $20 constitutes a life-member.

The payment of $100 constitutes an honorary life-manager.

The payment of $300 constitutes an honorary life-patron.

The payment of $30 supports an orphan for one year in India.

The payment of $40 supports an orphan for one year in Mexico.

The payment of $60 supports a Bible-reader for one year in India.

The payment of $24 supports a deaconess for one year in China.

The payment of $30 supports a scholarship for one year in India.

The payment of $40 supports a scholarship for one year in Japan.

N. B.—Yearly subscriptions must not be applied on *special* work.

FORM OF BEQUEST AND DEVISE TO WOMAN'S FOREIGN MISSIONARY SOCIETY.

BEQUEST. (*Personal Estate.*) — I give and bequeath to the Trustees of the Methodist Episcopal Church, incorporated under the General Laws of the State of Ohio, the sum of   dollars, in trust, to be held for the benefit and applied according to the direction of the Woman's Foreign Missionary Society of the Methodist Episcopal Church.

DEVISE. (*Real Estate.*)—I give and devise to the Trustees of the Methodist Episcopal Church, incorporated under the General Laws of the State of Ohio, all that certain [here insert a short description of the land, house, or other real estate,] with the appurtenances, in fee simple, in trust, the same to be held for the benefit and applied according to the directions of the Woman's Foreign Missionary Society of the Methodist Episcopal Church.

NOTE.—Prompt notice of all bequests and devises should be given to the Corresponding Secretary of the branch within whose territory the donor resides.

THE END.

www.ingramcontent.com/pod-product-compliance
Lightning Source LLC
Chambersburg PA
CBHW030326240426
43673CB00040B/1284